Second Look at First Things

Second Look at First Things
Case for Conservative Politics

THE HADLEY ARKES FESTSCHRIFT

Edited by
Francis J. Beckwith, Robert P. George, & Susan McWilliams

Introduction by
Francis J. Beckwith

Foreword by
Daniel Robinson

ST. AUGUSTINE'S PRESS
South Bend, Indiana

Manufactured in the United States of America

1 2 3 4 5 6   19 18 17 16 15 14 13

Library of Congress Cataloging in Publication Data
A second look at first things: a case for conservative politics:
the Hadley Arkes festschrift /edited by Francis J. Beckwith,
Robert P. George, and Susan McWilliams.
pages cm
ISBN 978-1-58731-759-0 (pbk.: alk. paper) –
ISBN 978-1-58731-761-3 (e-book)
1. Conservatism – United States – History. 2. Natural law – History.
3. Social justice – United States – History. 4. Political ethics – United
States – History. 5. Religion and politics – United States – History.
6. Federal government – United States—History. 7. Arkes, Hadley.
I. Arkes, Hadley. II. Beckwith, Francis. III. George, Robert P.
IV. McWilliams, Susan Jane, 1977–
JC573.2.U6S43 2013
320.520973 – dc23   2012040032

∞ The paper used in this publication meets the minimum requirements of the
American National Standard for Information Sciences Permanence of Paper
for Printed Materials, ANSI Z39.481984.

ST. AUGUSTINE'S PRESS
www.staugustine.net

Table of Contents

Foreword

My wife and I arrived in Amherst in 1968, but it was not until the following year that my friendship with Hadley Arkes took shape, a friendship born in the catered foxholes of academic politics. We agreed right off the bat that there would be long-term costs incurred by the politicization of academe; that a once collegiate and intellectual world would be transformed into parties ceaselessly engaged in ideological wrangles. Although we were right on this, we were wrong in our appraisal of the influence that the few but effective sullen and protesting students would come to have on our national life. Hadley and I sized them up as irremediably pathetic unless tamed by the realities of the marketplace. We never gave serious attention to the possibility that their raw habits of mind and indignant dispositions would come to shape what remained of the 20th Century. That is, we never imagined that our own later years would be lived in a world of their making.

There were, of course, other sources of the gravitational pull that found us ever more frequently in each other's company. Both of us had been groomed by the ethos of great cities; Hadley from the lesser one – Chicago – and I from the one that never sleeps. For us, "diversity" was not a shibboleth or cheap excuse; it constituted nothing less than the raiment of humanity: No two of us alike, but all of us comparably fitted out for lives of ordered liberty, ever mindful that our agentic powers carry with them very great obligations. And there was that wonderfully old world sense of family, with Hadley and Judy and the boys joining me and Ciny for sweet indulgences, happy reminiscences, sometimes wonderfully caustic commentaries on the little world in which we now found ourselves. We had our youth and the jauntiness that goes with it. Hadley, Judy and Ciny were not yet 30 and I was 31, so at least three of the four could be trusted according to the calculus of the SDS.

But for all the politics and maddening bumper-sticker "philosophy" of the time, the College did foster such friendships and we were happy beneficiaries.

Hadley honored me well beyond merit when, in dedicating *First Things* to me, he traced part of his concern for the moral foundations of politics to matters addressed on long walks and unhurried hours over coffee. If ever the alignment of celestial bodies ordained a future for a human being, it is clear that the very order of the heavens would have had Hadley Arkes exposing the world of law and politics to the light of moral criticism! It would have happened had all his walks been solitary or if, on our walks together, I had discussed nothing more than God's growing impatience with the White Sox. But we *did* talk. We talked about abortion and the special solicitude owed to the defenseless. We spoke about Kant and the plausibility of that "imperative" that might find us complicit with evil. We discussed the affairs of the College, lamenting the utterly political tone of discourse that had all but replaced collegial attention to what Matthew Arnold called "the best things said and done by the human race."

We left Amherst in 1971 but by then my friendship with Hadley had entered the plane of the enduring. E-mail was years away, but telephones had been invented and both of us had mastered the use of pen and paper – by which I mean *fountain pen* and paper. *Roe v. Wade* descended on the world of inchoate humanity and, as the body count quickly rose to more than a million annually, our letters and conversations became more frequent, more insistent. Each of us saw to it that our courses would make room for the issue. Each of us wrote on the issue. But Hadley would do more, much more. He would make a central part of his life's work . . . *life*. In its cause, he has traveled tens of thousands of miles, stood at countless lecterns, withstood often hateful criticism, and persisted in instructing the thinking part of the world that this newly won "right to choose" fails as both a right and a choice. *Bravo!,* dear friend, and, yes, that really *is* the choir of heaven singing a thankful acknowledgment.

There would be much more coming from Hadley, even if there is nothing more important. As the essays in this volume make clear, Hadley's published work and his teaching have addressed the very

foundations of constitutional jurisprudence. His critical appraisals of
major cases stand as paragons of scholarship and juridical reasoning.
He has mastered the text and now teaches the teachers. Hearing Hadley
on pivotal cases, I often form the picture of the judges of record reading Hadley's analysis and saying to themselves, "My God, is *that* what
we did?" A student of mine once asked me what, at bottom, was
Hadley's argument against granting a parade permit so the Nazis could
have day of mischief in Skokie. "At bottom?," I repeated. Well, at bottom, the argument is that the Second Amendment does not require that
I give you a gun with which you plan to shoot me! Kant is careful in his
Third Critique to distinguish between judgments of perception, judgments of experience and what he calls teleological judgments. I know
of no one who has applied that third category as deftly and instructive-
ly as Hadley has: He understands the ends and purposes of law as such,
and then is able to establish whether this or that law, this or that judgment makes the required contact with just those ends and purposes.

I turn briefly to something related to this, but something deeply
personal. I must be careful not to take liberties with our friendship and
so I tread delicately in approaching Hadley's reception into the Roman
Catholic Church. Those of us who are "born and bred" Catholic often
have some innocent fun with friends who have converted. "You mean
you *chose* this!" It should be clear to all, whatever one's own judgment
or sentiment might be regarding the claims of religion, that the House
of Faith has many mansions, various enough to accommodate those
whose longings are not all earthbound. Of the world's religions, surely
the Roman Catholic Church can lay claim to the longest continuing
record of critical, philosophical reflection worked out in sufficient
detail to fill whole libraries of books and manuscripts. Whatever else
one might wish to say about the doctrinal teaching of the Church, one
must grant that it arises from nothing less than the Long Debate. Had
the teaching been wrong when comprehended under the penetrating
lights of reason and moral criticism, then the Church would be wrong
for many, but not for all. In my own case, it would have been wrong for
me.

However, my sainted grandmother, Mary Elizabeth Burke from
County West Meath, never consulted the Vatican library, never to my

knowledge read a line of the *Summa Theologiae* or even saw a book on Canon Law. She loved God and loved the Mother of God, and said as much to them, seven days in the week, each day beginning with early Mass. It was her faith in Jesus Christ and in what she took to be His Church that grounded her acceptance of the teaching. With all due respect to Cole Porter, my grandmother's view was that fifty million Frenchmen *can* be wrong, but a thousand saints cannot.

There is, as I say, yet other mansions in this house. In one of them we find many books – books of words perhaps more than books of deeds. Here is the room in which human practices are subjected to moral appraisal, tested for their premises, weighed on the scales of justice. There are those summoned to the Roman Catholic Church in large measure by the fact that, on the enduring moral issues, it is the Roman Catholic Church that not only gets it right, but gets it right for the right reasons.

I can speak for no one other than myself – not even for a friend of more than forty years – in attempting to account for allegiance to a Faith. "Catholicism," after all, is not a univocal term. It refers to a venerable institution, brought into being when Jesus Christ uttered the words, "Thou art Peter. . . ." As an institution now in its third millennium, it has a mixed record, for in many if not most respects it is a human institution. It has fed the hungry but it has also burned witches. It should have fed the hungry, for many are hungry. It should not have burned witches, for there are no witches. There really aren't, you know. Well, so be it.

"Catholicism" as noted is also a body of doctrinal teaching; perhaps the most systematic body of teaching ever offered as an account of human nature, its needs and possibilities. The teaching is inspired but is less than perfect or it would never have changed. It is in the Church's very *culture* of thought that critics must be answered and, where no compelling answer can be framed, that same *culture* of thought requires reappraisals, even reforms. Holy Mother Church has not burned witches for a very long time. Finally, there is the "Catholicism" that is, for the believer, the body of Christ, existing on a mystical plane even as it sets about to do the work of the world.

Hadley Arkes knows a good argument when he hears one. He has a genius for finding small holes in large bodies of thought and illustrating how such porosity spells doom. He has studied the teaching of the Church and, if I am not mistaken, judged that it is *right* when it matters most. For a man such as my friend, to be drawn to this is not to abandon Judaism but to complete it. The path to Rome, though allowing traffic only in one direction, miraculously leaves nothing of value behind. We don't say "Judeo-Christian" to be polite! Had there not been the Hebrew there would not be the Christian. Jesus came, after all, to fulfill the prophesies. Long before my friend saw the Catechism he was on intimate terms with the one true God and with the elevating if terrifying fact that it is finally the *moral law* which gives human life its moorings. You see, he was in Rome all along.

A final word . . . Hadley, as we all know, is a great teacher. To many, that estimation is based on attendance at his often spell-binding lectures, his great humor, his equally thoughtful reflection on questions and issues advanced by senior scholars and first year students. What is often not noticed are the pages of comments he writes in response to essays submitted by his students; I mean *pages* of comments and addressed to enrollments of a hundred or more. He does not have post-doctoral students or graduate students doing his work. His students are not shunted off to teaching assistants or treated to useless generalities squeezed into the margins. Hadley would be an arresting teacher even if he let others do all this. But he would not be a *great* teacher, for he would not have commerce with each of the minds he has set out to refine, to challenge, to protect.

I hope this *Festschrift* pleases you, dear friend. It is a small gift from persons whose lives have been enriched by your vocation.

Daniel N. Robinson
Oxford University

Introduction:
A Second Look at First Things
Francis J. Beckwith

The political regime of the United States of America is one founded on three core philosophical ideas: natural rights, consent of the governed, and the rule of law. The American Founders put in place a structure – a federal constitutional government of divided powers consisting of states with their own republican governments – in order to ensure that these core philosophical ideas stood the best chance of surviving the tumult of human depravity. Thus, the Founders' government was a limited government, but it was not a libertine one. It offered what some call a regime of ordered liberty. That is, one in which the preservation and development of certain institutions and ways of life – already present in civil society – could be allowed to flourish for the sake of the common good.

The Declaration of Independence provides a philosophical snapshot of the grounds by which the infrastructure of this government was fashioned: "We hold these truths to be self-evident, that all men are created equal, that they are endowed by their Creator with certain unalienable Rights, that among these are Life, Liberty and the pursuit of Happiness." That is, human beings are rights bearers by nature, and these rights are given to them by God. And because the human being, in the words of Justice McLean, "bears the impress of his Maker,"[1] we are in fact creatures of equal dignity and immeasurable worth (even when our government did not live up to this truth).

Nevertheless, for well over a century the Founders' vision has been called into question by a variety of critics. Some have expressed doubts as to whether the Founders' framework – a divided government of

---

1   *Dred Scott v. Sandford*, 19 Howard 393, at 550 (1857) (McLean, J., dissenting).

checks and balances intended to protect fundamental liberties such as the right to property, due process, religious freedom – is based on a correct understanding of the progress of history and the different needs that citizens may have in an age of ever-changing circumstances and challenges unanticipated at the American Founding.

Others have raised questions about whether there is really such a thing as natural rights, while others who say they embrace natural rights reject the Founders' belief that such rights require a Divine Source. The consent of the governed too has been the target of critique, especially on questions of great moral controversy, such as abortion, the distribution of pornography, and same-sex marriage. In these three cases, courts have struck down laws passed by legislative and popular majorities on the grounds that these laws violated some deeper constitutional principles not apparent from the text of the Constitution itself.

Behind these developments and the political disputes that arise from them are philosophical beliefs about the nature of humanity, morality, law, and the common good. Hence, they are not, per se, political disputes, since they are the underlying reasons for our political disagreements. Take, for example, the issue of abortion, perhaps the issue over which Americans are the most deeply divided. Although there is in the academic world a wide spectrum of views on the morality of abortion, in the world of politics there are roughly two major positions: prolife and prochoice. Those who embrace the latter position generally believe that the right to abortion is a fundamental right. On the other hand, those who oppose abortion generally believe that abortion in every case is unjustified homicide because the unborn child is a full-fledged member of the human community and thus requires the protections of our laws. Thus, the abortion controversy hinges on a question of philosophical anthropology: who and what we are and can we know it? If the unborn child is not one of us, then it is entitled to no greater protections than we afford an appendix or a kidney. But if he or she is one of us, then it possesses an intrinsic dignity that all human beings have by nature, that just governments ought to recognize.

What is true of abortion is also true of other issues over which Americans disagree including the nature of marriage and family, the licitness of physician-assisted suicide, the scope and size of the welfare state, and whether the laws may be employed to support a particular moral vision of the good life. No matter how one answers these questions, whether one is for or against a particular position on each of them, the position one embraces will rely on a metaphysics of the human person. This is why our co-editor, Robert P. George, refers to these disagreement as a "clash of orthodoxies."[2]

I

It is rare today to find a young person who is aware of these distinctions and how they shape the ideas of those who call themselves "liberal" or "conservative." Instead, he or she is formed by a litany of slogans intended to cajole, prod, and shame. Conservative students, though their hearts are often in the right place, seem unaware of the philosophical roots of their own point of view. We have gone from Eric Voegelin saying "Don't immanentize the eschaton" to Hannity's, "Sean, you're a great American." To be sure, many conservative and liberal young people have firm opinions on issues along the conservative-liberal fault line. They can opine, and fiercely so, by blog, twitter, or email on issues as wide ranging as same-sex marriage, Constitutional interpretation, abortion, free markets, and the role of religion in the public square. But very few if any of them seem to be aware of the intellectual patrimony from which their views sprang, and the arguments and reasons that animated the proponents of the ideas they claim to sincerely and deeply hold. "Hope" and "change," though fine words in their own right, do not qualify as actual ideas that may guide presidents and prime ministers to excellence in statecraft.

There was a time when many of us while we were in college or graduate school would participate in robust discussions with friend and foe alike about the ideas and arguments we plumbed from the works authored by conservative luminaries as diverse as Hayek, Strauss, Voegelin, Buckley, Weaver, Friedman, Kirk, Lewis, Chesterton, and Anscombe, to name just a few. Sadly, there is very little of this going on today in our universities and colleges.

---

2   Robert P. George, *A Clash of Orthodoxies: Law, Religion, and Morality in Crisis* (Wilmington, DE: ISI Books, 2000).

A Second Look at First Things: A Case for Conservative Politics has two purposes. The first is to remedy this contemporary deficit by offering, in one volume, an intelligent, winsome, and readable articulation of conservative ideas on a variety of issues and questions. They range from the abstract ("Why the Natural Law Suggests a Divine Source" and "Natural Law and Contemporary Liberalism"), to the practical ("Natural Law and Policy" and "Lincoln and Justice for All"), and to the provocative ("Being Personal These Days: Designer Babies and the Future of Liberal Democracy").

The book's second, and most important, purpose is to honor the great conservative political philosopher, Hadley P. Arkes, the Edward Ney Professor of Jurisprudence and American Institutions at Amherst College. In 2010 he celebrated his 70th birthday, and 2011 marked the 25th anniversary of the publication of his highly influential monograph, *First Things: An Inquiry into the First Principles of Morals and Justice* (Princeton University Press, 1986). So, in celebration of these milestones, we have chosen to produce a work that is consistent with Hadley's vocation as an exceptional teacher of young people. Although most of those who have read Hadley's books and articles think of him as an engaging and productive scholar, which indeed he is, his students – including both those at Amherst as well as those of us who have had the privilege to hear his spell-binding lectures elsewhere – know him as an outstanding teacher. His ability to unpack a principle of jurisprudence by weaving together an analytical argument with an enthralling tale or insightful anecdote is truly magical to behold. (This is why we include a chapter by a former student of Hadley's, Susan McWilliams, "Moral Education and the Art of Storytelling." Professor McWilliams is also a co-editor of this volume.)

So, instead of just inviting a collection of colleagues and former students to contribute essays of their own choosing to celebrate the life and accomplishments of their dear friend and mentor, the editors envisioned a volume that truly honors Hadley as teacher. This is why this book – though consisting of separate chapters by different authors – is an organic whole that serves its second purpose by serving its first: it attempts to teach and to teach well. We cannot think of a better way to honor our friend Hadley while at the same time, as he would put it, advancing the argument.

II

This book is divided into four parts. Part I – Conservatism, Statecraft, and Soulcraft – contains four chapters. In Chapter 1 ("What is Political Conservatism?"), Larry Arnn impressively tackles the difficult task of explaining the meaning of "conservatism," and "American conservatism" in particular. He moves from the American Founding through the Progressive Era and into the presidency of Ronald W. Reagan. He explains how Progressive Era thinking – exemplified by the ideas of President Woodrow Wilson and effectively put into practice by President Franklin D. Roosevelt – stands in opposition to the principles of the American Founding and how that opposition helped bring about the modern conservative movement.

Abraham Lincoln figures prominently in Hadley Arkes's understanding of natural law and its application to statecraft. For this reason, we invited Allen C. Guelzo to author Chapter 2 ("Lincoln and Justice for All"). Guelzo offers a rich account of Lincoln's understanding of justice and how it shaped the way he understood his role as President during the most troubled times in the history of the American Republic.

In Chapter 3 ("Moral Education and the Art of Storytelling"), Susan McWilliams explains why storytelling is essential to the sort of moral education that a vibrant polity requires. For it does two things: it connects us to first principles (or "first things") on which the "moral" of every good story depends (e.g., the story of the Good Samaritan), while at the same time keeping us grounded by reminding us of our limitations and the particularity of the stories of our own lives. This is why one is more likely to remember, and learn from, the Story of the Good Samaritan than a highly abstract principle, such as a formulation of Immanuel Kant's Categorical Imperative. As the first two chapters tell us, the stories of the American Founding and Abraham Lincoln's burden of the American Civil War communicate to us in a more convincing fashion the first principles of the American regime than one would encounter reading John Locke's *Second Treatise on Government*.

On April 24, 2010, Hadley Arkes was received into the Catholic Church. One of the priests celebrating the Mass that evening was the Georgetown University political scientist Fr. James Schall, S. J. In chapter 4 ("On 'Eating the Last Pizza': The Wit of Hadley Arkes"), Fr. Schall provides a wonderful overview of how Hadley has effectively employed wit and humor in his serious academic work. But more than that, Fr. Schall suggests that Hadley's rhetorical moves – having their roots in Plato, Aristotle, and Cicero – can teach each of us, including the student, the professor, the politician, and the ordinary citizen, how to carefully and elegantly engage those with whom we disagree as well as teach our friends how to think more clearly and competently about the veracity and logic of our own beliefs.

The focus of Part II is Jurisprudence, which is an area of political and legal thought about which Hadley has written some of his most important works, including *First Things* and his 2010 monograph, *Constitutional Illusions and Anchoring Truths: The Touchstone of the Natural Law* (Cambridge University Press).

It is clear that the American Founders, like the man we are honoring, Hadley Arkes, believed that there exists a natural law, a collection of normative principles of human conduct that a government and its positive laws must reflect in order to be just. This is why the Declaration of Independence explicitly mentions natural rights in the portion of it quoted above. This natural law is not a human invention, but something that we can know when we carefully reflect on the nature of human persons, their proper ends, the goods by which they may flourish as individuals and in communities, and the institutions and practices in which these goods are embodied (however partially at times).

In Chapter 5, David Forte ("The Morality of Positive Law") explores the relationship between the natural law, constitutional government, and public policy. He argues that the principles that ground the positive law of the U. S. Constitution are themselves derived from the natural law. He then goes on to deal with several issues, one of which concerns the responsibilities of jurists in remaining faithful to the Constitution while doing justice.

If there is a natural law, and it includes principles by which to assess human conduct, both private and public, is it permissible for the government to "legislate morality"? If in fact there are real moral wrongs that citizens may commit in private, does the state have a legitimate power to proscribe such conduct? Micah Watson addresses this issue in Chapter 6 ("Statecraft as Soulcraft: the Case for Legislating Morality"). It is on this question that traditional conservatives (like Arkes and Watson) and libertarian conservatives part ways. The latter believe that the government should not prohibit self-regarding acts between consenting adults (e.g., ingesting narcotics, extra-marital intimacy, distribution of pornography) as long as third parties are not directly harmed. Watson offers a sophisticated and compelling response to the libertarians (as well as liberals who share that perspective).

Some contemporary political and legal philosophers often defend views that seem to be congenial to natural law thinking. Christopher Wolfe addresses this topic in Chapter 7 ("Natural Law and Contemporary Liberalism"). After presenting the different levels of natural law thinking, Wolfe assesses the thinking of liberal theorists John Rawls and Ronald Dworkin, concluding that they are only natural law thinkers in a very minimal sense, if at all. In his conclusion, Wolfe suggests that because of their minimalist nature, the liberalisms of Rawls and Dworkin may be incapable of sustaining liberal democracies in response to many internal and external challenges such as religiously based terrorism and economic instability. Only a rich natural law tradition, concludes Wolfe, can provide liberal democracies with the resilience such challenges demand.

Part III concerns the relationship between religion, liberal democracy, and the American project. In Chapter 8 ("Why the Natural Law Suggests a Divine Source"), J. Budziszewski offers a philosophical defense of what the American Founders believed is the source of the natural law on which our natural rights flow, namely, that they have their grounding in the Divine. Oftentimes, this understanding of natural law is credited to "civil religion" or reduced to some sociological phenomenon. What Budziszewski does is assess it as a philosophically serious account that can be robustly defended as true apart from the social facts and religious practices of the cultures that embrace it.

Vincent Phillip Muñoz explains the different ways that three

American Founders – James Madison, George Washington, and Thomas Jefferson – understood the relationship between church and state. In Chapter 9 ("The Place of Religion in the American Founding"), Muñoz also addresses the question of how these diverse understandings shape, and ought not to shape, originalism in constitutionalism interpretation. (*Originalism* is the view that the U.S. Constitution and its constituent parts should be interpreted in a way consistent with the plain meaning of how the language was understood at the time the Constitution and its amendments were made effective.)

Chapter 10 ("Freedom Under God: An American Understanding of Religious Liberty") is an explication of the American view of religious liberty for an Islamic audience curious about the West's practice of it, though skeptical of the aggressive secularism that many Muslims perceive is associated with religious liberty and religious disestablishment in some Western nations. In making his case, Michael Novak hopes to convince his Muslim readers that religious liberty is congenial to a robust and serious theism. In one place he shows the uncanny similarities between the Second Vatican Council's *Dignitatis Humanae* and two works on religious liberty penned by James Madison and Thomas Jefferson.

In Chapter 11 ("*Veritatis Splendor*: Exceptionless Norms, Human Rights, and the Common Good"), Gerard Bradley comes at the issue of church and state from an angle largely ignored in the professional literature. Instead of addressing the issue from the perspective of the state and its burdens, Bradley explores recent papal encyclicals and what they tell us about the state's moral authority and its obligations to the common good. His point of departure is a passage from *Veritatis Splendor*: "*When it is a matter of the moral norms prohibiting intrinsic evil, there are no privileges or exceptions for anyone. It makes no dif*ference whether one is the master of world or the 'poorest of the poor' on the face of the earth. Before the demands of morality we are all absolutely equal."[3] Sometimes called the "master of millions" passage,

3   John Paul II, *Veritatis Splendor* (August 3, 1993), 96, available at http://www.vatican.va/holy_father/john_paul_ii/encyclicals/documents/hf_jp-ii_enc_06081993_veritatis-splendor_en.html.

it tells us that the moral law applies equally to political officials as it does to individual citizens. Given that, Bradley explores what this may mean on a variety of policy matters in which the idea of "exceptionless moral norms," essential to the Catholic moral tradition, seems to hamper public officials from advancing the common good.

Communities, persons, and institutions are the focus of part IV. It concerns three central areas over which political conservatives part ways with some of their compatriots: the moral foundations of limited government, free markets and their relationship to constitutional government, and philosophical anthropology.

In Chapter 12 ("On the Moral Purposes of Law and Government"), Robert P. George makes a natural law case for limited government, arguing that a liberal democracy – in order to be just – must be grounded in certain basic goods, the dignity of the human person, and the intrinsic good of marriage as a one-flesh communion of one man and one woman. The bulk of this chapter is a philosophical defense of this understanding of marriage. In making in case, George also points out that the institutionalizing of same-sex "marriage" will have a deleterious impact on religious liberty and family autonomy, for it will result in the marginalizing of citizens who for reason of conscience cannot acquiesce to same-sex "marriage" as a good that ought to be celebrated.

In Chapter 13 ("The Justice of the Market and the Common Good: Justice Sutherland's Debate"), James R. Stoner, Jr. offers an analysis of the relationship between free markets, the Constitution, and public policy. His point of departure is several judicial opinions of the late U. S. Supreme Court Justice George Sutherland, a man whose work was the focus of Hadley Arkes's 1994 monograph, *The Return of George Sutherland: Restoring a Jurisprudence of Natural Rights* (Princeton University Press). Stoner explains how the issues that animated Justice Sutherland and his critics on the Court concerning the morality of markets and the scope of legislative limitations on those markets during the early to mid-20th century have resonance today, especially as Americans at the beginning of the second decade of the 21st century debate the wisdom of "Obamacare" and how to deal with the aftermath of the economic crisis of 2008.

Many converts to political conservatism were initially wooed to entertaining it by liberalism's abandonment of the unborn when it took the side of abortion rights in the early 1970s. I count myself as one of these converts. For me, my conservatism developed out of my liberalism. I was taught by my parents (both liberal Democrats when I was a youngster) that one of the roles of government was to protect the "little guy." But in my early twenties I began to notice that self-described liberals had no interest in protecting the littlest guy of all, the unborn. For many of us converts to conservatism, we want to conserve, and help develop more deeply and fully, a culture of life. In Chapter 14 ("The Unborn and the Scope of the Human Community"), Christopher Tollefsen provides a philosophically compelling defense for the intrinsic dignity and full personhood of the unborn human being. Throughout this chapter, Tollefsen draws our attention to Hadley's important academic work in which he has time and again given voice to the voiceless.

The focus of Chapter 15 is the promise of the revolution in biotechnology and how it has, and will, shape our understanding of what it means to be a person. In this chapter ("Being Personal These Days: Designer Babies and the Future of Liberal Democracy"), Peter Augustine Lawler explains how many scientific advances – especially those created to enhance, rather than merely heal, our natural powers – pose significant challenges to our understanding choice, autonomy, and the good life.

III

The editors and contributors offer this book as a small token of our love, gratitude and appreciation to our dear friend, Hadley Arkes. It is in his spirit as teacher that we attempt, however partially and modestly, to communicate to a wider audience something of the "first things" that Hadley has labored tirelessly to articulate and defend throughout his long and illustrious career. As the Angelic Doctor put it, "For even as it is better to enlighten than merely to shine, so is it better to give to others the fruits of one's contemplation than merely to contemplate."[4]

---

4   St. Thomas Aquinas, *Summa Theologiae* II.II, Q188, art6, 2nd and rev, literally translated by Fathers of the English Dominican Province [1920], online edition, http://www.newadvent.org/summa/3188.htm.

I. Conservatism, Statecraft, and Soulcraft

Chapter 1:
What is Political Conservatism?
Larry Arnn

To write about political conservatism is to involve oneself in several problems of definition and several disputes, all at once. To write about them for the young makes the matter worse, because being clear about a thing is a separate step with its own difficulty, after one has understood the thing himself. I undertake these serious difficulties because it is a chance to honor the author, the scholar and my friend Hadley Arkes, for whom this task would be simple. My first advice is that one should read Arkes's work if he wishes to understand political conservatism. Meanwhile, you are here, and I must do the best I can. I begin with definitions.

Definitions

Conservatism, obviously, is the wish or disposition to conserve something. What? Whatever is conserved must be in the past, and the past goes back a long way. Even traditions, things in the past that abide and attain dignity, speak with more than one voice about the priority of many good things. All conservatives are therefore picking some things from the past that they like and discarding others. They do not always pick the same things, which is one reason why there are disputes within conservatism.

The origins of conservatism shed some light. The word "conservative" was first used in a political context, according to the *Oxford English Dictionary*, by disciples of Edmund Burke. These disciples were French opponents of the French Revolution, to which Burke was also opposed. It was against the excesses of that revolution – and in particular its repudiation of old things, sometimes simply because they were old – that Burke and his disciples railed. The French Revolution was, in its own understanding, a liberal revolution, a revolution to secure liberty and equality. One might think that conservatives are always against these things. Edmund Burke, however, was very much a friend of the American Revolution, also famously a liberal revolution in favor of equality. Conservatives, apparently, can be in some sense liberals.

In the American context, conservatism was born in opposition to modern liberalism. It was born under the leadership, more than anyone else, of William F. Buckley, Jr. It was born, more than anywhere else, in his publication, *National Review*. A good place to look for a definition of American conservatism is the first issue of *National Review* published on November 19, 1955 – coincidentally the anniversary of the Gettysburg Address.

This first issue of *National Review* begins with a famous statement, a "Publisher's Statement," written by William Buckley. It contains one of his most famous passages in the second paragraph: "[National Review] stands athwart history, yelling Stop, at a time when no one is inclined to do so, or to have much patience with those who so urge it."[1] We shall see that Buckley identifies his enemy, the enemy of conservatism, with precision. It has to do with history. Conservatives must perforce like history, as there is something in it that they wish to conserve. This idea of history in motion, of history going somewhere, of history as causing things and becoming a cause to serve, is a different matter, about which more shortly.

Henceforth I will speak of conservatism as the American thing, born in the life and career of Buckley and his friends. It is well known that this conservatism is made up of several factions. Largest among these are the libertarians, much concerned with economics and personal freedom, and the traditionalists, much concerned with, well, tradition. By "tradition" they mean old things that have stood the test of time, including religion, the family, order and justice, and other things of fundamental importance. Conservatism, when it functions as a whole, is a union of these key ideas. When it functions well in politics,

1   *National Review* 1.1 (19 November 1955): 5.

it adds something else, something I will argue to be decisive. That thing is a wish to conserve the principles and institutions that gave their nation birth and operating form, the principles found in the Declaration of Independence, the institutions established in the Constitution.

By politics, I mean what Arkes has so often meant and explained. I mean the classical[2] definition. Politics is the most complete form of human community. It is born in the gift of speech, distinctive among humans, from which arise both our unique sociability and our moral sense. When we see things, we humans know what kind of things they are. We can compare one thing of a type with another. In a famous conversation in literature, Caroline says that a certain kind of party would be much more rational if there were conversation instead of dancing. Bingley replies, "Much more rational, my dear Caroline, I dare say, but it would not be near so much like a ball."[3] "Ball" then is a thing we can recognize and call by a name. To *be* a ball, then a thing must be in some sense a "*good*" ball; otherwise a conversation or a croquet match could be a ball. To have the *being* of a thing is to have the *good* of it.[4]

We humans first "see" this dimension of things as a simple act of perception. We are always seeing and figuring about the good and bad, the just and the unjust. And because we give names to things, we are able to talk about them in ways that transcend mere expressions of pleasure or pain, which brings us together in ways impossible in other animals. The community in which we work out the just and the unjust and live according to our conception of them – the community, in other words, where we express our full humanity – is the political community.

2   "Classical" here denotes not only the definition of politics accepted by the ancient Greek and Roman societies, but also the instance of something that comes closest to resembling its own nature – the one that establishes the class. The former sense is derived from the latter. So while the definition of politics used by Arkes and Aristotle is "classical," or Greek, it is more importantly "classical," or true. A classic does not have to be old, but it must be good.

3   Jane Austen, *Pride and Prejudice* (New York: Alfred A. Knopf, 1991), 51.

4   I copy this example from Harry Jaffa, who used it first in my hearing in class about 35 years ago. It took me some years to figure why he was telling that story in a class on Aristotle's *Nicomachean Ethics*. If I still do not have it right, he will doubtless correct me.

Political communities are always particular things, formed by individual human beings working together. There is a wide variety of them. They require the citizens and their statesmen to be able to talk together and to share a common sense was of justice. A universal or global state is hard to imagine when one considers that we must talk with one another and agree about certain things, and there are so many languages and so many points of view in the world. It is a fact of politics that each of us belongs to a particular political community demanding of us particular loyalties. The laws of that community have vital things to do with how we live, and our membership in that community implies some agreement with its central ideas. Indeed the fiercest disputes inside political communities concern those central ideas.

The wide variety of political communities around the world, and thus the wide variety in conceptions of justice around the world, lead some to claim that there is no "real" meaning to the term "justice" itself. They argue that if justice were a fixed or objective thing, there would be no disagreements among human beings about what constitutes justice. Conservatives by and large respond that human error is no refutation of the idea of right: the problem is in the error and not in the conception of right. Humans betray commonly, even amidst their worst errors, that they themselves have a sense of right and wrong different from the errors. Murderers usually claim they did not do it, and when they admit to committing murders, usually they cite the many reasons why their actions were compelled upon them, or justified by the circumstances, or not deserving of the punishment they suffer. All of these are assertions about justice. Conservatives notice things like this and think that there is some knowledge of the good that sits in judgment upon everything we do, even our own actions, and even when they are wrong. Human beings are the creatures capable of blushing. This thing that makes us blush is our perception of right and wrong. And, as Hadley Arkes has explained beautifully and often, what we are perceiving, when we perceive right and wrong in that way, is a natural standard of right, available to this rational faculty, the same faculty that permits us to talk.

The American is a member of a special political community, the first in history founded in dedication to the natural rights of man, including civil and religious freedom. This makes the American nation different from the classical cities, in reference to which the classical authors defined justice. The relation between the American nation and those classical cities is different specifically in matters of religion, because their religions were particular to each city. The United States, by contrast, was founded after the birth of universal monotheism. Because of this, the American founders concluded that religion must be free. People in every country can claim to be Christians, for example, but the laws differ greatly from one country to the next. Christianity, which is explicit in claiming to set up no political system of its own, implies and requires therefore a limit on the law, a limit to prevent the law from obstructing the freedom to worship. The American founders conceived it a fundamental right of every human being to worship as he pleases, so long as he, in the words of George Washington, "demeans himself as a good citizen."[5]

Many conservatives have thought that the American regime was correct in making this arrangement. Some have not. Whoever is right about this, notice that it changes things very much if a thing so important as religion is to be free, a private matter for individual citizens to control as they please. The limit on the reach of the law implicit in this fact is of the first importance. It means that other things, like the ability to speak one's mind, or hold one's own property secure against unreasonable taking, or petition the government, also follow from the same idea. Our particular political regime is one of limited government, in which government is conceived to get its authority from the consent of the governed. We may not be governed rightly except on the basis of that consent.

---

5   Washington, "Letter to the Hebrew Congregation in Newport, Rhode Island 18 August 1790," in *The Papers of George Washington. Presidential Series*, Vol. 6, ed. Dorothy Twohig (Charlottesville: University Press of Virginia, 1996), 285: "It is now no more that toleration is spoken of, as if it were the indulgence of one class of people, that another enjoyed the exercise of their inherent natural rights. For happily the Government of the United States, which gives to bigotry no sanction, to persecution no assistance requires only that they who live under its protection should demean themselves as good citizens, in giving it on all occasions their effectual support." This is probably the first time, except in Israel, that Jews are addressed as equal citizens by a chief of state.

Liberalism Old and New

American conservatism begins, we have said, in opposition to modern American liberalism, and it is with the political form of this liberalism that American conservatism must contend when it enters politics. Therefore, to understand conservatism, we must understand this liberalism. This will involve us in understanding how this liberalism relates to the liberalism of the American Revolution, the liberalism to which Edmund Burke, whose followers became the first conservatives, was a friend. American conservatism does not, we have said, begin with its roots firmly, or anyway explicitly and by consensus, in the American Revolution. How does modern liberalism relate to the liberalism of the American Revolution?

In his "Publisher's Statement" in the founding issue of *National Review*, William Buckley identifies modern liberalism with history. This is apt. We may say that modern liberalism begins with a movement very much concerned with history, a movement called Progressivism that was born in the nineteenth century. The progressives had an insight, made available to them by the power of modern science. This insight is that history is a process, a process that changes everything. John Dewey, one of the leading progressives, writes:

> If we employ the conception of historic relativity, nothing is clearer than that the conception of liberty is always relative to forces that at a given time and place are increasingly felt to be oppressive.[6]

In other words, what we mean by liberty depends upon where and when we live, and what is pressing upon us in ways we do not like. Liberty in one time and place may not be the same as liberty in another. It depends upon what presses upon us and upon how we feel about it. Already we can see a certain contrast between the thought of John Dewey and the thought of Thomas Jefferson.

For progressives, these historical forces come to seem very powerful, so powerful in fact as to be commanding of human thought, even

---

6　John Dewey, *Liberalism and Social Action* (New York: Capricorn Books. 1963), 48.

of academic thought. This belief is made clear in the writings of Frank Goodnow, one of the founders of the American Political Science Association, a professor of politics at Columbia and later president of Johns Hopkins:

> We teachers perhaps take ourselves too seriously at times. That I am willing to admit. We may not have nearly the influence which we think we have. Changes in economic conditions, for which we are in no way responsible, bring in their train, regardless of what we teach, changes in beliefs and opinions. But if we are unable to exercise great influence in the institution of positive changes, we can, by acquainting ourselves with the changes in conditions and by endeavoring to accommodate our teaching to those changes, certainly refrain from impeding progress.[7]

See the struggle in this passage. Just before the passage Goodnow writes that educators have a "solemn responsibility," and he himself was one of the most influential educators of his age. But then he wonders whether "economic conditions" are so powerful as to be the real determinant of beliefs and opinions. His students may read what he assigns and hear as he lectures, but maybe they–and if they, then why not he? –will instead get their opinions from the experiences they have in getting their living. This is no certain endorsement of the freedom of the soul. It might even be read to diminish the value of all the observations of Professor Goodnow, himself. I said above that murderers have a voice of conscience in them that condemns the murder in their own mind. Professor Goodnow thinks it best for the teacher to accommodate his teaching to "conditions," so as not to impede "progress." "Conditions" seem to take the place of conscience and of truth. "Progress" seems to be whatever happens to be happening.

Mark the difference between these passages and, say, the Declaration of Independence. That document ends with a very particular and local

---

7   "The American Conception of Liberty" in *American Progressivism: A Reader*, eds. Ronald J. Pestritto and William J. Atto (Plymouth, UK: Lexington Books, 2008), 63.

kind of intensity: "In support of this Declaration we mutually pledge to each other our lives, our fortunes, and our sacred honor." People sometimes miss that this famous pledge is made by each person signing the Declaration, to each other person, and by all of them on behalf of the people they represent. This part reads, then, like a battlefield statement among soldiers, who do so often come to love one another in their adversity and find one part of their courage in that love. At the end the Declaration reads like the poetry of war.

The sentiments of Progressivism also differ from the sentiments expressed at the beginning of the Declaration, which is almost shy in speaking of any of the people involved in writing it, or even of their particular cause or country. "When in the course of human events," is a phrase transcending time. "It becomes necessary for one people," is a phrase transcending any particular place or people. The American people are taking up their cause at risk to themselves, to their lives, fortunes, and sacred honor. After all the King of England is among the most powerful of living men, and the Declaration is an act of treason against him, a hanging offense. As they do this, they think it necessary to pay a "decent respect to the opinions of mankind." In other words, they say that they must respect the opinions even of people who do not share their immediate circumstances nor feel their immediate pressures. They are long past justifying their actions under British law. They are repudiating that law. And so they find a kind of law often spoken of in the works of Hadley Arkes, "the laws of nature and of nature's God." This is the moral law, known to reason and to faith, claiming to apply everywhere that nature subsists and God reigns.

The "laws of nature and of nature's God" are not a subjective law, consisting in the way we feel about things, nor are they derived from the "conditions" we find around us, except in a very grand sense of that term "conditions." Rather, we have certain ways of feeling about things because we have this nature, this human nature. Our natural equality consists in the fact that we share this nature, however different we may be one from another in all other obvious respects. Horses, with a little training, get used to being ridden and even delight in it. Thomas Jefferson writes in his last letter, by way of explanation of the Declaration, that "Some men are not born with saddles on their backs, nor others booted and spurred to ride them by the grace of God."[8] Men do not get used to being ridden. It is not in our nature. "It is at once the glory and the safeguard of mankind," writes Winston Churchill, "that they are easy to lead and hard to drive."[9] It is then a provision of the "laws of nature and of nature's God" that one does not treat a man like a horse.

The Declaration is much concerned with the "conditions" or the circumstances in which the Founders are living, but it sees them in a universal and eternal light. Abraham Lincoln, one of the Declaration's greatest disciples, says of its author:

> All honor to Jefferson–to the man who, in the concrete pressure of a struggle for national independence by a single people, had the coolness, forecast, and capacity to introduce into a merely revolutionary document, an abstract truth, applicable to all men and all times, and so to embalm it there, that to-day, and in all coming days, it shall be a rebuke and a stumbling-block to the very harbingers of re-appearing tyranny and oppression.[10]

These progressives have a different outlook than the Founders, then, about the meaning of nature. For them, nature is a thing subject to the rules of history. One might say that for them history *is* nature. Nature is a process by which men struggle: struggle with their circumstances, struggle with the material nature from which they must get their living, and struggle with one another. In this struggle they change nature, and nature changes them. All things are in a state of development. Moreover, we humans, very much included in this process, have also gained a

8   "Letter to Roger C. Weightman, Monticello, June 24, 1826" in *Thomas Jefferson: Writings* (Merrill Peterson, ed., New York: The Library of America, 1984), 1517: "All eyes are opened, or are opening, to the rights of man. The general spread of the light of science has already laid open to every view the palpable truth, that the mass of mankind has not been born with saddles on their backs, nor a favored few booted and spurred, ready to ride them legitimately, by the grace of God. These are grounds of hope for others."
9   "Mass Effects in Modern Life" in Winston Churchill, *Thoughts and Adventures: Churchill Reflects on Spies, Cartoons, Flying, and the Future*, ed. James Muller, (Wilmington, DE: ISI Books, 2009), 273.
10   "To Henry L. Pierce and Others, Springfield, Ills. April 6, 1859" in *The Collected Works of Abraham Lincoln. Vol. 3*, ed. Roy Basler (New Brunswick, NJ: Rutgers University Press, 1953), 376.

power to stand outside it. Now we know, in a decisive discovery, the "nature" of the process. Now we know for example that when the Founders talked of the "laws of nature and of nature's God," they were really only saying something about their own time and circumstances.

Further, Progressivism teaches that the science that gives us an insight into the historical process also gives us a way to deal with it. We can alter it in our favor if we use the tools of science. If we apply the great discoveries of natural science to the organization of human affairs, we can make a better world for ourselves. This will require that we have a much more united, a much better organized, and much better directed effort than has been possible under the American form of government so far. Our Constitution itself is out of date. We have to find new ways to meet the new dangers arising in our age of science and industry, to meet the new knowledge arising in our age of scientific inquiry, and to meet the new opportunity arising in our ability to apply the tools of science to the way we live and are organized.

I say, "alter things in our favor." That raises a point that must be considered. It is not so hard to see how one might define what is "in our favor," if one thinks that a human being is a thing with a nature, a different nature from a horse, which also has a nature. It is also not so hard to see a definition of "in our favor" if he thinks "the fear of the LORD is clean, enduring for ever: the judgments of the LORD are true and righteous altogether."[11] In the one case, what favors us is what is in accord with our nature. In the other case, what favors us is the judgment of the Lord. In both cases, what favors us is the thing good for us, the thing that accords with our being, with our nature.

What if one thinks, as the progressives do, that history is a process of indeterminate end, a process that we ourselves can ultimately command? What then is the standard of right? Is it that we may do as please? Burke said once, "The effect of liberty to individuals is, that they do what they please: We ought to see what it will please them to do, before we risk congratulations."[12] Or consider the darkest possibilities: adherents of

11   Psalm 19:9 (KJV).
12   *Reflections on the Revolution in France* (New Rochelle, NY: Arlington House, 1965), 20.

the historical process in the Soviet Union, in the Third Reich, and in the Confederacy have all read history to command slavery and two of them genocide. These things were called "progress" and hailed as scientific in their basis. By what standard does one criticize these claims, if he confines himself to the historical process for his rules?

Woodrow Wilson, one of the most effective of the progressives in politics and the only man holding a doctorate to be elected president, was much trained in this new conception of history. He concluded from his studies that much about the American Revolution required alteration. Much of the altering needed to be done to things that are fundamental. He writes:

> The makers of our Federal Constitution read Montesquieu with true scientific enthusiasm. They were scientists in their way, – the best way of their age, – those fathers of the nation. Jefferson wrote of "the laws of Nature," – and then by way of afterthought, – "and of Nature's God." And they constructed a government as they would have constructed an orrery, – to display the laws of nature. Politics in their thought was a variety of mechanics. The Constitution was founded on the law of gravitation. The government was to exist and move by virtue of the efficacy of "checks and balances."
>
> The trouble with the theory is that government is not a machine, but a living thing. It falls, not under the theory of the universe, but under the theory of organic life. It is accountable to Darwin, not to Newton. It is modified by its environment, necessitated by its tasks, shaped to its functions by the sheer pressure of life. No living thing can have its organs offset against each other, as checks, and live.[13]

Here we reach the second major difference between these progressives and the American founders. They do not like checks and balances that restrain the operations of government. It is obvious, and the progressives by and large admit that it is obvious, that these checks and balances are for the Founders somewhere near the heart of the matter.

Moreover the Founders do not say that they are making a machine

---

13   *The New Freedom* (New York: Doubleday, Page & Company, 1918), 46–47.

nor describe the Constitution as a machine or a mechanism. It is nearer the truth to say that they see it as a microcosm for the order of nature, and they see its purpose to reflect in human affairs the way nature works particularly as it regards human beings. And how does nature regard human beings? Here we can turn to James Madison, one of the most important of the Founders.

Madison begins the 49th *Federalist Paper* by taking issue with a constitutional plan proposed by Thomas Jefferson for the state of Virginia. Jefferson wanted his constitution to be easy to amend. With great respect, Madison objects: every appeal to the people on a constitutional point would "carry an implication of some defect in the government." He writes, "Frequent appeals would, in a great measure, deprive the government of that veneration which time bestows on everything."[14] This, notice, is rather a conservative point, even if it comes from a revolutionary.

In other words, the Constitution is to be respected not only by those in the government, but by the people who have made the Constitution. The Founders took pride in the fact that ours is the first truly representative system. The sovereign, the people, is located outside government, and they rule only through representatives. They make directly but one law, the Constitution itself, and they make that by a ratification process that disappears after one use. The Constitution is then outside the ordinary will both of its servants in the government and the sovereign outside the government. It can be altered only by an amendment process that is difficult to complete and has, as was intended, been rarely used.

The fundamental reason for this arrangement is explained by Madison toward the end of the 49th *Federalist*. If appeals were made to the people constantly to decide constitutional matters, then those contending would have reason to stir up the people. And then, Madison writes, the "*passions*, therefore, not the *reason*, of the public would sit in judgment. But it is the reason, alone, of the public, that ought to control and regulate the government. The passions ought to be controlled and regulated by the government."[15]

14   *The Federalist Papers, ed.* Clinton Rossiter (New York: Penguin, 2003), 311.
15   Ibid. 314.

This formulation is little other than the classical prescription for the good order of the soul, reason commanding the passions until ultimately they come to work together. One can see then that the purpose of the Constitution is not only effective action. There are many passages in the document designed to produce, for example, energy in the executive, the ability to act suddenly and with effect particularly in war. The document is also balanced so as to constrain every use of power, whether by the government or even by the people, so as to achieve so far as possible the direction of power toward the good alone. In this, Madison's view seems both to anticipate Wilson's argument and refute it. This disjunction between the founding position and the progressive position is evident.

Not only the proper ordering of the human soul, but also the proper order in nature, is reflected in the design of the Constitution. Madison writes that in organizing the departments of government and maintaining their separateness, "the interest of the man must be connected with the constitutional rights of the place."[16] Human beings have interests, and government must be arranged so that their interests, especially when connected to their passions, do not undermine the "permanent and aggregate"[17] interest of the public. This Madison says is a "reflection on human nature."[18] And he continues in a famous passage:

> But what is government itself, but the greatest of all reflections on human nature? If men were angels, no government would be necessary. If angels were to govern men, neither external nor internal controls on government would be necessary.[19]

This enriches our picture of the Constitution and also of the meaning of human equality. We have seen that men are not like horses, and they may not be ridden without their consent. Also they are not angels, and they may not then be trusted with the powers that would be safe only in the hands of angels. (In the Declaration of Independence God is mentioned four times, including once in each of the branches of

16   Ibid. *Federalist* 51, 319.
17   Ibid. *Federalist* 10, 72.
18   Ibid. *Federalist* 51, 319.
19   Ibid. *Federalist* 51, 319.

government. The implication is that the powers of government could all be combined in the hands of God, but not in the hands of any king, not indeed in the hands of any man.)

Franklin Roosevelt and Patriotic Progressivism

This also points up the essential weakness in American progressivism. It was born in opposition to the great doctrines of the American Revolution, to the doctrines under which the first truly self-governing people became also the most powerful and also the most influential people on earth. It was born in opposition to the Constitution under which those people lived, the most successful of all written constitutions. The American people have not been quick, not even today, to abandon this heritage.

Progressivism began to find its success in politics when it began to find ways to cope with this problem. The key was fashioned by the master locksmith, the longest serving of our presidents, the president most commonly ranked by historians along with Washington and Lincoln as the best and most influential. The key was made by Franklin Delano Roosevelt, and the lock he sought to fit protected the Founding from his influence. Or, as his advocates might say, it liberated the ideas of the Founding to persevere in the modern age when they might have been extinguished, indeed even to rise to heights unimagined by the Founders. He fashioned the key for its first use in the fall of 1932, just more than a month before he was elected President of the United States for the first time. It appears first in his famous Commonwealth Club Address,[20] a campaign address in that well-known club in San Francisco. This speech forms the challenge that conservatism must face if it is to conserve, in their original meaning, the political ideas and practices of America.

The Commonwealth Address tells a story of history, just as so many progressive tracts do. In this story, the American people and the

---

20 "'New Conditions Impose New Requirements on Government and Those Who Conduct Government.' Campaign Address on Progressive Government at the Commonwealth Club, San Francisco, Calif. September 23, 1932" in *The Public Papers and Addresses of Franklin D. Roosevelt. Vol. 1* (New York: Russell & Russell, 1969), 742–756.

people of Europe before them have been coping with obstacles to their freedom and security. At each stage they have required a different kind of government, and a different kind of leader, in order to cope. Frequently "ruthless men"[21] have been required to secure as much of the well being of the people as was available. The great advance of the American Revolution, Roosevelt continues, was to secure for the people their rights of "personal competency,"[22] meaning their civil rights, freedom of speech and of worship, for example. These rights help them to solve the problem of oppressive government, of the individual against the system. For a long time, these rights were sufficient.

Now we live, continues Roosevelt, in the industrial age. Now accumulations of private wealth have raised up a new form of oppression. Now we understand that our right to our property, which is fundamental, requires the protection of the government. "Every man has a right to his property; which means the right to be assured, to the fullest extent attainable, in the safety of his savings."[23] No longer can a citizen exercise self-government by safeguarding his own property; it must be protected, and regulated, by academic and bureaucratic officials. In order to ensure its safety, wealth must be distributed more equitably, and the influence of malefactors of great wealth must be restricted.

Here we have the language of the American Revolution retained, deployed, but also adapted. The rights of "personal competency" are still treasured, but they will be surpassed. The right to property takes on, at least at first glance, a greater security. The government must have greater latitude to protect this right than it has previously held or exercised. This means that the property in the hands of an individual American may be taken for equitable distribution by the government, but in the name of security of the property of all. Roosevelt was speaking to a group including many rich men, and he is speaking during the great Depression. They have grown accustomed to such references as "malefactors of great wealth"[24] (Roosevelt is quoting his distant cousin,

---

21 Ibid., 744. Various forms of the word ruthless are used four times in the speech; it has an atmosphere, let us say, of a certain determination.
22 Ibid., 746.
23 Ibid., 754.
24 Ibid., 749.

Republican president Theodore Roosevelt). They will have seen this as a warning of what may be coming. But his talk of the security of their property must also have been reassuring. Roosevelt closes:

> Faith in America, faith in our tradition of personal responsibility, faith in our institutions, faith in ourselves demand that we recognize the new terms of the old social contract. We shall fulfill them, as we fulfilled the obligation of the apparent Utopia which Jefferson imagined for us in 1776, and which Jefferson, Roosevelt and Wilson sought to bring to realization. We must do so, lest a rising tide of misery, engendered by our common failure, engulf us all. But failure is not an American habit; and in the strength of great hope we must all shoulder our common load.[25]

If Jefferson were alive, Roosevelt implies, he would do what Roosevelt does. If property is to be protected, it must also be surrendered in part to the government. If the Constitution is to abide, it must adapt. The government must have new powers to achieve old ends. This is made necessary by the impending collapse of the old practices, overwhelmed by the challenges of the new day. It is justified by the grand opportunity available now in the present to seize a brighter future.

It is not hard to see why this effort would have been so successful. It is one of those brilliant things that others might later wonder why it did not come to them. We do not have to upend the successes before us; we must build upon them. This was latent in the idea of progressivism from the beginning, but now it is developed into an explicit political strategy. The strength of the American regime becomes the foundation of change. Winston Churchill notices how much better the European cousins of progressivism are able to do in politics when they get nearer the real basis of politics.

> As long as Socialists present themselves in an international guise as creators of a new world order, like the beehive or the ant heap, with a new human heart to fit these noble conceptions, they could

---

25   Ibid. 756.

easily be beaten, and have been very effectively beaten both by argument and by nature. But when new forms of socialism arose which were grafted not upon world ideals but upon the strongest forms of nationalism, their success was remarkable.[26]

The language of the nation is powerful among its citizens, at least in any nation not decaying. It is more powerful still if that country happens to be the United States, the majesty of whose political vocabulary and the success of whose political practices have been "a stumbling block to the harbingers of reappearing tyranny" in every age since they were first made known.

Roosevelt was presented with a crisis, and like his followers today he did not let it go to waste. His plans for addressing it were sweeping, but they were described as ordinary and regular, in keeping with the best that had gone before, but somehow also a significant and necessary change. This change would sacrifice nothing good that we have held dear, but rather expand and improve all that and make it finally secure. Whereas, if new policies were not adopted and new rights secured, the old ones, including our property, would be sacrificed.

Thoughtful progressivism still dwells upon these ideas today, and it makes its final redoubt at the life and career of Roosevelt. This is well-chosen, and it makes contemporary liberalism formidable to political conservatism in ways that are apparent in politics all around us. This

---

26 Winston S. Churchill, "What Good Is a Constitution?" in *Collier's* 98.8 (August 22, 1936): 22, 39–40. Churchill was an admirer and for years a close partner with Roosevelt in their most monumental of tasks, the prosecution of the greatest war in history as partners. Churchill does not in the speech call Roosevelt a socialist, nor I think intend that. He publishes this essay in the United States during the controversy with the Supreme Court that would lead Roosevelt to propose his court-packing plan in the following year. Churchill takes sides with the fixity of the American Constitution in this article and with the court. He also writes: "In the United States, also, economic crisis has led to an extension of the activities of the Executive and to the pillorying, by irresponsible agitators, of certain groups and sections of the population as enemies of the rest. There have been efforts to exalt the power of the central government and to limit the rights of individuals. It has been sought to mobilize behind this reversal of the American tradition, at once the selfishness of the pensioners, or would-be pensioners, of Washington, and the patriotism of all who wish to see their country prosperous once more."

argument, the argument of Roosevelt, is likely to be the battleground upon which the future of the nation is decided.

The student of politics in America today would do well to focus his attention here, upon this question. Has Roosevelt succeeded in making the principles of America compatible with modern, centralized, bureaucratic government? Is such a government necessary to achieve justice in the conditions that prevail today? Or is it rather still the case that, men not being angels, and angels not governing men, internal and external controls on the government are urgently required and must not be left to the ebb and flow of the politics of the day. Political conservatives answer this question in the affirmative. This makes them followers of the Founding in a more literal or strict sense than modern liberals.

Ronald Reagan

Politics requires not only thinking, but especially doing. The great question is always how to proceed. The essence of politics is choosing. What is political conservatism to do? The answer might be found in its own greatest success.

Interestingly, the first issue of *National Review* does not take a position upon the American principles, or Roosevelt's still recent redefinition of them. It contains a litany, written with power and foresight, of the evils of liberalism and the tendencies it sets up in government. These include the destruction of the free market, the inability to oppose communist tyrannies, and the threat to individual rights constituted by "Social Engineers, who seek to adjust mankind to conform with scientific utopias."[27]

Neither in the "Publisher's Statement," nor in another statement immediately following entitled "The Magazine's Credenda," is there any explicit reference to American institutions in particular, or mention of any idea or institution, as being exclusively American. Conservatives have reached a wide agreement on the principles expounded in this first issue of *National Review*, but this agreement has not always extended to things fundamentally American. This is a significant problem for

27   *National Review* 1.1 (19 November 1955): 6.

understanding political conservatism in general and understanding American conservatism in American politics.

But while conservatism in America may not have begun with its focus upon the principles and institutions of the United States, the political debate has a way of directing attention there. One need only look at the phenomenon of the "Tea Party" to see how the ideas of the Founding can rise to the surface suddenly and capture the imagination of millions. Political conservatism has been able, at the peak of its influence, to seize upon this phenomenon and give voice to it. It did this especially in the person of Ronald Reagan, the president closest to the conservative movement and one of the most successful presidents of any persuasion of the modern era. He is the supreme expression of conservatism in politics. As with Roosevelt, so with Reagan, we can find the key elements of his strategy in a single speech. Consider Reagan's first speech as president, his First Inaugural Address.

An inaugural address is a high public occasion. It has a constitutional standing similar to the State of the Union, or Annual, messages of the president. State of the Union messages are called for explicitly in the Constitution; inaugural addresses have emerged naturally from the fact that the Constitution requires the president to take an oath before he commences his office. The oath is important. In Article II, the Constitution provides its text verbatim:

> Before he [the president] enter on the Execution of his Office, he shall take the following Oath or Affirmation: – "I do solemnly swear (or affirm) that I will faithfully execute the Office of President of the United States, and will to the best of my Ability, preserve, protect and defend the Constitution of the United States."[28]

The oath is a separate requirement, in addition to the requirements of age, citizenship, residence, native birth, and election stated in the Constitution. Its effect is to enroll the personal honor of the president in the execution of his office and to give him distinct, personal and separate commitments to the Constitution. Because the oath is a condition

28 Article II. Section 1.

of holding the office, its taking must be witnessed. If there is to be a ceremony of witnessing, then it follows that the man taking the oath might give a speech, the speech influenced by the constitutional act for which the witnesses have assembled. In practice all presidents have given such a speech,[29] and the speeches are remarkably similar in length and scope. For this reason, a line of continuity runs from George Washington to the inauguration of Barack Obama. Because of this, the United States, so young in many ways, is also the oldest of countries, possessed of the oldest continuous constitutional practices.

Reagan was inaugurated on January 20, 1981. He was the first president to hold his inauguration on the west side of the capital, the side looking out upon the National Mall. It has become a more common practice since then. Reagan's speech is from the first word to the last a speech about the greatness of self-government, and so he begins as portraying himself as a servant. Consider this opening:

> To a few of us here today this is a solemn and most momentous occasion, and yet in the history of our nation it is a commonplace occurrence. The orderly transfer of authority as called for in the Constitution routinely takes place, as it has for almost two centuries, and few of us stop to think how unique we really are. In the eyes of many in the world, this every-four-year ceremony we accept as normal is nothing less than a miracle.[30]

The point of the ceremony is not "his" presidency. For Reagan, his family, and his friends the occasion is "solemn and momentous"; in the life of the nation, and to the glory of the nation, it is a commonplace. Reagan succeeds others; others still will come later to succeed him.

As so many of our recent presidents have done, Reagan begins by describing economic difficulty. His point about them refers to self-government: "The economic ills we suffer . . . will go away because we as Americans have the capacity now, as we've had in the past, to do whatever needs to be done to preserve this last and greatest bastion of freedom." Government, he says, is not "in this present crisis" "the solution

---

29   Except, of course, for those presidents without an Inauguration: John Tyler, Millard Fillmore, Chester Arthur and Gerald Ford.

30   Reagan, Ronald. *Speaking My Mind* (New York: Simon and Schuster, 1989), 60.

to our problem." "Society has [not] become too complex to be managed by self-rule."[31]

Then, a paraphrase of Lincoln[32]: ". . . If no one among us is capable of governing himself, who among us has the capacity to govern someone else?"

In the name of this idea of self-government, Reagan takes on directly the policy of progressivism to expand the federal government as an instrument of scientific management. "It is my intention to curb the size and influence of the federal establishment and to demand recognition of the distinction between the powers granted to the federal government and those reserved to the states or to the people."[33] Reagan will return to the constitutional forms. They will command us today as they commanded our fathers. They are not superseded by the new conditions; on the contrary, they are the key to coping with the new conditions. It is not in the expertise of the elite, but in the energy of the ordinary, that the genius of America lies: "If we look to the answer as to why, for so many years, which you so much, prospered as no other people on earth, it was because here, in this land, we unleash the energy and individual genius of man to a greater extent than has ever been done before."[34]

The power of self-government is the key to American foreign-policy as well. "As we renew ourselves here in our own land, we will be seen as having greater strength throughout the world. We will again be the exemplar of freedom and a beacon of hope for those who do not now have freedom."[35] And "above all, we must realize that no arsenal or no weapon in the arsenals of the world is so formidable as the will and moral courage of free men and women. It is a weapon our adversaries in today's world do not have."[36]

From this, Reagan proceeds to the task that led him to move

31 Ibid., 61.
32 Lincoln: "As I would not be a slave, so I would not be a master. This expresses my idea of democracy." (*The Collected Works of Abraham Lincoln*, Vol. 2, 532).
33 Reagan, 62.
34 Ibid., 62–3.
35 Ibid., 64.
36 Ibid., 65.

ceremony around to the side of the Capitol commanding a view of the National Mall. He takes us on a tour.

First he speaks of George Washington: "Father of our country, a man of humility who came to greatness reluctantly"; Then he says of Thomas Jefferson: "The Declaration of Independence flames with his eloquence"; and of Abraham Lincoln: "Whoever would understand in his heart the meaning of America will find it in the life of Abraham Lincoln."[37]

Then we cross the Potomac to the Arlington National Cemetery. There we see "row on row of simple white markers bearing crosses or Stars of David," which add up to only "a tiny fraction of the price that has been paid for our freedom." Each one of these markers "is a monument to the kind of hero I spoke of earlier." Reagan to this point has spoken of two kinds of heroes, everyday Americans working, producing, raising families, and those to whom the great monuments are dedicated. In naming his last hero, Reagan connects the two.

Under one of the markers at Arlington, Reagan continues, lies a young man "who left his job in a small town barbershop in 1917 to go to France with the famed Rainbow Division. There, on the western front, he was killed. . . ." On his body was found a diary, and on the flyleaf a pledge entitled "My Pledge." Reagan reads it:

> America must win this war. Therefore I will work, I will save, I will sacrifice, I will endure, I will fight cheerfully and do my utmost, as if the issue of the whole struggle depended on me alone.[38]

Here Reagan uses words from the heart of a citizen soldier to reach into the heart of every citizen. Its power comes from the longing of every man to serve the good intrinsic to his own being; as the Philosopher writes: "It has been beautifully said that the good is that at which all things aim."[39] We are the beings empowered to carry this knowledge and act upon it of our own volition, responsible under God for the goodness

---

37   Ibid., 65–66.
38   Ibid., 660.
39   Aristotle, *Nichomachean Ethics*, trans. Joe Sachs (Newburyport, MA: Focus Publishing, 2002), 1.

of our works. This is the appeal of self-government. It does not regiment according to a human contrivance from science or administration. It forms an army of volunteers. The success of Reagan wells up from the place where the original and the essential in man are first identified.

This is American political conservatism operating at its peak. It thrives by recovering the first things about this country. It finds both the freedom and the dignity of man in the same place, in his natural equality below the angels and above the beasts. As the Declaration of Independence is the greatest proclamation of this truth, so the Constitution is its greatest shield. Conservatism must smite with that truth and guard with that shield. There is the calling for which it was appointed, even before its knowledge became full with the wisdom of experience.

Chapter 2:
Lincoln and Justice for All
Allen C. Guelzo

Justice is the concern of everyone, but the property of no one, at least humanly speaking. It is, fundamentally, a relationship – of people to each other, of parts to a whole, of balance between people and parts – in which the two great goals in view are that of *satisfaction* and that of *harmony*. In a putatively just world, people are satisfied with what they have (either by use or possession or both), what they do (in terms of love and work), and where they are (both as physical location and where they perceive themselves in relation to other people's social and economic standing). But satisfaction is not the whole story; it is, after all, possible to be satisfied and at the same time disgruntled, if we feel that our satisfactions are simply compromises with a reality we do not otherwise applaud. Nor is satisfaction permanent – what satisfies at one point in the life of an individual or a society may pale and disintegrate at another. What is required for justice is, alongside satisfaction, *harmony*. It is a kind of universal aesthetic, a species of beauty and complacency whose ultimate location is in the being of God. We must have the sense that the arrangements of justice are not only satisfactory for ourselves, but satisfactory to us in what is granted to, or achieved by, others. Our own satisfactions may mean little if we perceive that others' satisfactions are promoted beyond our own, and we will soon begin to regard as unjust the arrangements which allowed this to happen; at that moment, we will begin to agitate for some kind of redress, and there will go harmony out the window. Or, we will begin to fear that, if others' satisfactions have been discounted to a level lower than our own, these "others" will one day take some action to reverse the situation, such as robbery or revolution. The first victim of this fear, likewise, is harmony.

Unhappily for any political order, both satisfaction and harmony have subjective and objective aspects. The wealthy miser may be tormented by the anxiety for acquiring more wealth, and his perception that his increasing wealth is being threatened by some external force leads him into suspicion and litigation, leaving him with neither satisfaction nor harmony, but an abiding sense of the injustice of things. The operator of the village smithy, on the other hand, whose

> . . . brow is wet with honest sweat,
> He earns whate'er he can,
> And looks the whole world in the face,
> For he owes not any man. . . .[1]

may be blithely content with his "flaming forge" and his daily routine of "something attempted, something done," and this gives him his "night's repose" – irrespective of the greater engines of finance, acquisition and consumption all around him which have been fleecing the blacksmith (and his kind) of the true value of their labor. The miser looks at his own over-compensated life, and calls it injustice; the blacksmith looks at his under-compensated one, and enjoys both satisfaction and harmony. And above them both floats the philosopher, who tells them, alternately:

(a) that the world (or the nation, or the society, or the neighbor hood) is a conspiracy to defraud which he and the miser have both rightly descried;

(b) that the world (and so forth) is a conspiracy to defraud whichever one of them is too stupid and blinded by hegemonic false-consciousness to perceive without the epiphany of revolutionary self-consciousness, or

(c) that the world (yet again) is a conspiracy to defraud about which nothing can really be done, but the denunciation of which the philosopher can use as a means of achieving his own version of satisfaction and harmony, preferably as the occupant of an endowed chair in political or economic theory.

1   Henry Wadsworth Longfellow, "The Village Blacksmith," in *Ballads and Other Poems* (Cambridge, MA: John Owen, 1841), 100.

With such subjectivity standing like a veil between justice and the experience of injustice, we might well consign all hope of recognizing justice to the same category as that other famous item which we can't define, but which we know when we see it.

But only if we ourselves are also philosophers. There are at least two practical ways of cutting the subjective knot and confecting a universal solution to this dilemma of what makes for justice. One is by *power*. We may erect a structural standard of justice, without any particular regard for anything inherently consistent, limiting or painful about its parts or its application, and compel a submission to this standard so overwhelming that there will be no choice but to find in it satisfaction and harmony. This is the justice of the straitjacket, in which dissatisfaction is regarded as a trait of mental illness and dissonance as a crime. It requires endless labor, because it is entirely reactive in nature, but no work, because everyone is satisfied and everything is in harmony. In this environment, injustice eventually becomes impossible because it has been definitionally abolished. Ordinarily, given the fissiparous nature of human behavior, this might not strike us as very "practical," but in fact, modern technology (not to mention pharmacology) is making it more achievable, and our lives less human, day-by-day.

The other method is by *law*: we may create a functional standard of justice which requires only logical adherence, and then walk away, resorting only to power for the deployment and enforcement of the legal code. A society cannot dispense entirely with power in its government; otherwise, law becomes shredded by those who worship *mere* power. Let the law and its officers operate, and in a predictable and routine pattern, and let what results from that operation be deemed *harmony*. In that way, even the worst examples of law-codes produce more harmony than does mere power. The fundamental problem is that law frequently falls far short of granting *satisfaction*. Of course, one out of two ain't bad; and sometimes and in some societies, you do succeed in getting both. Unhappily, law also depends for its application on that same fissiparous human nature, to the point where law can become merely a mask for power. One can get Cincinnatus, using an emergency donation of power to restore law; or one can get Caesar, using an emergency donation of power to destroy it. At that moment, vexed and righteous souls become convinced that law is a crook, and that they need to invoke power in order to provide satisfaction and harmony. True, there has been more than enough evil done by power; but power, some believe, can be de-fanged if it is exercised on behalf of *fairness*, an even more subjective precept which suggests that power, in the right hands, can work miracles of justice which law cannot.

There is a third way, which is not a solution, but rather an intellectual palliative, and that is *anarchy*, which fears power, and yet also nurses deep suspicions of law. But anarchy (and its milder, libertarian forms) only has the appearance of justice – it secures only the immediate satisfaction of having no restraint, and the immediate harmony of having no one but yourself to enjoy it with. After the first 24 hours, or the first 24 visitors with semi-automatic weapons, either power or law get called into service, simply in the interest of taking a secure breath – or any breath at all.

This, in less than a thousand words, is the history of thought about justice. Thrasymachus (in Plato's *Republic*), Calhoun, Marx and Hobbes believed that justice was the operation of power, and lived entirely within history. They were suspicious. Locke, J.S. Mill and Hayek believed it was the operation of law, based on an overarching natural law which was eternal. They were earnest. As for American thinkers, power has held more attraction than we might imagine, especially when its aim can be designated as "fairness" and its harmony identified with "disinterested benevolence" or "the Beloved Community." But Americans have always been people of two souls, one the soul of the Puritan and the other the soul of the Enlightenment, at once both suspicious and earnest. Speaking for law and the Enlightenment and the containment of power were the Founders of the Republic, and the "second founder" who saved it from self-destruction, Abraham Lincoln.

Abraham Lincoln certainly had more than a little to say about justice. Frequently, he used the word to mean something like a rough-and-ready tit-for-tat. In dealing out political patronage, he promised Lyman Trumbull, his fellow Illinois Republican, that "I will, myself, take care of the question of 'corrupt jobs' and see that justice is done to all, our friends, of whom you write, as well as others."[2] In hailing the Union victory at the battle of Antietam in 1862, he praised how "bravely, skillfully and successfully fought the battle had been," but because he did not yet "know the particulars," he wanted to be "sure that in giving praise to particular individuals, we do no injustice to others."[3] And a few weeks later, he had to assure the laggardly Major-General George B. McClellan that "I intend no injustice to any" for sarcastically querying why McClellan's "cavalry horses were too much fatigued to move." McClellan's inertia "presented a very cheerless, almost hopeless, prospect for the future; and it may have forced something of impatience into my despatches."[4] Justice, in this *petit* sense, was about decorum, politeness, and giving newsworthy credit to the nation's servants.

Sometimes, however, the tit-for-tat could rise to something more than the rough-and-ready. Massachusetts Congressman John B. Alley remembered presenting Lincoln with a petition from his district to pardon the master of a "vessel engaged in the slave- trade" who had "served out his term of imprisonment, but could not pay his fine." The prisoner added his own "urgent and pathetic appeal, . . . acknowledging the crime and the justice of the sentence, and declaring that he must spend his life in prison if the condition of freedom was the payment of that fine, for he had not a cent in the world." Lincoln read the documents over, and pushed them back at Alley. "I believe I am kindly enough in nature . . . to pardon the perpetrator of almost the worst creme that the mind of man can conceive," Lincoln said, "but any man . . . who can rob Africa of her children to sell into interminable bondage, I never will pardon, and he may stay and rot in jail before he will get relief from me."[5]

But justice could also mean a more universal, all-embracing balancing of what was right and what was wrong. The presidential action

---

2   "To Lyman Trumbull" (December 8, 1860), in *Collected Works of Abraham Lincoln*, ed. Roy P. Basler et al (New Brunswick: Rutgers University Press, 1953), 4:148.

3   "Reply to Serenade in Honor of Emancipation Proclamation" (September 24, 1862), in *C.W.*, 5:438.

4   "To George B. McClellan" (October 27, 1862), in *C.W.*, 5:479.

5   John B. Alley, in Rice, *Reminiscences of Abraham Lincoln*, 583.

he deemed "the central act of my administration and the great event
of the nineteenth century" – namely, the Emancipation Proclamation
of January 1, 1863 – was declared by him to be "an act of justice" on
whibch he confidently invoked "the considerate judgment of
mankind, and the gracious favor of Almighty God."[6] He aggressively
defended the use of military tribunals and suspending the writ of
habeas corpus as legitimate acts of justice because the ordinary civil
courts were unequal to the tasks presented by full-scale insurrection
and sedition:

> Nothing is better known to history than that courts of justice are
> utterly incompetent to such cases. Civil courts are organized
> chiefly for trials of individuals, or, at most, a few individuals act-
> ing in concert; and this in quiet times, and on charges of crimes
> well defined in the law. Even in times of peace, bands of horse-
> thieves and robbers frequently grow too numerous and powerful
> for the ordinary courts of justice. But what comparison, in num-
> bers, have such bands ever borne to the insurgent sympathizers
> even in many of the loyal states?

In time of peace, interference with political dissent would be an injustice; in time of war, not to interfere with political dissent would be
treachery. "He who dissuades one man from volunteering, or induces
one soldier to desert, weakens the Union cause as much as he who kills
a union soldier in battle. Yet this dissuasion, or inducement, may be so
conducted as to be no defined crime of which any civil court would
take cognizance." Lincoln would be obligated under military law to
"shoot a simple-minded solider boy who deserts," while the civil courts
insist "I must not touch a hair of a wiley aligator who induces him to
desert." In the time of war, he asked, was this justice?[7]

Questions about the varying levels of justice came readily to Lincoln
because he was, after all, a lawyer by profession, so that determining the
justice or injustice of human affairs was a daily responsibility. "My way

6   Francis B. Carpenter, *Six Months at the White House with Abraham Lincoln: The
     Story of a Picture* (New York: Hurd & Houghton, 1867), 90; "Emancipation
     Proclamation" (January 1, 1863), in *C.W.*, 6:30.
7   "To Erastus Corning and Others" (June 12, 1863), in *C.W.*, 6:264.

of living leads me to be about the courts of justice," he said in 1848, although he admitted that not everything he saw there actually lived up to the name of justice. "There, I have sometimes seen a good lawyer, struggling for his client's neck, in a desperate case, employing every artifice to work round, befog, and cover up, with many words, some point arising in the case, which he dared not admit, and yet could not deny."[8] Lincoln was also, by avocation, a politician, and there, too, he had more than a few opportunities to see the making of laws fall far short of the glory of justice. In the proceedings of legislatures (and Lincoln sat in the Illinois state legislature from 1834 to 1842, so he spoke with authority), it was too often the case that "the immutable principles of justice are to make way for party interests, and the bonds of social order are to be rent in twain, in order that a desperate faction may be sustained at the expense of the people."[9]

In 1841, Illinois Democrats tried to ram a restructuring of the state judiciary through the state Assembly. Lincoln found the intention of the restructuring so nakedly self-serving (and so little interested in the establishment of justice) that even members of the Democratic caucus rebelled against stacking "the temples of justice and the seats of independent judges" with "the tools of faction." Lincoln saw this for what it was, even on that comparatively small-scale stage – the substitution of power for law. The pursuit of justice was being swept aside to make way for "an arbitrary exercise of power which may soon become the precedent for still more flagrant violations of right and justice." The most "baneful and miserable . . . tendencies of this measure," however, would be the way the taint of power, exercised in one branch of government, would soon infect them all. Politically stacked courts were politically predictable courts, where verdicts were obtained first and evidence mustered later, so that nothing they decided could really be trusted to be just. Without the restraint of the courts, the legislature would feel free to open the floodgates to self-interest, corruption, and a lethal fog of cynicism which would spread over all of the body politic, "since

8   "Speech in United States House of Representatives: The War with Mexico" (January 12, 1848), in *C.W.*, 1:438.
9   "Circular from Whig Committee Against the Judiciary Bill" (February [8?], 1841), in *C.W.*, 1: 246.

our courts, if not corrupt, must be suspected, and the streams of justice tinged, if not by the impurity of the fountain, by the jaundiced vision of the beholder."[10]

But the ultimate threat posed to the health of a democracy by the "jaundice" of power was not merely a lapsing into indifference (although in a democracy, where sovereignty lay in the hands of the people, popular cynicism and indifference certainly promised a slow erosion of the vigor necessary to sustain it). Where power replaced the operation of justice, then the victimized would themselves resort to power in self-defense (or self-justification), and the operation of a democracy would all-too-rapidly degenerate into the violence and anarchy of armed mobs. "I hope I am over wary," he warned in 1838, after a series of high-profile mob actions in the towns of the upper Mississippi valley, but it was no sign of robust health in a democracy

> whenever the vicious portion of population shall be permitted to gather in bands of hundreds and thousands, and burn churches, ravage and rob provision stores, throw printing presses into rivers, shoot editors, and hang and burn obnoxious persons at pleasure, and with impunity.

"Depend on it," Lincoln predicted: when power supplants law, "this Government cannot last." When a popular government shows that it is incapable of governing itself by law, and "in lieu of the sober judgement of Courts" allows "worse than savage mobs" to function as "the executive ministers of justice," then "the feelings of the best citizens will become more or less alienated from it; and thus it will be left without friends, or with too few, and those few too weak, to make their friendship effectual." It has the effect of a fall of dominoes: let the rulers govern themselves by self-interest rather than law, then do not be surprised when the people in the streets decide to do the same thing, whether as vigilantes or as rioters. And do not be surprised, either, that "the best citizens," recoiling from the unrestrained tumult in the streets, turn their backs on popular government itself and turn to "men of sufficient talent and ambition" who will be happy to restore order through their own

10   Ibid, 1:236, 247.

exercise of power, "and overturn that fair fabric, which for the last half century, has been the fondest hope, of the lovers of freedom, throughout the world." Law, in effect, became a religion for Lincoln.

> Let reverence for the laws, be breathed by every American mother, to the lisping babe, that prattles on her lap – let it be taught in schools, in seminaries, and in colleges; – let it be written in Primmers, spelling books, and in Almanacs; – let it be preached from the pulpit, proclaimed in legislative halls, and enforced in courts of justice. And, in short, let it become the political religion of the nation; and let the old and the young, the rich and the poor, the grave and the gay, of all sexes and tongues, and colors and conditions, sacrifice unceasingly upon its altars.[11]

For all of his anxieties about the allure of power, Lincoln never lost his faith in either law or politics to light the way to justice. John P. Usher, who sat in Lincoln's cabinet as Secretary of the Interior, believed that "Mr. Lincoln's greatness was founded upon his devotion to truth, his humanity and his innate sense of justice to all."[12] He had little in the way of religious faith apart from what looked to most observers like a form of secularized Calvinism; but like many of the Founders, Lincoln made up for this loss with an intensified commitment to natural honor and obligation. Joseph Gillespie, his longtime political ally in Illinois, thought that "Mr. Lincoln's love of justice & fair play was his predominating trait." This was especially true inside the courtroom, where it was no legend that Lincoln was nearly incapable of defending a position he was convinced was not just. "It was not in his nature to assume or attempt to bolster up a false position. He would abandon his case first," Gillespie wrote in 1866; in fact, Gillespie had "often listened to him when I thought he would certainly state his case out of court." Judge David Davis, who presided over Lincoln's old 8th Judicial Circuit in Illinois, recalled that Lincoln "thought that his duty to his client Extended to what was honorable and high minded – just and noble – nothing further." He was no more

11   "Address Before the Young Men's Lyceum of Springfield, Illinois" (January 27, 1838), in *C.W.*, 1:109.
12   J.P. Usher, "Lincoln and Slavery," in Rice, *Reminiscences of Abraham Lincoln*, 77.

likely to attempt lawyerly sleights-of-hand on his opponents, either. Judge Davis said that "the meanest man in the bar would always pay great deference & respect to Lincoln" because "he never took advantage of a man's low character to prejudice the Jury."[13]

This pursuit of legal rectitude won Lincoln widespread respect, but not necessarily widespread affection, especially among friends and clients who wanted to win in either law or politics – and expected him to resort to any tricks available to do so – rather than merely to be right. Being right, as Gillespie remarked, meant that Lincoln "was by some considered cold hearted or at least indifferent towards his friends" because he "He would rather disoblige a friend than do an act of injustice to a political opponent."[14] The ordinary lawyer, observed another long-time legal associate on the 8th Circuit, Henry Clay Whitney, would allow "the current of details and exigencies" to "jostle" him one way or the other, but Lincoln "stood upright through all contingencies, and nothing could swerve him from the observance of rigid, exact, unerring justice." This did not mean that Lincoln believed he possessed some godlike perception of justice in all circumstances and all cases, and "of course," added Whitney, "if there was a margin for doubt, he used the usual advantages incident to his side as any other lawyer would."[15] But in what Whitney called "conclusive cases," Lincoln seemed almost morally unable to make dark appear light. "The main question with Mr. Lincoln was: 'Is the thing right, is it just?'" remembered Lincoln's law partner of 14 years, William Henry Herndon.

> If a man was the subject of his attention, the question which he put to himself was: "What great truth, what principle, do you represent in this world?" If the thing was just, he approved of it, and if the man was a sham, he said: "Begone." He was a man of great moral

---

13 Joseph Gillespie to William H. Herndon (January 31, 1866) and David Davis (September 20, 1866), in *Herndon's Informants: Letters, Interviews and Statements About Abraham Lincoln*, eds. R.O. Davis and D.L. Wilson (Urbana: University of Illinois Press, 1998), 182, 351.

14 Joseph Gillespie to William H. Herndon (December 8, 1866), in *Herndon's Informants*, 507.

15 Whitney, *Life on the Circuit with Lincoln*, ed. Paul Angle (Caldwell, ID: Caxton Printers, 1940), 240.

and physical courage and had the valor and bravery of his convictions and dared cautiously to do what he thought was right and just.[16]

And when Lincoln was convinced of the justice of a plea or a policy, that conviction animated him as nothing else would. "I will say here that, in such moments, I have never heard his equal," recalled Horace White, who accompanied Lincoln around Illinois during Lincoln's debates with Stephen A. Douglas in 1858 as a cub reporter for the *Chicago Tribune.* "I believe I have listened at times to nearly all the public speakers of considerable reputation in this country," but "I cannot conceive that Patrick Henry, Mirabeau, or Vergniaud ever surpassed him on those occasions when his great soul was inspired with the thought of human rights and Divine justice."[17] Anyone who met Lincoln casually was likely to see only a homely-looking country lawyer whose "flesh was dark, wrinkled, and folded . . . dry and leathery, tough and everlasting," with a "head small and forehead receding." But, interposed Herndon, "when this great man was moved by some great or good feeling – by some idea of liberty or justice or right," then Lincoln was transformed. The eyes brightened, the stature straightened, and the arms were flung energetically upward, and "then he seemed an inspired man."[18]

The standard of justice to which Lincoln held the world began with recognizing the existence of a fundamental natural law. Like many of the liberal political theorists of the nineteenth century, Lincoln was tempted to endorse a variety of utilitarian nostrums about law, starting with Jeremy Bentham's dictum that law should be guided by the principle of "the greatest happiness for the greatest number."[19] So, for Lincoln, our "duty to . . . assist in ameliorating mankind" inclined him,

16   Herndon to C. O. Poole (January 5, 1886), in Emmanuel Hertz, ed., *The Hidden Lincoln From the Letters and Papers of William H. Herndon* (New York: Viking, 1938), 121.

17   Horace White to William H. Herndon (May 17, 1865), in *Herndon's Informants*, 4.

18   Herndon (June 24, 1887), in Hertz, *The Hidden Lincoln*, 185.

19   On the "greatest happiness" formula, see Bentham, *Deontology together with A Table of the Springs of Moral Action,* ed. Amnon Goldworth (Oxford, 1983), 60.

"without entering upon the details of the question," to "simply say, that I am for those means which will give the greatest good to the greatest number."[20] One reason he could not endorse the Bible without reservation was, as he told Isaac Cogdal in 1860, that he "could not believe in the endless punishment of anyone of the human race" because this made justice operate in a retributive fashion, whereas he preferred to think, like Bentham, that "punishment was parental in its object, aim, and design, and intended for the good of the offender; hence it must cease when justice is satisfied."[21] Had he wanted to be a consistent Benthamite, he might have joined Bentham in dismissing any connection between statutory law-codes and natural law as "nonsense on stilts." And Lincoln actually advised one young lawyer to train himself to "listen well to all the evidence" and "Hear the lawyers make their argument as patiently as you can." But after that,

> stripping yourself of all prejudice, if any you have, and throwing away, if you can, all technical law knowledge . . . then stop one moment and ask yourself: what is justice in this case, and let that sense of justice be your decision. Law is nothing else but the best reason of wise men applied for ages to the transactions and business of mankind.[22]

But Lincoln was not a theorist or a philosopher, and liberal democrats in the nineteenth century were far from unanimous in embracing Bentham's rejection of natural law, and when Lincoln came to confront the issue of slavery in both law and politics, he fell back almost at once on an appeal to natural law.

Lincoln described his aversion to slavery as virtually an instinct, a natural moral default. "I am naturally anti-slavery. If slavery is not wrong, nothing is wrong. I can not remember when I did not so think, and feel."[23] This was not just Romantic sentimentality. There were

---

20 "Speech to Germans at Cincinnati, Ohio" (February 12, 1861), in *C.W.*, 4:202.
21 Cogdal, in Don and Virginia Fehrenbacher, eds., *Recollected Words of Abraham Lincoln* (Stanford, CA: Stanford University Press, 1996), 110; William Lee Miller, *Lincoln's Virtues: An Ethical Biography* (New York: Knopf, 2002), 87.
22 Herndon, in Fehrenbacher, *Recollected Words of Abraham Lincoln*, 243.
23 "To Albert G. Hodges" (April 4, 1864), in *C.W.*, 7:281.

certain "immutable principles of justice" grafted onto nature, and among these were the natural rights enumerated by Thomas Jefferson in the Declaration of Independence (to "life, liberty, and the pursuit of happiness") and found in the universal behavior of all creatures. Slavery clashed inharmoniously with all of them. "All feel and understand it, even down to brutes and creeping insects." At its root, slavery was nothing more than "the same old serpent that says you work and I eat, you toil and I will enjoy the fruits of it."[24] That much, even the ant recoiled from. An "ant, who has toiled and dragged a crumb to his nest, will furiously defend the fruit of his labor, against whatever robber assails him," and by the same token, even "the most dumb and stupid slave that ever toiled for a master, does constantly know that he is wronged."[25] Lincoln's own experience was to feel an automatic revulsion against anyone who tried to steal from others the fruit of their labor. "My faith in the proposition that each man should do precisely as he pleases with all which is exclusively his own, lies at the foundation of the sense of justice there is in me." And in their heart of hearts, slaveholders knew that this was a natural axiom of justice: "Your sense of justice, and human sympathy" is "continually telling you, that the poor negro has some natural right to himself – that those who deny it, and make mere merchandise of him, deserve kickings, contempt and death." What trampled across this inherent sense of the injustice of slavery was nothing but self-interest, which had to be summoned-up in order to "repress all tendencies in the human heart to justice and mercy" on the part of slaveholders.[26] "Slavery is founded in the selfishness of man's nature – opposition to it, in his love of justice," and when these are "brought into collision so fiercely, as slavery extension brings them, shocks, and throes, and convulsions must ceaselessly follow."[27]

The besetting problem for Lincoln and his generation was that slavery was also founded in statute law. The majority of states in the Union at the time of the Constitution legalized chattel slavery, and even those which subsequently emancipated their slaves still provided for the ren-

---

24 "Speech at Chicago, Illinois" (July 10, 1858), in *C.W.*, 2:500.
25 "Fragment on Slavery" [July 1, 1854?], in *C.W.*, 2:222.
26 "Speech at Carlinville, Illinois" (August 31, 1858), 3:80.
27 "Speech at Peoria, Illinois" (October 16, 1854), in *C.W.*, 2:265, 271.

dition of fugitive slaves by state law, as well as by the requirement of Article IV, section three of the federal Constitution, and the federal fugitive slave laws of 1793 and 1850. In the face of slavery's protections under federal and state law, the response of slavery's most radical opponents was to dismiss the standing of law as a mere disguise for Southern political power, and to offset "the Slave Power" with the power of non-compliance and even outright law-breaking. Ralph Waldo Emerson saw, like Lincoln, that slavery was based on "the love of power, the voluptuousness of holding a human being in . . . absolute control." But his solution in 1851 was to disobey the Fugitive Slave Law of 1850: "This filthy enactment was made in the nineteenth century, by people who could read and write. I will not obey it by God."[28] The abolitionist minister, Owen Lovejoy, who represented one of Illinois' seven Congressional districts, roared his defiance of the Fugitive Slave Law in 1859 on the floor of the House of Representatives: "Owen Lovejoy lives at Princeton, Illinois, three-quarters of a mile east of the village, and he aids every fugitive that comes to his door and asks it. Proclaim it then from the housetops. Write it on every leaf that trembles in the forest, make it blaze from the sun at high noon."[29]

Emerson, Lovejoy, and every other abolitionist worth reckoning believed that they could appeal directly to divine or natural law, and use that sanction to shoulder aside the inequities and half-truths of human statute. In principle, Lincoln did not disagree that there was a "higher law" than statute law, and that it flatly obliterated any argument in favor of slavery. The Declaration of Independence, and its enunciation of a universal equality based on the natural rights of life, liberty and the pursuit of happiness was a "majestic interpretation of the economy of the Universe," filled with a "lofty, and wise, and noble understanding of the justice of the Creator to His creatures" in "nothing stamped with the Divine image and likeness was sent into the world to be trodden on, and

---

28 Robert D. Richardson, *Emerson: The Mind on Fire* (Berkeley: University of California Press, 1995), 397, 498.

29 Lovejoy, "Speech on the Fanaticism of the Democratic Party" (February 21, 1859), in *His Brother's Blood: Owen Lovejoy, Speeches and Writings, 1838–1864*, ed. William F. & Jane Ann Moore (Urbana: University of Illinois Press, 2004), 178.

degraded, and imbruted by its fellows."[30] But he also understood that evil, in the process of being humanly institutionalized, wraps up with itself bits and percentages of good, which it would be fool's wisdom to destroy along with the evil in one righteous smash. "The true rule, in determining to embrace, or reject any thing, is not whether it have any evil in it; but whether it have more of evil, than of good," Lincoln said in Congress in 1848. "There are few things wholly evil, or wholly good. Almost everything, especially of governmental policy, is an inseparable compound of the two; so that our best judgment of the preponderance between them is continually demanded."[31] Lincoln could not believe that there was no pathway around the shortcomings of human institutions but that of anarchy and power. It mortified him that the Taney Court could breeze so cheerfully past both natural law and the will of the people, as it did in *Dred Scott v. Sanford* in 1857. Still, the solution was not defiance, but "obedience to, and respect for, the judicial department of government," because even a mistaken Court is better than no Court at all:

> We think its decisions on Constitutional questions, when fully settled, should control, not only the particular cases decided, but the general policy of the country, subject to be disturbed only by amendments of the Constitution as provided in that instrument itself. More than this would be revolution. But we think the Dred Scott decision is erroneous. We know the court that made it, has often over-ruled its own decisions, and we shall do what we can to have it to over-rule this. We offer no resistance to it.[32]

There was no foreshadowing of Gandhian civil disobedience in Lincoln, if only because disobedience of any sort, for whatever noble motive, acted like dry-rot on the rule of law, and eventually persuaded people that the restraints of law are the enemy, rather than the basis of human freedom.

"The injustice of men" is not righted by compensatory displays of

---

30   "Speech at Lewistown, Illinois" (August 17, 1858), in *C.W.*, 2:246–247.
31   "Speech in United States House of Representatives on Internal Improvements" (June 20, 1848), in *C.W.*, 1:484.

well-intentioned power, judicial, legislative or executive, but by faithful adherence to the rule of law, which included both statutes and the mechanisms for altering statutes. It is only within the framework and expectations of the rule of law that power can be deployed with enough certainty to relax. In his first public protest against slavery, registered in 1837 in the Illinois legislature, Lincoln announced that "the institution of slavery is founded on both injustice and bad policy." But by challenging the law, "the promulgation of abolition doctrines tends rather to increase than to abate its evils." When a mob lynched some riverboat gamblers in Vicksburg in 1837, Lincoln thought that "Its direct consequences are, comparatively speaking, but a small evil," since the community as a whole was going to shed few tears over the reduction of the gaming population. But what it tended toward was the suggestion that power was the only effective antidote to evil. "By instances of the perpetrators of such acts going unpunished, the lawless in spirit, are encouraged to become lawless in practice; and having been used to no restraint, but dread of punishment, they thus become, absolutely unrestrained." Slavery, likewise, was an evil , but the resort to power to disrupt its operation reduced the moral authority of its opponents to the same level as the slaveholders and, in the case of fugitive slaves, the slave hunters.[33] Much as the abolitionists insisted that they had a mandate which relieved them of any responsibility for the consequences of public disobedience, Lincoln shot back that the claim

> that they would "do their duty and leave the consequences to God," merely gave an excuse for taking a course that they were not able to maintain by a fair and full argument. To make this declaration did not show what their duty was. If it did we should have no use for judgment, we might as well be made without intellect, and when divine or human law does not clearly point out what is our duty, we have no means of finding out what it is by using our most intelligent judgment of the consequences.

32 "Speech at Springfield, Illinois" (June 26, 1857), in *C.W.*, 2:401.
33 "Protest in Illinois Legislature on Slavery," (March 3, 1837) and "Address Before the Young Men's Lyceum of Springfield, Illinois" (January 27, 1838)in *C.W.*, 1:75, 109.

He did not dispute, any more than the abolitionists, that "slavery was an evil," but given the fact that slavery was a state enactment, until those state legislatures where slavery was legal chose to abolish it or to emancipate their slaves in some gradual fashion, "we . . . cannot affect it in States of this Union where we do not live." That was simply in the nature of a federal Constitution which strictly divided the jurisdictions of the state and the national government. Of course, if the question was not about slavery in the states, but whether slavery should be legalized in the western territories, this would be another matter, because Congress had direct jurisdiction over the organization of the territories and their preparation for statehood, and could take legislative action there concerning slavery which it could not take in the states. "The question of the extension of slavery to new territories of this country, is a part of our responsibility and care, and is under our control."[34]

For whatever purpose the abolitionists thought government was intended, Lincoln did not believe that it was intended for the purpose of righting all wrongs, at all times, by all means. "The legitimate object of government is to do for the people what needs to be done, but which they can not, by individual effort, do at all, or do so well, for themselves." This included matters which had little or nothing to do with justice and "exist independently of the injustice in the world" – for instance, the "Making and maintaining roads, bridges, and the like; providing for the helpless young and afflicted; common schools; and disposing of deceased men's property." There were two places the government did have a clear and unambiguous responsibility to address injustice. One was in national self-defense against the outrages and aggressions of warlike powers. "If one people will make war upon another, it is a necessity with that other to unite and cooperate for defense. Hence the military department." The other situation in which government brought its attention to bear on injustice was when "some men will kill, or beat, or constrain others, or despoil them of property, by force, fraud, or noncompliance with contracts, it is a common object with peaceful and just men to prevent it. Hence the criminal and civil departments."

---

34 "Speech at Worcester, Massachusetts" (September 12, 1848), in *C.W.*, 2:2; Miller, *Lincoln's Virtues*, 192–197.

The bulk of Lincoln's legal practice was civil in nature, and it is useful to remember that this is what he deemed a concern of justice: the largest component of his practice was property disputes, and fully half of the 3,400 cases he and Herndon handled between 1844 and 1861 involved debt collections.[35] A debt collector is not often thought of as an agent of justice. But Lincoln was by no means a legal Robin Hood: he wrote opinions for the Illinois Central Railroad on the dispossession of squatter and pre-emption rights to land the railroad claimed, and defended the Illinois Central in tax-exemption suits. Olivier Fraysse, commenting on Lincoln's record as a lawyer and a politician on property-ownership issues, remarked that "the small landowner threatened with seizure, the squatter who sold his clothes to keep his rights of pre-emption from falling into the hands of speculators, had trouble recognizing one of their own kind in Lincoln."[36] If anything, Lincoln saw his role as a lawyer less as a progressive crusader than as mediating facilitator who could "resolve disputes peacefully."[37]

Lincoln was not oblivious to economic or social unfairness. How could he be, having been born poor himself? But "he submitted to adversity and injustice with as much real patience as any Man I Ever knew," wrote Illinois governor Richard J. Oglesby, "because he had an abiding belief that all would yet come out right or that the right would appear and Justice finally be awarded to him."[38] What inclined Lincoln to such confidence in the ultimate swing of justice was its claim on human nature and the unobstructed arc it enjoyed in an environment of governmental minimalism and the rule of law, not the mandating of fairness. To create law and to walk away from further intervention in people's lives was to invent a zone of openness and opportunity for self-transformation. Under a government of laws, "it is best for all to leave each man free to acquire property as fast as he can." And the best evidence of how this worked was Lincoln's own history. "Twenty-five

---

35 Mark E. Steiner, *An Honest Calling: The Law Practice of Abraham Lincoln* (DeKalb, IL: Northern Illinois University Press, 2006), 100.

36 Olivier Fraysse, *Lincoln Land, and Labor, 1809–60*, trans. Sylvia Neely (Urbana: University of Illinois Press, 1994), 78.

37 Brian Dirck, *Lincoln the Lawyer* (Urbana: University of Illinois Press, 2007), 164.

38 R.J. Oglesby (January 5, 1866), in *Herndon's Informants*, 152.

years ago, I was a hired laborer," he said in 1859. But "the hired labor-er of yesterday, labors on his own account today; and will hire others to labor for him tomorrow." Of course, Lincoln could not (and did not) deny that there were hired men who never became more than hired men. But that was not because some titanic injustice deliberately hand-icapped them. "If any continue through life in the condition of the hired laborer, it is not the fault of the system, but because of either a depend-ent nature which prefers it, or improvidence, folly, or singular misfor-tune."[39] The role of law – whether in the legislature or the courts – was to ensure that every man would "have the chance – and I believe a black man is entitled to it – in which he can better his condition. . . . That is the true system . . . and so it may go on and on in one ceaseless round so long as man exists on the face of the earth!"[40] That was why he would, in 1861, describe the Civil War as "a People's contest" – not a popular uprising of the masses, but a battle to stave off the imposition of a slave-based aristocracy on America and preserve a system that encouraged economic and social mobility, a

> struggle for maintaining in the world, that form, and substance of
> a government, whose leading object is, to elevate the condition of
> men – to lift artificial weights from all shoulders – to clear the
> paths of laudable pursuit for all – to afford all, an unfettered start,
> and a fair chance, in the race of life. . . . This is the leading object
> of the government for whose existence we contend.[41]

In no sense did he imagine that justice was simply a question of who had the power and who could manipulate the laws. Justice had not arrived because the sword had been crossed by the pitchfork, or because monarchy had been replaced by the commune. Justice was what happened when laws were popularly adopted, and the rule of law even-handedly enforced. That will not guarantee the same results for everyone. "Some will get wealthy" and will "accumulate capital," then

---

39   "Address before the Wisconsin State Agricultural Society, Milwaukee, Wisconsin"
      (September 30, 1859), in *C.W.*, 3:478–479; John Channing Briggs, *Lincoln's
      Speeches Reconsidered* (Baltimore: Johns Hopkins University Press, 2005), 234.
40   "Speech at New Haven, Connecticut" (March 6, 1860), in *C.W.*, 4:24–25.
41   "Message to Congress in Special Session" (July 4, 1861), in *C.W.*, 4:438.

"to use it to save themselves from actual labor and hire other people to labor for them."[42] In the case of those who did not, the solution was not a policy of spread-the-wealth or soak-the-rich by interposing the hand of power. If justice really is a matter of achieving both satisfaction and harmony, it will not come from

> a war upon property, or the owners of property. Property is the fruit of labor – property is desirable – is a positive good in the world. That some should be rich, shows that others may become rich, and hence is just encouragement to industry and enterprize. Let not him who is houseless pull down the house of another; but let him labor diligently and build one for himself, thus by example assuring that his own shall be safe from violence when built.[43]

Not every complaint about fairness is really a protest against injustice; and not every complaint about injustice can be satisfied without running some risk that its real motive is the will-to-power. "Inequality is certainly never to be embraced for its own sake," Lincoln admitted. But that was no sanction for "the pernicious principle . . . that no one shall have any, for fear all shall not have some." Those who appealed to governmental power as the catch-all source of justice would find that governments can develop a nasty appetite for power, especially if it can be disguised as the dispensing goddess of fairness.[44] He warned the young Illinois state legislator Shelby Cullom in 1862 that

> there is this difference between dealing with the government and dealing between individuals. If you deal with an individual and he doesn't do right you can sue him in court and make him pay damages. But if you are dealing with the government you are helpless.[45]

Even his decision to append the claim that the Emancipation Proclamation was an "act of justice" was a last-minute addition to a

---

42 "Speech at Cincinnati, Ohio" (September 17, 1859), in *C.W.*, 3:459.
43 "Reply to New York Workingmen's Democratic Republican Association" (March 21, 1864), in *C.W.*, 7:259–60.
44 "Fragment on Government" [July 1, 1854?], in *C.W.*, 2:221–222.
45 Cullom (March 22, 1908), in Fehrenbacher, *Recollected Words of Abraham Lincoln*, 125.

document whose foundation was otherwise laid in a scrupulous, almost plodding, application of whatever could be construed as a legal exercise of presidential "war powers" under the president's constitutional rubric of "commander-in-chief of the army and navy in time of war or rebellion."

Ironically, even after using those governmental "war powers" to hand down "an act of justice" in the Proclamation, Lincoln actually grew *less* confident about the ability of government to achieve justice. He worried that immediate emancipation would prove inferior to "some practical system by which the two races could gradually live themselves out of their old relation to each other, and both come out better prepared for the new."[46] And he worried that that the federal courts might strike down the Proclamation as unconstitutional. "I think it is valid in law, and will be so held by the courts," he wrote General Stephen Hurlbut in 1863, but in any case "I think I shall not retract or repudiate it." Two years later, he was less sure: at the Hampton Roads Conference in February, 1865, he admitted to Alexander H. Stephens that he did not know how "the Courts would decide it . . . and [he] could give no answer."

> His own opinion was that as the proclamation was a war measure and would have effect only from its being an exercise of the war power, as soon as the war ceased, it would be inoperative for the future. It would be held to apply only to such slaves as had come under its operation while it was in active exercise. This was his individual opinion, but the Courts might decide the other way and hold that it effectually emancipated all the slaves in the States to which it applied at the time. So far as he was concerned, he should leave it to the Courts to decide. He never would change or modify the terms of the Proclamation in the slightest particular.[47]

Strikingly, his recourse in that case was not to the accumulation of more power, but a determination to settle the end of slavery by statute – which

---

46   "To Nathaniel P. Banks" (August 5, 1863), in *C.W.*, 6:365.
47   Stephens, *A Constitutional View of the Late War Between the States* (Philadelphia: National Publishing Co., 1870), 2:610–11.

in this case took the form of the Thirteenth Amendment. And he warned radical Republicans not to be over-confident that Union victory in the war was a sign that justice had become a Northern political property. "If we shall suppose that American Slavery is one of those offences which, in the providence of God, must needs come," Lincoln said in his Second Inaugural Address, then it has come because no nation, being human, can avoid such offenses. But let it be clear that this particular offense was shared by both North as well as South, since both had colluded historically in fastening the blight of slavery on the republic. Now, through the instrument of "this terrible war," the blight is being removed; but the judgment, like the collusion, comes down on "both North and South . . . as the woe due to those by whom the offence came." This may rasp unpleasantly on the sensibilities of the over-righteous among the antislavery radicals; but who can gainsay the justice of the Almighty? "Shall we discern therein any departure from those divine attributes which the believers in a Living God always ascribe to Him?" Much as Lincoln hoped that "this mighty scourge of war may speedily pass away," yet there was still justice in the punishment it assessed:

> Yet, if God wills that it continue, until all the wealth piled by the bond-man's two hundred and fifty years of unrequited toil shall be sunk, and until every drop of blood drawn with the lash, shall be paid by another drawn with the sword, as was said three thousand years ago, so still it must be said "the judgments of the Lord, are true and righteous altogether."[48]

We yield haltingly to the justice of God, because yielding to it means that we have admitted at last that ultimately justice is not our property, and that we have finally met the perfect balance of law and power. But, whether we wanted to yield or not, Lincoln believed "that He will compel us to do right in order that He may do these things, not so much because we desire them as that they accord with His plans of dealing with this nation, in the midst of which He means to establish justice."[49]

48   "Second Inaugural Address" (March 4, 1865), in *C.W.*, 8:332.
49   James F. Wilson, "Some Memories of Lincoln," *North American Review* 163 (December 1896), 668.

So if, by means of the war, "God now wills the removal of a great wrong, and wills also that we of the North as well as you of the South, shall pay fairly for our complicity in that wrong," then "impartial history will find therein new cause to attest and revere the justice and goodness of God."[50] Justice would indeed concern everyone, whether they liked its shape or not; but no one would own it as their property, to play with as the cat's-paw of power. Over two hundred years after Lincoln's birth, it might be well to remind ourselves that the real enemy of both fairness and justice is not the weakness of our satisfactions or an unwillingness to bear shared sacrifice, but the dark temptation of power, luring us to the abyss with our own desires.

50   "To Albert G. Hodges" (April 4, 1864), in *C.W.*, 7:282.

Chapter 3:
Moral Education
and the Art of Storytelling
Susan McWilliams[*]

Give ear, O my people, to my law:
incline your ears to the words of my mouth.
I will open my mouth in a parable.
— Psalm 78[1]

In the course of his travels, the Greek lawgiver Solon once visited Lydia, where he was invited into the palace of King Croesus. For days, the Lydian king entertained Solon in grand fashion, showing him what it means to be "as rich as Croesus." They ate lavishly, had servants tend to their every need, and explored the palace's vast stores of treasure and wealth. Then, after all this great feasting and excess, Croesus pulled Solon aside and said something to the effect of: "Solon, you have traveled the world and seen many things, and everyone considers you to be an incredibly wise man. So I must ask you: of all the men you have encountered, who is the most blessed of all?" Croesus smiled, certain that after such an extravagant display, Solon would be compelled to bestow the honor upon him.

But Solon didn't flatter Croesus, and he didn't miss a beat. "Tellus the Athenian," he said, going on to tell the story of Tellus's life: how he had good and beautiful sons who themselves beget good and beautiful

---

*   In writing this essay I have had the help of many friends and colleagues, to whom I owe great thanks. But this essay owes most substantially to the influence of my teacher Hadley Arkes, who – although he will not quite agree with everything I say here – is a truly gifted moral educator, in no small part because he is a man who can tell a story with the best of them.

1   The King James Bible, Psalm 78:1–2.

children; how he brought immense prosperity to his city; and how he died in a moment of great glory, routing the enemy Eleusinians as they tried to attack Athens. To round out the story, Solon described the lavish public funeral that the grateful Athenians had held in Tellus' honor.

Croesus sat quietly through the story, but at its completion he asked if maybe Solon wouldn't mind identifying the *second* most blessed man he had ever met – certain, in asking the question, that he would at least be awarded this honorable mention. But Solon disappointed Croesus again. "Cleobis and Biton," he said, going to tell the life stories of those Argive brothers known for their great athleticism and vigor. Solon described how, when their mother needed a ride to the festival of Hera but could not find any oxen to pull her cart, Cleobis and Biton harnessed themselves beneath the yoke and pulled their mother the 45 stades to the temple. Arriving there, the two men collapsed from exhaustion and died. But for their selflessness and devotion, they were rewarded with one of the greatest funerals that anyone had ever seen, a magnificent banquet and affair at which their mother was bestowed with honors, and at which the Argives erected statues of the young men to stand for eternity.

After sitting through this story, Croesus became irritated. "My Athenian friend," he asked Solon, "is the happiness that is mine so entirely set at naught by you that you do not make me the equal of even private men?"

Solon answered, articulating the principle that lay beneath the stories he just told. Men have lives that are subject to great vicissitudes of fortune, he told Croesus, and until you have seen the full scope of a man's life – that is, until you have seen a man's life through to its end – you cannot estimate how blessed a life it is. Further, material wealth cannot be used as a judge of a man's fortune, since "many very rich men are unblessed, and many who have a moderate competence are fortunate," especially in the manner and terms of their demise. "One must look always at the end of everything – how it will come out finally," said Solon, "for many the god has shown a glimpse of blessedness only to extirpate them in the end."[2]

---

2   Herodotus, *The History*, trans. David Greene (Chicago: The University of Chicago Press, 1987), 45–47 [1.29–1.32].

For Herodotus, who tells this story in the first book of his *History*, this exchange with Croesus demonstrates the true extent of Solon's moral and political wisdom. For one thing, Solon turns out to be right to refrain from calling Croesus blessed; not too long after this conversation, Croesus befriends a foreigner who then kills Croesus's son, causing the king much grief and sadness. And ultimately, Croesus makes a great mistake that causes his own downfall: he misinterprets an oracle and goes to war against Persia, a decision that results in the collapse of the Lydian empire. In the process he loses most of his material fortune, and it becomes unlikely that Croesus will ever be celebrated by his fellows in death the way that Tellus or Cleobis and Biton were. The principles Solon articulated – that one cannot take the full measure of a man's life until that life has been lived in full, and that material wealth is not equivalent to true fortune – clearly apply to Croesus' life. Moreover, as the rest of the *History* demonstrates, those principles stand the test of human experience more broadly, across time and place. That Solon understands and can articulate such principles, fundamental principles in the realm of moral and political judgment, testifies to his wisdom. But so, too, does the artfulness with which Solon answers Croesus' initial question. Even though Croesus wishes Solon had responded to his question differently, he is drawn in by the care and craft of the stories Solon tells. Despite his misgivings, Croesus cannot help but consider Solon's teaching. And eventually, Croesus sees the truthfulness and merit of those fundamental principles. Later in his life, Croesus tells others that Solon was the wisest person he ever met; he even becomes a kind of moral educator himself, passing the principles he learned from Solon down to other political leaders.[3]

In this exchange, Herodotus allows us to see Solon, not just as a man with substantial insight and principled judgment, but also as a clever and able storyteller. And Herodotus suggests that the two traits might be importantly related – especially to the extent that we can regard Solon as a great educator, or a great lawgiver.

---

3   Ibid., 74 [1.86]; 127 [1.207]; 227 [3.36]. See also Thomas Harrison, *Greeks and Barbarians* (New York: Routledge, 2002), 30.

* * *

By their very nature, statements of moral and political principle get formulated in abstract terms. The reason for this is apparent: to speak at the level of principle means to speak beyond the level of particularity and to make a claim that applies to more than a single situation. There is thus inevitable abstractness to any proposition of principle, an abstraction from particular details and circumstances. When we say that someone has principled judgment, we are saying that this person has a firm under-standing of broad standards, standards that transcend the details of indi-vidual cases even as those standards may be applied to individual cases. We might even say that statements of principle have a universalizing cast, at least among human beings; when we encounter Immanuel Kant's cat-egorical imperative, or Solon's statement that material wealth should not be equated with true fortune, we understand it as a rule meant to adhere not just to some people some of the time, but to all people in general.

Consequently, then, moral education is an education in principled reasoning and judgment; it involves the cultivation of this kind of abstract thinking and speech.[4] But at the same time, as Herodotus' description of Solon begins to indicate, moral education has long been tied not only to the articulation of principles in the abstract, but also to a different kind of linguistic expression: storytelling. The great moral educators have often been great storytellers – people who speak in alle-gory and parable – and this correlation has not gone without notice in the annals of history. Far beyond the casual connections that we make between moral education and storytelling when we refer to "the moral of the story," we can discern in the history of Western political theoriz-ing a sustained and serious defense of the place of storytelling in moral education, particularly as it relates to cultivating people for rule and self-government.

And in this long tradition of thought, we can identify two distinct but complementary threads of argument, each of which asserts a criti-cal role for storytelling in moral education. First, beginning with the ancient Greeks, one line of thinkers has emphasized the *engaging*

---

4   See Norman J. Bull, *Moral Judgment from Childhood to Adolescence* (London: Routledge & Kegan Paul Limited, 1969), 22.

power of storytelling: the ways in which stories can draw in a listener and artfully expand the terms of his or her thought, encouraging broad reflection and thereby laying the groundwork for the clear articulation and consideration of moral principles. At the same time, other thinkers have described storytelling as a *moderating* force in moral education. They stress the way in which stories trade on detail, circumstance, and accident. Stories are thus, the argument goes, a means by which we remind ourselves of the inherent particularity and imperfection of the human animal, thereby chastening our pretensions to moral faultlessness and our fantasies of achieving moral completion in practice.

These argumentative threads may seem, in some respects, to run counter to each other. The first sees storytelling as a vehicle for intellectual and imaginative expansion; the second portrays storytelling as a means of intellectual and imaginative temperance. How can storytelling be at once a tool of growth and a tool of restraint? The answer, I think, is clear: the tension between these two threads of argument is only an apparent tension, a tension at the surface of things. Indeed, if we take these two depictions of storytelling in concert, it is possible to discern the grander and more holistic purpose that storytelling may play when it is employed as part of moral education.

That is: despite what may at first seem to be a contradiction on the surface, these accounts of storytelling are merely different sides of the same coin. Both accounts underscore the extent to which storytelling is a form that draws on and speaks to the human condition, thus locating moral education within an appropriate structure for its invariably human students. The first line of thought draws attention to the ways in which storytelling is a familiar communicative form that does not need explanation, a framework by which people naturally tend to recount events and share information. As Alasdair MacIntyre puts it, humans experience themselves as living a "narratable life," such that storytelling itself is the primary form by which human beings learn to give and compare accounts, to provide frameworks for justification.[5] Stories may therefore be used to effect a move from the surface-level human

---

5   Alasdair MacIntyre, *After Virtue: A Study in Moral Theory* (Notre Dame, IN: University of Notre Dame Press, 1981), 202.

experience of the world to the abstract language of principle and morality. The second line of thought focuses on the fact that storytelling highlights the human experience of partiality; stories play on our own status as incomplete beings. Storytelling therefore helps to temper abstract and uniform linguistic formulations of moral principle with the acknowledgment that human life is, in practice, neither abstract nor uniform. Thus, it teaches that the application of moral principle to human practice or regulation requires some consideration of detail and circumstance.[6] In both these lines of thought, then, storytelling is presented as valuable because it recurs to (and imbues moral education with) what we often call "common sense." But storytelling reinforces a particular kind of common sense, one that encourages us, as Hannah Arendt claims, to think through and reconsider experience in the service of greater and more comprehensive understanding. The storyteller, says Arendt, helps to transform human experiences by bringing them from the realm of intimate emotion into the realm of reason-giving and discussion, making them "fit for public appearance."[7]

In this way, I argue that it is proper to regard storytelling as indispensible for moral education, particularly as that moral education relates to the formation of political knowledge and judgment. Within the context of moral education, storytelling reminds us humans about what kind of creatures we truly are: mortal beings who live somewhere between the beasts and the gods, in Aristotle's formulation, and who are capable of reaching levels of perfection in speech and thought that we are unable to achieve in deed.[8] This is an especially critical service to the extent that moral education is undertaken as part of a project of civic education: education about rule, law, and self-governance in preparation for action. Justice requires that lawmakers, whether they be kings or citizens, ·recognize that the world is not "infinitely malleable," as Arlene

6   This should not be taken to imply any kind of thoroughgoing relativism, as I will mention later.

7   Hannah Arendt, "The Public Realm and the Private Realm," in *The Portable Hannah Arendt*, ed. Peter R. Baehr (New York: Penguin Putnam, 2000), 199. See also Carol A. Gould, "Hannah Arendt," in *Approaches to Political Thought*, ed. William L. Richter (Lanham, MD: Rowman and Littlefield Publishers, 2009), 72.

8   Aristotle, *The Politics*, in *The Politics and the Constitution of Athens*, ed. Stephen Everson (Cambridge: Cambridge University Press, 1996), 14 [1253].

Saxonhouse says, even "by a human intellect capable of abstracting from all particulars and from bodily creation."[9] Even as moral principles must take their purest form in phrases that are general and abstract, lawmakers must learn to apply them to beings and situations that are neither. In legislating, for instance, we must be cautious about being too vague or applying too ambitious a law on the imperfect creatures we are. By schooling us in both our human capacities and limits, storytelling is a means of orienting moral education toward prudential civic action.

To be clear, I do not mean to imply that all endeavors in storytelling serve the purpose of moral education or good citizenship; I am dubious of Strabo's often-cited notion that to be a good storyteller one must necessarily be a good man.[10] It seems clear to me, by contrast, that Socrates is correct in *The Republic* when he argues that that in moral terms, not all storytelling is equal, and moral guardians must consider seriously the stories they tell. If we are considering stories within the context of moral education, one must evaluate stories in terms of the ends they serve: a task for those already schooled in philosophical and moral wisdom.[11] But making such distinctions among stories, as important as they are, is not my task here. Rather, here I want to reclaim and reassert the long tradition of thought that sees the art of mindful storytelling as an integral part of moral education.

For the most part, such a view is not the norm in our own times. As William Kirk Kilpatrick observes, the telling of stories does not seem to play much of a role in contemporary moral education – at least, moral education in its most formal, academic incarnations. More frequently, such education tends to involve the contemplation of disembodied and nonspecific "moral dilemmas" that relate only tangentially to human experience.[12] Such "dilemmas," as Kilpatrick notes, may help to

9   Arlene W. Saxonhouse, *Fear of Diversity: The Birth of Political Science in Ancient Greek Thought* (Chicago: The University of Chicago Press, 1992), 74.

10   Strabo, *The Geography of Strabo, Volume I,* trans. Horace Leonard Jones (London: William Heinemann, 1917), 63 [1.5].

11   Plato, *The Republic*, trans. Allan Bloom (New York: Basic Books, 1968), 55–76 [377b-398b].

12   Kilpatrick is thinking about the kinds of hypothetical problems that tend to involve imagining faceless people in a lifeboat that is taking on water, in a nuclear fallout shelter with limited resources, and so on.

illustrate clashes between various principles, but they imply that "particular loves and loyalties" are "largely irrelevant" to moral issues, that "one can somehow dispense from moral particularities and leap right into the area of universal principles." In this model of moral education, human life is portrayed as a "disconnected set of ethical and other dilemmas, all of which are amenable to rational solution" – in other words, as life without specific attachments and affections.[13] For whatever its virtues, such training leaves something wanting, lacking as it does the complication and nuance that are inherent to political decision-making. Storytelling, by contrast, is a form that retains a connection with the fundamental complications of human experience and thus grounds moral education firmly in what Herodotus called the proper realm of political inquiry: the realm of "human things."[14] It helps to elevate the wisdom inherent in common sense even as it brings moral abstractions down to earth – a fact the ancient Greeks, among others, knew.

* * *

For the ancient Greeks, the discovery and articulation of the principles that underlie politics – what Christian Meier has called "the Greek discovery of politics," and what we might term the discovery of political philosophy – emerged largely as part of a particular kind of storytelling.[15] This kind of storytelling found its first formal expression in the practice of *theoria* (θεωρία), the word from which our own word "theory" derives. *Theoria* was largely an exercise on the Solonic model. During the Attic period, many of the Greek city-states employed a *theoros* (θεορός) – a theorist – to travel to visit foreign city-states or religious

---

13 William Kirk Kilpatrick, "Moral Character: Story-telling and Virtue," in *Psychological Foundations of Moral Education and Character Development: An Integrated Theory of Moral Development*, ed. Richard T. Knowles and George F. McLean (Washington, DC: The Council for Research in Values and Philosophy, 1992), 169–170.

14 Herodotus, *The History* ,132 [2.4].

15 Christian Meier, *The Greek Discovery of Politics*, trans. David McLintock (Cambridge: Harvard University Press, 1990).

16 See J. Peter Euben, *The Tragedy of Political Theory: The Road Not Taken* (Princeton: Princeton University Press, 1990), 232–233; and Sheldon Wolin, *Tocqueville Between Two Worlds: The Making of a Political and Theoretical Life* (Princeton: Princeton University Press, 2001), 34.

oracles.[16] The *theoros* was expected to study the variety of customs exist-ing in the world; the *theoros* traveled to accumulate a wealth of experi-ence. But perhaps the most important part of his job took place when the *theoros* returned to his home city. Upon his arrival, he was expected to report on what he had seen, giving particular attention to the principles that lay behind specific foreign conventions.

For the *theoros*, this charge involved two related tasks, intellectual-ly speaking. The first, as Peter Euben has written, is that the *theoros* had to learn to think and speak at the level of human universals or ideals. To be successful in his role, the *theoros* had to move beyond a simple recounting of experiences and into a search for elements of the ideal that could be found in other places. And in order to understand his own travels as a search for elements of the ideal in specific foreign places, the *theoros* had to be able to conceive of an ideal that escaped the grasp of all present conventional systems. The activity of the *theoros* could not only "issue in a critical sense toward the particularity, even arbi-trariness, of his own culture" but also "stimulate a drive to find a high-er unity or reality beneath the particularity of appearances, whether in nature, Being, or human nature." As Euben notes, it is easy to see how the task of the *theoros* could incline him to question or repudiate con-ventional wisdom and make a plea for "superior understanding."[17] And to make that plea, he needed to be able to speak in terms that transcend-ed the particularity of specific times and places, to be able to speak at the level of principles – "first principles," even, or "first things."[18]

But at the same time, the *theoros* could not dispense with the par-ticularities of the conventional world altogether. In speaking with his fellow citizens, he could not merely offer some abstract formulation of principles or moral ideals. Such a bald articulation was likely to con-fuse his audience or strike them as foreign – and as the Athenian

17 J. Peter Euben, "Creatures of a Day: Thought and Action in Thucydides," in *Political Theory and Praxis: New Perspectives*, ed. Terence Ball (Minneapolis: University of Minnesota Press, 1977), 34–35.

18 In accordance with the subject and spirit of this volume, I am happy to invoke terms made popular by Hadley Arkes, most notably in *First Things: An Inquiry Into the First Principles of Morals and Justice* (Princeton: Princeton University Press, 1986).

Stranger makes clear in Plato's *Laws*, that would make them unlikely to listen, and possibly make them hostile or suspicious of the *theoros'* intent.[19] Rather, the *theoros* had to draw his fellows into this new way of seeing and thinking about standards of rule. He had to begin by standing where they stood, by standing from within the community he sought to teach.[20] And so he had to take them on a kind of intellectual journey, one that mirrored his own experience of transformation. That is, the *theoros* had to draw his fellows in by telling them stories from his travels, stories that illustrated and exemplified the broader principles of judgment at stake. Then eventually, as Solon did in his exchange with Croesus, the *theoros* could translate the stories into more abstract, principled language. In public, the *theoros* could not harness and employ the power of principled wisdom without first making recourse to storytelling. If the *theoros* were to be successful in changing or altering the laws of his city-state – the laws themselves being the central means by which a polity teaches moral behavior to its citizens – he had to first convince his fellows to listen to him.[21]

The storytelling of the *theoros*, then, prefigures Socrates' description in *The Republic* of moral education as "the art of turning around." Rather than trying to "put into the soul knowledge that isn't in it, as though they were putting sight into blind eyes," Socrates says, those who are incisive philosophers and moral educators approach people with greater care. They assume that all people have the capacity to acquire theoretical insight but must be convinced to see in expanded terms, since initially those terms are unfamiliar and even may seem frightening.[22] The philosopher does not merely proclaim something like "I have seen the light of truth!" and expect others to join his parade, subscribe to his

19   Plato, *Laws*, trans. Benjamin Jowett (Amherst, NY: Prometheus Books, 2000), 286–290 [950–953].
20   To some degree, I am echoing Michael Walzer's argument in *Interpretation and Social Criticism* (Cambridge: Harvard University Press, 1987), 39. In Walzer's formulation, if the social critic "has picked up new ideas on his travels, he tries to connect them to the local culture, building on his own intimate knowledge; he is not intellectually detached."
21   For a more extensive argument on the point that a polity teaches morality through its laws, see Arkes, *First Things*, 26.
22   Plato, *The Republic*, 197 [518b-d].

newsletter, or otherwise follow his intellectual lead. Rather, he speaks with a kind of indirection, employing his speech with care and craft. His is a mode of enticement rather than a mode of exhortation. It is a process of persuasion, a seduction that works by calculated increments rather than sudden force. The philosopher, as Douglas Kries writes, is involved in "turning the *desire* of the student toward a higher end in addition to explaining what that heretofore undesired end is."[23]

With that in mind, it is critical to remember that when Socrates issues this description of education, he does so right after *telling his own students a story*: the Allegory of the Cave.[24] And, as Martin Heidegger among others has noticed, the Allegory of the Cave clearly seems intended to help effect the "turning around" of those who hear it; it is an alluring story that points from the level of observation and appearances to the level of truth and fundamentals. With his own attempt at storytelling so neatly juxtaposed with this description of philosophical education, Socrates seems to be suggesting that a certain kind of careful storytelling – the storytelling that, in Heideggerian terms, leads from the realm of experience to that of essence – is a critical part of "turning around the whole human being," of "removing human beings from the region where they first encounter things and transferring and accustoming them to another realm where beings appear."[25] There is a deep and abiding – perhaps even a necessary – link, Socrates indicates, between the telling of stories and education in abstract principles.

In the overlapping Solonic and Socratic traditions of ancient Greek thought, then, storytelling is understood as a necessary component of education in principled thought and judgment in large part because storytelling is more likely to *engage* people – especially people with no prior philosophical training – than direct statements made at the level of abstraction. Storytelling, in this account, is presented as having the

---

23   Douglas Kries, *The Problem of Natural Law* (Lanham, MD: Lexington Books, 2007), 147.

24   We also might regard the city in speech, with which Socrates and his interlocutors have been busying themselves, as an exercise in communal storytelling.

25   Martin Heidegger, "Plato's Doctrine of Truth," in *Pathmarks*, ed. William McNeill (Cambridge: Cambridge University Press, 1998), 167.

kind of transformative or erotic power that Friedrich Nietzsche seems to have in mind when he writes that "the more abstract the truth is that you would teach, the more you have to seduce the senses to it."[26] Stories, which draw people in, help them to begin the slow ascension toward the apprehension and appreciation of abstract principles.

Stories have that capacity, the argument goes, because they are such a familiar means of communication.[27] People are accustomed to hearing and sharing stories; many have argued, persuasively, that storytelling is the most common mode of human exchange.[28] (One thinks of Robert Penn Warren's line that in the American South, only copulation is as common as storytelling, both being inexpensive and easy to procure.)[29] People are habituated to comprehending events through stories in a way that they are not habituated to comprehending events through statements of principle, and thus they are not threatened or confused by stories in the way they may be threatened or confused by abstract linguistic formulations. As MacIntyre argues, people are used to thinking in the form that narrated stories provide. And even more importantly, people are accustomed to engaging narrated stories with questioning and reflection. He writes:

> To be the subject of a narrative that runs from one's birth to one's death is . . . to be accountable for the actions and experiences which compose a narratable life. It is, that is, to be open to being asked to give a certain kind of account of what one did or what happened to one or what one witnessed at any earlier point in one's life the time at which the question was posed. . . . Asking you what you did and why, saying what I did and why, pondering the differences between your account of what I did and my account of what

26   Friedrich Nietzsche, "Beyond Good and Evil," in *Basic Writings of Nietzsche*, ed. Peter Gay, trans. Walter Kaufmann (New York: Random House, 2000), 277.

27   In the present day, this argument occasionally appears in the most general literature of higher education. See, for instance, Janice McDrury and Maxine Alfredo, *Learning through Storytelling in Higher Education: Using Reflection and Experience to Improve Learning* (London: Kogan Page Limited, 2003), 171.

28   See, for instance: Wendy Doniger O'Flaherty, *Other People's Myths: The Cave of Echoes* (Chicago: The University of Chicago Press, 1988).

29   Cited in Robert Andrews, ed., *The Columbia Dictionary of Quotations* (New York: Columbia University Press, 1993), 860.

I did, and *vice versa*, these are essential constituents of all but the very simplest and barest of narratives.[30]

In other words, people are accustomed to responding to stories with precisely the kind of reflection that underpins moral reasoning. To respond to a story by asking why a character did something, or why a character would want to do something, is to move into the realm of reason-giving and justification. And this, of course, is the realm of thought that disposes itself to conversation at the level of abstraction. Solon's response to Croesus models this pattern almost perfectly; Croesus responds to Solon's stories with a question that brings the exchange to the fundamentals. Solon essentially sets Croesus up to ask a question that lends itself to a principled answer. His stories compel Croesus to ask *why*, drawing him from a realm of rather limited and self-interested concern into a level of inquiry that is more abstract and intellectual. Through enticement and indirection, Solon's stories help Croesus, almost literally, to see past himself and to another level of contemplation. Solon's storytelling helps make a transition from the world of perception and opinion to the world of abstraction and principle, making the push past conventional ways of thinking. It demonstrates an awareness of Aristotle's teaching that many need to be persuaded or even compelled to consider philosophical principles in the first place.[31]

The fact that people tend to regard storytelling as familiar, and thus engage storytellers with a degree of ease, seems to matter for moral education especially when unfamiliar teachings are at stake. Without a doubt, people are in particular attracted to "new" stories in a way that they are not attracted to "new" principles, baldly stated. As far as most people are concerned, a new or unfamiliar story promises excitement, while a new or unfamiliar statement of principle bespeaks change and even danger. Thomas More underscores that teaching in his *Utopia*; in that book, the character Raphael Hythloday reports that people seem unwilling to listen to his proposals for principled social and political change when they are stated as such, but it is clear that everyone wants to listen to him when he

---

30   MacIntyre, *After Virtue*, 202–203.31 Aristotle, *Metaphysics,* trans. W.D. Ross (Stilwell, KS: Digireads, 2006), 40 [3.5].

31   Aristotle, *Metaphysics,* trans. W.D. Ross (Stilwell, KS: Digireads, 2006), 40 [3.5].

tells stories about the island of Utopia (though of course those stories point toward the same social and political principles which Hythloday had trouble propagating when he stated them in the abstract).[32] This phenomenon, so well illustrated by More, is of critical interest to the moral educator, since, as Leo Strauss has echoed Socrates in saying, all philosophical or moral truth is somewhat at odds with or "unfamiliar" within the boundaries of conventional society.[33] Stories seem to be a means by which the unfamiliar may be introduced into a conversation, subtly and slowly, to prepare people for the unfamiliar ways of thinking that are part and parcel of philosophical expression and moral education. Stories, in those terms, open people's minds to the unfamiliar that is the philosophical.

Along these lines, Strauss observes that there is a particular genius to the way the Athenian Stranger approaches his conversation with Kleinias and Megillus in Plato's *Laws*. Very shortly after the three men meet, the Athenian Stranger leads the younger men in a long conversation about wine-drinking, a conversation which involves the exchange of many stories and observations. The effect of the conversation about wine, Strauss notes, is to loosen the tongues and minds of the men almost as if they had been drinking. It lowers their inhibitions about speaking beyond the boundaries of familiarity. It serves as a kind of liberation from convention, a platform from which the men may embark on a true philosophical discussion. Rather than leap immediately into an abstract discussion of politics and laws, the Athenian Stranger induces his interlocutors to that discussion through the indirection and enticement of storytelling.[34] Their shared storytelling helps the men to ease from the realm of convention and surfaces to the relatively unfamiliar realm of fundamentals. Storytelling serves as a tool of ascent to the philosophic and abstract.

Among political philosophers, Montesquieu perhaps makes the most direct defense of storytelling along these lines. Montesquieu, of course, experimented with a variety of literary forms and styles, in his

---

32 See Thomas More, *Utopia*, ed. George M. Logan and Robert M. Adams (Cambridge: Cambridge University Press, 1989).

33 Leo Strauss, *What Is Political Philosophy: And Other Studies* (Chicago: The University of Chicago Press, 1959), 221.

34 Ibid., 31.

own philosophical writing. But in reflections composed late in his life, Montesquieu reveals that he preferred the form of his *Persian Letters*, a novel, to the form of *The Spirit of the Laws*, an abstract treatise. He explains that in storytelling, "where accident selects the characters, and the subjects dealt with are independent of any design or preconceived plan, the author is entitled to mingle philosophy, politics, and morality with romance, and to connect the whole by a hidden, and somewhat novel, bond."[35] Montesquieu goes on to suggest that stories make it possible to entice readers into complicated and intricate modes of thought because they lure people in with drama and intrigue. Stories trade on the essentials of human emotional life, making them not only a familiar but also poignant form. For Montesquieu, this enhances a story's power to move people to deeper thought. One of his characters in the *Persian Letters* puts it this way: "With truths of a certain kind, it is not enough to make them appear convincing: one must also make them felt."[36] Storytelling, by speaking to people's passions along with their capacity for reason, provide multiple paths by which people may be led to engage in principled or abstract thought.

This is an argument echoed by many thinkers, including Bertrand de Jouvenel, who observes that a "mere explanation of the principles" is rarely as intriguing or compelling as some kind of "traveller's account" or story that is imbued with "the semblance of reality." As a practical matter, Jouvenel writes, storytelling engages more people than does an abstract treatise because it begins with what is familiar and credible at the same time that it excites.[37] Stories, to borrow Herodotus' term, have "color."[38] Phillip Sidney puts a slightly different cast on the matter; a story, he argues, "yields to the powers of the mind an image of that whereof the philosopher bestows but a wordish description, which does neither strike, pierce, nor possess the sight of the soul so

---

35 Montesquieu, "Some Reflections on the *Persian Letters*," in *Persian Letters*, trans. John Davidson (New York: E. P. Dutton, 1923), 32.

36 Montesquieu, *Persian Letters*, trans. C. J. Betts (New York: Penguin Books, 1993), 53 [Letter 11].

37 Bertrand de Jouvenel, "Utopia for Practical Purposes," *Daedalus* 94 (Spring 1965): 438.

38 Herodotus, *History*, 33 [1.1].

much as the other does."[39] But no matter which tinge the argument is given, the general case is the same: storytelling is a form of communication that is likely to unsettle or move people who would not be stirred by purely abstract articulations and forms. Put another way, storytelling is a means by which the moral educator demonstrates a kind of care for his students and the way they think; in telling his listener a story, the philosopher temporarily descends to conventional speech in the "interest of the elevation of the other," as Wilson Carey McWilliams writes.[40]

In short, there is a long thread in the history of Western political thought that sees storytelling as critical for moral education because of its power to engage people – and by engaging them, encouraging broad reflection and thereby laying the groundwork for the clear articulation and consideration of a principle. Storytellers have the capability to draw in a listener and artfully expand the terms of his or her thought, subtly shifting the ground from what is seen in the world to what might truly be, or shifting the ground from the *is* in human life to the *ought*. In these accounts, we see storytelling as the means by which people may be convinced to ascend from thinking in terms of the familiar and episodic into thinking in terms of the unfamiliar and universal. Storytelling, that is to say, is an erotic means of moving people upward, toward the abstract light of philosophic discourse and toward an apprehension of first principles.

* * *

While the arguments so far described present storytelling as a means of ascent to the realm of philosophic, abstract, or moral discourse, there is another line in the history of Western political thought that moves in a different direction. According to this second way of

---

39 Philip Sidney, *A Defence of Poetry* (Oxford: Oxford University Press, 1966), 32. In this and subsequent citations, I have replaced the laborious "–eth" verb endings with the more familiar "-s."

40 McWilliams notes that this is in fact a gesture of great love. "Love moves us to sacrifice at least a considerable measure of dignity and rank in the interest of the elevation of the other: parents clown with children, philosophers come back to the cave, God descends to man. And in that descent, love finds its own excellence and its higher nobility, as in Paul's grand cadence." See "Minstrels, Kings, and Citizens: Mark Twain's Political Thought," in *Democracy and Excellence: Concord or Conflict?*, ed. Joseph Romance and Neal Riemer (Westport, CT: Praeger, 2005), 44.

thinking, storytelling is critical for moral education because it is a force of moderation. Rather than being portrayed as a vehicle of ascent to the philosophic or abstract realm, here storytelling is portrayed as a vehicle of descent, chastening our pretensions to moral perfectibility and correcting our most excessive philosophic aspirations. In this view, storytelling tempers moral abstractions by drawing attention to the particularity and imperfection inherent to human existence. This process of moderation and temperance, the argument goes, is especially important to the extent that moral education is pursued as part of training for the political sphere, since as Thomas Aquinas contends, we must be cautious of trying to impose too ambitious a law on imperfect creatures – and aware that any law conceived by humans is itself necessarily imperfect.[41] In other words, for moral education to have proper purchase in the world of action, it must be tethered to an understanding of human limits, and storytelling helps to provide that understanding.

In the modern age, perhaps the thinker who makes this argument most directly is Arendt, who propagates a view of political education in which storytelling is central. According to Arendt, "the political function of the storyteller – historian or novelist – is to teach acceptance of things as they are."[42] Storytelling is a communicative form that captures the particularity of human action, the fact that different humans see and decide and proceed differently in the world, and each in an imperfect way. Storytellers serve to remind human beings of our limited capacities as mortal beings; storytellers must be "loyal to life," says Arendt, in the sense that to work, stories must take account of the partial sight of human beings, of human frailty and imperfection.[43] (On this count, we might think of the Nigerian writer Ben Okri's statement that "where there is perfection there is no story to tell.")[44] Stories trade on detail, circumstance, and accident: those elements of human experience that are as fixed as they are limiting. And those elements, without doubt, set

---

41 Saint Thomas Aquinas, *Summa Theologiae,* trans. Fathers of the English Dominican Province, 1912 (Raleigh, NC: Hayes Barton Press, 2006), 1870.
42 Hannah Arendt, *Between Past and Future: Eight Exercises in Political Thought* (New York: Penguin Books, 1993), 262.
43 Hannah Arendt, *Men in Dark Times* (New York: Harcourt Brace, 1993), 97.
44 Ben Okri, *Birds of Heaven* (London: Orion Books, 1996), 22.

boundaries on the political actualities and possibilities of the world. Without an appreciation of human particularity, Arendt argues that political judgment may become not only indifferent but brutal; as Kimberly Curtis notes, for Arendt the "unbearable pain" of the concentration campus, and more generally of life in totalitarian society, was its "radical rendering superfluous of human particularity."[45] In Arendt's estimation, as Lisa Disch says, storytelling involves a mode of judgment that is taking "a stand in full recognition of the complexity and ambiguity of the real situations in which judgments are made," and holding "oneself responsible to argue with and speak not only to those with whom one agrees but to those with whom one disagrees." Storytelling reminds us, therefore, that in human life, some amount of conflict is inevitable.[46] Stories are therefore anti-totalitarian, in the practical and philosophical senses. Human beings are situated partially, seeing through our glasses darkly, who in mortal life can never achieve the levels of perfection that we can envisage or even establish in speech. As Augustine has it, the city of God cannot be fully realized by men on earth.[47]

In one of his most illuminating essays, Ralph Waldo Emerson makes a strong case that storytelling thrives in the distance between Augustine's two cities – the distance between the divine and the human, or the whole and the part. The "radical joke of life and literature," writes Emerson, lies in the "intellect's perception of discrepancy" between the ideal in the philosophical sense and the delinquencies of human practice. Stories move us to laughter or tears largely, Emerson says, because they expose "the contrast between the idea and the false performance." Great storytelling reminds us of what Emerson calls our "halfness," our incompleteness and imperfection as living creatures – and the pathos and humor that lie in our pretentions to wholeness. The laughter or the tears that a story can provoke are the mark of

45 Kimberly F. Curtis, "Aesthetic Foundations of Democratic Politics in the Work of Hannah Arendt," in *Hannah Arendt and the Meaning of Politics*, ed. Craig Calhoun and John McGowan (Minneapolis: The University of Minnesota Press, 1997), 33.

46 Lisa Disch, "More Truth Than Fact: Storytelling as Critical Understanding in the Writings of Hannah Arendt," *Political Theory* 21.4 (November 1993): 688.

47 Saint Augustine, *The City of God Against the Pagans*, ed. R. W. Dyson (Cambridge: Cambridge University Press, 1998), 80ff.

recognition that something fundamental about ourselves is being made manifest. In providing this opportunity for tragicomic recognition, Emerson says, storytelling lends to the philosopher a more truthful kind of "integrity," providing a "balance-wheel in our metaphysical structure" that is "an essential element in a fine character."[48] By reminding us to be honest about who we are, storytelling ennobles us even though it may at first lower or impugn our most substantial ambitions.

Within the context of moral education, therefore, storytelling serves to chasten the most abstract and perfected linguistic formulations with the recognition that in reality, human life is neither abstract nor perfectible. By drawing attention to human experience, and the limitations that experience entails, storytelling helps to correct the philosopher's temptation to overlook those limitations and perform what Donna Haraway calls the "god trick" of professing to see everywhere from nowhere, or of purporting to have infinite vision (which can include the infinite vision of "easy relativism").[49] They chasten, that is, the philosopher's temptation to radically divorce thought from the complex experience of the world, or to imagine that in political philosophy, the "displacement of politics," as Bonnie Honig calls it, is a desirable or even viable goal.[50] Storytelling teaches that an awareness of the limitations of human experience – an awareness of human partiality – is necessary for informed and sagacious political thought. Even if moral propositions may be stated and understood in abstract language, in politics those principles need to be translated into regulation. And that regulation must rest on some recognition of the kind of (mortal, imperfect, partial) beings whom that regulation is intended to serve and address.

It should be clear that this argument draws on the old proposition, most powerfully articulated by Edmund Burke, that political judgment

48 Ralph Waldo Emerson, "The Comic," in *Emerson's Complete Works: Letters and Social Aims*, ed. Edward Waldo Emerson (Boston: Houghton Mifflin, 1917), 159–161.

49 Donna Haraway, "Situated Knowledges: The Science Question in Feminism and the Privilege of Partial Perspective," *Feminist Studies* 14 (1988): 581–582; Donna Haraway, *When Species Meet* (Minneapolis: University of Minnesota Press, 2008), 296.

50 Bonnie Honig, *Political Theory and the Displacement of Politics* (Ithaca: Cornell University Press, 1993).

requires more than mere familiarity with moral principle in the abstract. "The nakedness and solitude of metaphysical abstraction," Burke writes, can never serve as a sole source of political knowledge, since "circumstances (which with some gentlemen pass for nothing) give in reality to every political principle its distinguishing colour, and discriminating effect," and "the circumstances are what render every civil and political scheme beneficial or noxious to mankind."[51] Burke's famous formulation, of course, is not unique in its sentiment; many serious political thinkers have made the case that political wisdom rests on an awareness of human existence that is not merely abstract. A better good, says Plato, is as close as humans may get to the best; even if we can imagine an ideal form, we can never reach it, but only approach it in fits and starts.[52] Aristotle argues that because "the best is often unattainable," political wisdom depends on an acquaintance "not only with that which is best in the abstract" but also with particular conditions and forms of governance.[53] Even Georg W.F. Hegel contends that "abstraction from every aspect," when applied to politics, becomes a kind of destructive "fanaticism"; political thinking, he argued, must regard the inherent particularity of institutions even as it aspires to a certain kind of detachment.[54] (Elsewhere, Hegel makes the claim more generally, maintaining that "people who are too fastidious towards the finite never reach actuality, but linger lost in abstraction, and their light dies away.")[55] There is inescapable imperfection in human life, and to

---

51   Edmund Burke, *Reflections on the Revolution in France* (London: Seeley, Jackson, and Halliday, 1872), 11.

52   Plato reveals his understanding of this fact in the discussion of the Form of the Good in *The Republic*. The Form of the Good provides the ultimate standard by which it is possible to judge the value of particular objects, but systematic knowledge of the Good – though it be the highest goal in education – is not the Good itself. "As for knowledge and truth," Socrates says, "just as in the other region it is right to hold light and sight sunlike, but to believe them to be sun is not right; so, too, here, to hold these two to be like the good is right, but to believe that either of them is the good is not right." See Plato, *The Republic*, 189 [508e-509a].

53   Aristotle, *Politics*, 92 [1288b].

54   G. W. F. Hegel, *Philosophy of Right*, trans. S. W. Dyde (London: George Bell and Sons, 1896), 14; 16.

55   G. W. F. Hegel, *The Logic of Hegel*, trans. William Wallace (Oxford: Oxford University Press, 1904), 173.

neglect that fact – as straightforward formulations of moral abstraction may do – is to risk a kind of recklessness in the realm of action. Of course, it bears emphasis that none of these thinkers believes in dispensing with abstractions or universals altogether – all assume that that there are universal standards of better and worse, good and bad, right and wrong, that can be apprehended by humans as rational beings – but they believe, rather, that an awareness of human imperfection helps us to inform the way those universal standards should be translated into practical rules.

This sense of the moderating role of storytelling in particular – of the role of storytelling in helping to translate moral principle into prudent political regulation – finds expression in the work of a number of Western political thinkers. It is the sense that underlies Niccolo Machiavelli's description of himself not as a political scientist or philosopher, but as a storyteller; as Michael Harvey says, Machiavelli saw storytelling as a way to expose the "tragic strain" of human inconstancy and imperfection that he thought needed to be taken into account in any political vision.[56] And it is the sense underpinning Walter Benjamin's assertion that "an orientation toward practical interests is characteristic of many born storytellers." As Benjamin describes, storytelling is a form of counsel that makes use of "the fabric of real life," drawing on individual and communal human experience in order to guide proper political action.[57] To a great degree, Solon's answer to Croesus exemplifies this feature of storytelling; part of the power of his response is that it draws on particular experiences and names particular mortal beings. Their stories interest Croesus in part because they deal with real communities and real people, people to whom Croesus can compare himself readily. What makes Solon's answer to Croesus powerful, in other words, is that it demonstrates forcefully, with tangible examples, man's ultimate frailty and mortal incompletion.

---

56   Michael Harvey, "Love and Longing in *L'Asino*," in *The Comedy and Tragedy of Machiavelli: Essays on the Literary Works*, ed. Vickie B. Sullivan (New Haven: Yale University Press, 2000), 134–135.

57   Walter Benjamin, "The Storyteller," in *Theory of the Novel: A Historical Approach*, ed. Michael McKeon (Baltimore: The Johns Hopkins University Press, 2000), 79.

Another cast on this argument about the moderating force of storytelling emphasizes the way in which, as an educational tool, stories provide tangible and particular examples of general principles. (A story "couples the general notion with the particular example," as Sidney puts it.)[58] Just as a physics professor might roll a ball down an inverted plane to provide an example of the principle of acceleration, a moral educator tells stories to provide illustration, to tie the greater principle at stake to its expression in the world. In both cases, the abstract statement and the particular example work together to provide a more comprehensive view of the subject. Along those lines, stories thus may remind us principles are only made manifest in particular instances – much in the way, say, that the United States Supreme Court expresses principles for judging only through its rulings in specific cases.[59] As Aquinas says, citing Aristotle, "prudence does not deal with universals only, but needs to take cognizance of singulars also." Therefore, "it is necessary for the prudent man to know both the universal principles of reason, and the singulars about which actions are concerned." Even the knowledge of a few particular cases – the knowledge that can be gleaned from exposure to a certain number of stories – "suffices for human prudence," says Aquinas.[60] A complete moral education cannot neglect the particulars, which are precisely what storytelling may provide.

For his part, MacIntyre offers a powerful summation of this argument in favor of storytelling as a moderating and particularizing force in moral education. Storytelling reminds us, he says, that

> particularity can never be simply left behind or obliterated. The notion of escaping from it into a realm of entirely universal maxims which belong to man as such, whether in its eighteenth-century Kantian form or in the presentation of some modern analytical

---

58   Sidney, *A Defence of Poetry*, 32.

59   Paul Gewirtz notes, somewhat along the same lines, that the common-law legal method "celebrates case-by-case and fact-dependent decision-making" and thus "reflects a certain distrust of the ability of general legal rules to regulate a complex and ever changing reality." See "Narrative and Rhetoric in the Law," in *Law's Stories: Narrative and Rhetoric in the Law*, ed. Peter Brooks and Paul Gewirtz (New Haven: Yale University Press, 1996), 6.

60   Aquinas, *Summa Theologiae*, 2529.

moral philosophies, is an illusion and an illusion with painful consequences. When men and women identify what are in fact their partial and particular causes too easily and too completely with the cause of some universal principle, they usually behave worse than they would otherwise do.

Even if we acknowledge, as MacIntyre does, that it is "in moving forward from such particularity that the search for the good, for the universal, consists," we must acknowledge that prudential and wise political action must attend to detail and circumstance. Thus, "the chief means of moral education is the telling of stories."[61]

Notably, as a number of thinkers have made clear, there tends to be a strong conservative strain to this argument about the relationship between storytelling and moral education. Arendt, Benjamin, and MacIntyre all stress the fact that storytelling is a powerful connective and intergenerational force within communities, helping to preserve traditions and modes of understanding. That is, storytelling not only involves itself with particular details in the most general sense; storytelling often involves itself with particular details that are "ours," that focus on the specific experiences of a given community of human beings. For Arendt, stories are important largely because they are a means of cultural transmission across the generations that add depth and meaning to political judgment; "depth cannot be reached by man except through remembrance," she writes, and storytelling is a means by which people remember from whence they have come.[62] A story, says Benjamin, "preserves and concentrates" wisdom across the generations, and is capable of releasing that wisdom "even after a long time."[63] MacIntyre puts it this way: those who listen to a storyteller are best understood as "heirs." It is through stories, says MacIntyre, that people learn "what the cast of characters may be in the drama into which they have been born and what the ways of the world are."[64] Storytelling tethers people not just to an understanding of human

61   MacIntyre, *After Virtue*, 205–206; 121.
62   Arendt, *Between Past and Future,* 94.
63   Benjamin, "The Storyteller," 81.
64   MacIntyre, *After Virtue*, 201.

beings as partial creatures in the general case, but to those particular attachments and loyalties that attend being a member of some given society. In this way, too, storytelling moderates the highest moral abstraction, reminding us that our duties and obligations apply to us as members of particular families, communities, and polities.[65]

In general, this strain of argumentation rests on the understanding that politics itself is an endeavor where particularity matters deeply, and matters at all times, since politics itself is the necessary craft of in-between beings who have some capacity for transcendence, imagination and liberation but are in other ways limited, beings who have capacities for abstracting intellectually from their own condition but who exist within bodies and boundaries. These accounts emphasize that politics is predicated on human in-betweenness, on the expansive visions of incomplete beings. As the *Symposium* speeches of both Socrates and Aristophanes illustrate, as soon as you imagine humans in a state removed from particularity and partiality, a state of completion, the need for politics disappears.[66] Without an account of particularity in human experience, politics itself stops making sense – or becomes unrecognizable. "Completion makes the city irrelevant," as Saxonhouse writes. "The city arises to satisfy our incompletion, our failure to reach our *eidos*, our form, our own."[67] James Madison captures this notion in his well-known locution that "if men were angels, no government" – no city, no politics – "would be necessary."[68] In addition, political activity

65   Of course, conventions and traditions can be morally dubious or just plain wrong, as in the tradition of slavery within the American South. This suggests why the Arendtian notion of storytelling in political life is incomplete, at least as far as moral education goes; this kind of awareness needs to itself be filtered through and tested by more abstract and universal formulations of good and bad, right and wrong. Just as an account of morality that neglects particularity is incomplete, an account of morality that neglects universals is incomplete.

66   See Plato, *Symposium*, trans. Candace Ward (New York: Dover Publications, 1993).

67   Arlene W. Saxonhouse, "Eros and the Female in Greek Political Thought: An Interpretation of Plato's *Symposium*," *Political Theory* 12.1 (February 1984): 19.

68   James Madison, "Federalist 51," in *The Federalist Papers* by James Madison, Alexander Hamilton, and John Jay, ed. Isaac Kramnick (New York: Penguin Books, 1987), 319.

itself – as a human activity – does not transcend that human incompletion; "like the human beings who inhabit them," Mary Nichols writes, "cities are not isolated units, closed to the outside and perfect within themselves."[69] Political life does not represent the triumph over the human condition but merely reflects it, a truth that Madison captured in his rhetorical question: "What is government itself but the greatest of all reflections on human nature?"[70] Political action, like the human animal, is imperfect, particular, and complex. With that in mind, it seems evident that wise political judgment – political judgment that is properly called moral – cannot exist without an awareness of human partiality and imperfection.

In this second mode of thought about the role that storytelling may play in moral education, especially as that moral education is part and parcel of civic or political preparation, storytelling is critical because it keeps us bound to ourselves, and bound to the earth on which we reside. Storytelling is a means by which we remind ourselves that even if moral propositions are properly formulated at the level of abstraction, they are properly applied in particular circumstances and instances. If a complete moral education involves attention both to the grandest philosophical constructs and the inevitable imperfections of human experience, storytelling may be its most essential tool.

* * *

It should be clear at this point that although these two major strains of thought about the place of storytelling in moral education seem to point in different directions, they are in fact quite complementary strains of argumentation. Put together, they remind us of the need for moral education to be informed by an awareness of who we really are – of our human nature. And, as Aristotle says, "our nature is not simple."[71] We are creatures both of nature and convention, creatures who by nature live under conventional regulations. We are political

---

69   Mary P. Nichols, *Citizens and Statesmen: A Study of Aristotle's* Politics (Lanham, MD: Rowman & Littlefield, 1992), 136.
70   Madison, "Federalist 51," 319.
71   Aristotle, *Nichomachean Ethics*, trans. J.E.C. Welldon (London: Macmillan and Co., 1912), 243 [7.15].

creatures. With that in mind, perhaps the greatest task of the moral educator is to find ways to help his students access the higher and more fundamental truths – to cultivate their philosophical capacities – while at the same time reminding them of their essential imperfections, and the essential imperfections of all creatures to whom conventional rules and regulations are intended to speak. No moral education is complete without attention to both of these dimensions. It is thus the great virtue of storytelling, that it can elevate the grounds of our contemplation even as it tethers us to the truth about ourselves.

The role of storytelling in moral education might on these terms be compared to Socrates' account of the pursuit of the Beautiful – what Allan Bloom calls the "ladder of love" – in Plato's *Symposium*. There, Socrates, while recounting a conversation with a woman named Diotima, says that the philosopher must begin his ascent toward the Beautiful by rooting himself in particularity; it is only through gazing upon one body that he realizes that all bodies are beautiful. This rootedness is a necessary component in ascending the "ladder of love" that allows the philosopher, or lover, to view the particular, worldly, forms of Beauty before eventually gazing upon Beauty itself.[72] Yet even then, there is no transcendence of particularity; a ladder must stand firmly on the ground for us to be able to ascend it, and it must remain grounded for us to see long into the heights. Similarly, we might say storytelling is a means of moral education that assists our ascent toward the fundamental and universal truths while remaining grounded in an awareness of the particularity and imperfection of human nature. Both the transcendence and the rootedness are necessary for the pursuit of moral goodness and virtuous action, a reflection of the fact that love is both the greatest of human universals and the most intimate and partial of attachments.

One of the best moral educators I know is fond of recounting a story that appeared in the "Metropolitan Diary" column of *The New York Times*. "It was midway through Act III of 'La Traviata' by Verdi at the New York City Opera," the story begins:

---

72   Plato, *Symposium*, 30–33 [210–211]; Allan Bloom, "The Ladder of Love," *Plato's Symposium: A Translation by Seth Benardete with Commentaries by Allan Bloom and Seth Benardete* (Chicago: University of Chicago Press, 2001).

After witnessing Alfredo's confession of love, Violetta's rejection of the carefree life of Paris, their retreat to the country, Giorgio's plea to release Alfredo for the benefit of his sister's marriage prospects, Violetta's compliance and pretended deceit, Alfredo's jealous rage, Violetta's reversal, Giorgio's sympathy, an illness, the lovers' tragic reunion and Violetta's death, I heard the woman directly behind me say to her companion, "The same thing happened to my friend Gloria."[73]

One of the things that story reminds us is that the grand and the prosaic exist together in our world, the high mingled with the low. And for human beings, the low is always speaking to the high, and vice versa. What connects us – what connects Verdi's Violetta to the audience member's friend Gloria, what connects each to another – is that our stories are recognizable to each other on both the high and the low registers. Stories, as John Steinbeck once told a friend, make us less lonesome.[74] In learning to recognize each other through stories, we learn to recognize that we are beings who can appeal to a nature that transcends our partial selves, even as we remain to some extent partial beings. Moral education can never stray far from that kind of recognition, for such is the recognition of our own humanity, and moral education is the craft of cultivating a better human life. In its careful attention to the kind of creatures we are, storytelling helps to provoke and preserve that recognition, just as the moral educator who tells stories demonstrates careful attention to – demonstrates the most basic kind of care for – the creatures his students are and might be. Such storytelling, we might say, is the manifestation of the special kind of love that undergirds the greatest moral education. For it is only when people are made to contemplate who we really are that we may begin to contemplate who we might truly become.

---

73 Stanley H. Kreitman, in "Metropolitan Diary" by Ron Alexander, *The New York Times* (May 17, 1995), C2.
74 John Steinbeck, "To Peter Benchley (1956)," in *Steinbeck: A Life in Letters*, ed. Elaine Steinbeck and Robert Wallsten (New York: Penguin Books, 1989), 523.

Chapter 4:
On "Eating the Last Pizza":
The Wit of Hadley Arkes
James V. Schall, S. J.

As Justice Holmes taught us, it was the purpose of the modern project in law to remove the connection between morality and law. And yet that connection between the logic of morals and the logic of law cannot be removed. We convey the point to students in part in this way: If we come to the recognition that any act stands in the class of a 'wrong' – that it is wrong, say, for parents to torture their infants – our next move is not to say, 'therefore let us offer them tax incentives to induce them to stop.' Or 'let us offer them a DVD player.' It strikes people, at once, as laughably obscene to make contracts or appeal to self-interest here.

— Hadley Arkes, The Catholic Thing.[1]

But have you ever supposed . . . that men who could not render and exact an account of opinions in discussion would ever know anything of the things we say must be known?

— Plato, The Republic, 531e[2]

The law of contradiction expresses a necessary truth, and all efforts to refute it will fall into the embarrassment of self-contradiction. . . .

---

1   Hadley Arkes, "The Melting of the Pro-Life Democrats," *The Catholic Thing* (January 4, 2010), available at http://www.thecatholicthing.org/columns/2010/the-melting-of-the-pro-life-democrats.html.
2   (trans. Paul Shorey). *The Collected Dialogues of Plato, Including The Letters*, eds. Edith Hamilton and Huntington Cairns (Princeton, NJ: Princeton University Press, 1961).

The law of contradiction is something we must be able to grasp on our own before we are capable of understanding or assessing definitions.

– Hadley Arkes, First Things.[3]

I.

Near the beginning of his *Rhetoric*, Aristotle tells us that "things that are true and things that are better are, by their nature, practically always easier to prove and easier to believe in." (1355a).[4] He goes on to remark, in a profound passage, "it is absurd to hold that a man ought to be ashamed of being unable to defend himself with his limbs, but not of being unable to defend himself with speech and reason, when the use of rational speech is more distinctive of a human being than the use of his limbs." Someone may object that the powers of reason and speech can be badly used, "but that is a charge which may be made in common against all good things except virtue, and above all against the things that are most useful, as strength, health, wealth, generalship. A man can confer the greatest benefits by a right use of these and inflict the greatest injuries by using them wrongly" (1355b). The philosopher of common sense always makes common sense.

These famous words of Aristotle bring to mind the oratorical skills and earnestness of purpose of Hadley Arkes. They recall his clarity about the things that are true, his ability to defend and explain that truth with words even before those who will not listen to it, before those who use sophistical and convoluted speech to persuade themselves. They often choose not to see the truth when it is spelled out before them. As Yves Simon once remarked, it can be difficult for a man to give up a pet scientific theory of his even after it is proved to be wrong.[5]

The case of correcting one's own errors is both more serious and

3 Hadley Arkes, *First Things: An Inquiry into the First Principles of Morals and Justice* (Princeton: Princeton University Press, 1986), 51.

4 (trans. W. Rhys Roberts). Available at http://www2.iastate.edu/~honeyl/Rhetoric /rhet1–1.html#1355a.

5 Yves Simon, *A General Theory of Authority* (Notre Dame, IN: University of Notre Dame Press, 1980).

more dangerous in moral practice than in science. But once men have to give reasons for how they live and how they explain their actions, these reasons are no longer merely "private." They become public, subject to the logic that reduces them to principle. In the public order today, no one does this explication better, or with more wit, than Hadley Arkes. In his writings and lectures, Arkes shows us the wonder of seeing any issue at hand in its order or disorder. He delights in seeing the sheer truth of the thing against the background of the errors that surround it.

When I am asked to "prove" the implicit existence of a natural law among us, I resort to two strategies. Well, actually, I resort to a single strategy made manifest in two examples, one in C. S. Lewis, the other in Hadley Arkes. Lewis, in *Mere Christianity*, shows that the natural law works in each of us. We use it whether we are aware of using it or not. We implicitly understand its force and use it. Lewis asks us to think of almost any folks "quarrelling" over something.[6] The argument will go back and forth. One person will be accused of doing something wrong. The other person will deny that it is wrong, or he will give a reason why it was right. The two will exchange fine points of logic. Both sides, Lewis notes, will appeal to a standard. No one will simply say, "I am more powerful than you; therefore, shut up." This standard is binding on both. Each has to give a reason. Each side insists that his act was reasonable and right according to an objective standard.

Arkes uses a similar example in his "Provisional Summary," in *First Things*.[7] He tells of working as a young man in a Chicago precinct police station. (The life as lived in Chicago, his hometown, is much in evidence in all that Arkes writes. He knows both what goes on and what should go on there but often doesn't.) Somehow, Arkes found himself in charge of recording the crimes as they were reported to the police on an average Saturday night in the summer. After some time in this post, Arkes became bemused. He reflected on the meaning of what he was seeing. He set down the reasons given for murder on those Saturday nights in Chicago. He lists several. One was that "the man would not

---

6   C. S. Lewis, *Mere Christianity* (New York: Macmillan, 1952), 17–18.
7   Arkes, *First Things*, 165.

shut off the radio." Another, my favorite, was that "he ate the last pizza." How incongruous! But how do these bloody incidents "prove" the existence of a natural law?

Suppose we tell this story, as I have often done, to an ordinary group of students or others. Invariably, on hearing what happens, on hearing the paltry reasons given in Chicago for shootings on a Saturday night, the listeners laugh at such preposterous justifications. They understand the disproportion between killing a man because "he ate the last pizza" and what might be called an "ordinary" motivation to murder. The issue is not the killing itself and its rationale, but the disproportion between the normal reason and the crime's given frivolous reason.

This exaggeration is what makes us laugh. This laughter is a sign of working intelligence seeing the relation of things to each other. It is an implicit awareness that something, some law of proportion, has been violated. Ordinary people see its absurdity. Laughter is caused in us by our reason. We see an unexpected imbalance or irony presented as "reasonable." We get it. We do not have to have it explained in detail to us. Our minds already understand by holding the two acts before each other.

As I have known and read Hadley Arkes over the years, one thing above all strikes me. This capacity of wit makes him dangerous in public discourse. He sees contradictions. As I cited Arkes in the beginning, "The law of contradiction exercises a necessary truth, and all efforts to refute it will fall into the embarrassment of self-contradiction." He sees absurdities. He spells them out in their logic. Arkes enjoys the foolish mind in its foolishness and self-deception. It is not a vice, but a kind of redemption of the foibles of our kind. Laughter is the one thing that the proud man who refused to examine his own errors cannot stand. In this sense, the bemused philosopher is especially provocative. But for the same reason, he is particularly necessary for human sanity.

In many ways, in philosophical things, laughter is the only thing that will suggest to us the absurdities of our souls. I have often compared Hadley Arkes to Groucho Marx; both see the absurdity of things and are pleasantly bemused by it. Groucho was famous for "A Day at the Races." I might say that Hadley Arkes is famous for "A Day in the Classroom."

Ideas are to him what "Duck Soup" was to the Marx Brothers. But Arkes's humor, like all humor, stands on a foundation of the "serious." It stands on the abiding permanence of the truth of *what is*. It stands solidly on truth as seen in paradox and wit and contradiction.

II.

Philosophy exists primarily in discussion, not in books. Truth is only known when an active mind knows it. And that active mind has to be revolving about something, not just itself. Truth is when the mind corresponds with reality and knows that it does. In the beginning we not merely are, but we are with minds. The mind is not our invention. It is already given to us and makes us what we are. We discover that we have it by first using it and by hearing others use their minds. A man ought to be able to defend himself not only with arms but with speech, with his mind, as Aristotle told us.

We cannot "prove" the existence of, say, the natural law, its first principles. But we can indicate that we use it all the time, even when we deny that we are doing so. Much of the delight in existence consists in spelling out what those principles – Arkes's felicitous *first things* – that we use all the time are, even if we do not know or acknowledge that we are using them. It is from this point of view that I approach the work and mind of Hadley Arkes. He has seen and identified terrible things wrought by the confused minds of men. He sees what Aristotle saw, how small errors in the beginning lead to huge errors in the end. These erroneous things can be redeemed, at least in part, when we can laugh at the things that are but still ought not to be. This laughter is the first step of intelligence restored.

C. S. Lewis, as I mentioned, asked us to pay attention to any quarrel that we have overheard taking place among most any existing people. We will notice, he said, that those who argue with one another always appeal to a standard. They do not know that they do this. They just do it as if this is the way the mind works. This is how Lewis puts it:

> Now what interests me about all these remarks is that the man who
> makes them is not merely saying that the other man's behavior

does not happen to please him. He is appealing to some kind of standard of behaviour which he expects the other man to know about. And the other man very seldom replies: "To hell with your standard." Nearly always he tries to make out that what he has been doing does not really go against the standard, or that if it does there is some special excuse.[8]

What is remarkable in all the controversial work of Hadley Arkes is the presence of this standard of reason that informs his argument and lets him see absurdities. He may not suffer fools gladly, but I venture to say that he suffers them laughingly. He does not present truth as if he invented it. He presents it as that which is found in the thing at hand, itself waiting to be spelled out in clarity and logic.

In the beginning, I cited a passage from Plato's *Republic*. It reads: "But have you ever supposed . . . that men who could not render and exact an account of opinions in discussion would ever know anything of the things we say must be known?" The ability to examine and explain one's views in discussion is what the art of rhetoric is about. Implied here is the fact that many people do not consistently examine or explain their views. If they cannot, it looks like they will never see the illogic of their own views, even when that illogic is spelled out for them.

It is the function of what I might call "rhetorical charity" to point these things out. Often this pointing out can only be done with humor. Men are very loathe to acknowledge they were wrong in moral affairs when their logic is spelled out. They can easily, as Aristotle said, blind themselves through their bad habits so that they will not use first principles of action or draw prudential conclusions.[9] Hence, they look aside from the erroneousness of their stated position. They learn how to deflect their very own principles.

Take the following example from a column that Arkes penned in the summer of 2008.[10] Arkes had been largely responsible for promot-

---

8   Lewis, 17.
9   Aristotle, *Nicomachean Ethics*, Bk. II.
10   Hadley Arkes, "The Born-Alive Act and the Undoing of Obama," *The Catholic Thing* (August 18, 2008), available at http://www.thecatholicthing.org/columns/2008/the-born-alive-act-and-the-undoing-of-obama.html.

ing in Congress the enactment of the "born-alive infant protection" bill. This bill sought to protect the life of a child who has somehow managed to be born alive in spite of the abortionist's attempt to kill it.

The purpose of the bill was to establish a principle–namely that a live child, however it survived, was itself subject to the protection of the Constitution as a human being. Such a child is obviously a real human child, alive before us. This bill was a minimal step, but it could perhaps be an opening to a broader principle of human life protection in all its stages. Arkes knew what he was doing, one step at a time.

The current American president was asked about this issue when he was campaigning for that office. His response, as Arkes analyzed it, shows how the mind of Hadley Arkes works. "Barack Obama was asked about abortion, and he remarked that it was a serious, vexing 'moral' question. On the matter of when human life began, he said, that 'whether you're looking at it from a theological perspective or a scientific perspective, answering that question with specificity . . . is above my pay grade.'" Obviously, for an American president to admit that something so central is "above his pay grade" is in itself amusing. Arkes would not let this odd expression pass. We wonder what, in the president's view, his "pay grade" allows him to know.

Arkes next examines the logic of this presidential statement. "In the hands of Obama the meaning of 'moral' is recast: What does it mean to say that this is a 'moral' question and yet it must depend on judgments that are wholly subjective and personal, and which cannot be judged as true or false? For Obama, a 'moral' question is one for which reason can supply no judgment, and the judgment may finally turn on nothing more than self-interest." A moral judgment must precisely be not subjective. It must depend on logic and facts available to all, including a president. Arkes is right that implicitly Obama changes the definition of "morals" to suit his agenda. Going back to Plato, we wonder if he knows what he is doing here.

Next, Arkes takes up the question of whether the beginning of life is beyond anyone's "pay grade," especially a president. Arkes begins with an analogy. Take global warming. Not unlike the issue of when human life begins, this evidence for warming is also a "tangled, scientific question." However, in this area, the president has no trouble consulting authorities on the topic. The issue is not "above his pay grade." So, "what prevents him from consulting the textbooks of embryology or obstetric gynecology, or asking anyone who knows, in an effort to inform his judgment about human life?"

In fact, the textbooks are quite clear on the topic. "Human life begins with the merger of male and female gametes to form a zygote, a unique being with a genetic definition quite different from that of either parent." Why should a president not know this, at least by equivalent authority as he knows of, say, earth warming, though, in fact, the scientific status of the latter is far less established than the former?

Arkes continues: "If that is too much to absorb, he (the president) may retreat to the point readily understood, even by people without a college education: A pregnancy test is a sufficient and telling sign that new life is present and growing." Arkes adds: "We know now that this life does not undergo any change of species from its beginning to its end. Conceived by humans, it cannot be anything other than a human life."

Arkes makes his conclusion with humor: "If there was nothing there alive and growing, an abortion would no more be indicated or relevant than a tonsillectomy." But, of course, there is something alive there and growing in its own nature, and it is not the tonsils which grow in a different way. We draw this conclusion itself from the premises that Arkes has given us.

But this is not the final word of argument. If such evidence "is truly above Mr. Obama's 'pay grade,'" then the presidency must surely be beyond his competence and his pay grade." That is, the presidential office itself requires a man who can follow ordinary evidence and logic. He cannot avoid the "logic" in what he is doing by redefining morals subjectively and then propose that the matter is over his head, over his "pay grade."

All that needs to be added is that Obama, in the Illinois legislature, on the same sort of bill, did not vote to protect the child born in spite of the abortionist. "For Obama, the right to abortion is nothing less than the right to an 'effective abortion' or a dead child." Obviously, any "right to a dead child" makes mockery of our tradition's understanding that the purpose of constitutional rule is based on a "right to life." The two are contradictory. It is well that we see it spelled out.

In a related column,[11] Arkes makes this same point in another way, again with benefit of a bit of humor. "In that famous old joke, a lawyer is told by the Devil that he can have all the women and money he would ever want – and in return? He would give the Devil his soul. The lawyer, ever wary, ponders the offer and finally asks, 'What's the catch?'" The lawyer does not know of his own soul. Arkes sees in this old joke the same principle.

"But now large numbers of people with a college education learn that Barack Obama would withhold the protection of the law and medical care from a child who survives an abortion and they say, 'And so?' Why should that make a difference in *this* election?" Arkes proceeds to spell out why it would make a difference. "In this way, without the least strain or awareness, the soul of a democratic people is gently altered."

The altered soul sees no problem with the killing of the innocent in its beginnings. Human life is not protected by the law. Human life is now itself subject to the law, the law not of the Constitution, but of the jungle. The Socratic foundations of our civilization are based on the premise that "it is never right to do wrong." We now do wrong by denying that what we do is wrong. "The soul of a democratic people is gently altered." The lives of the most innocent are ruthlessly destroyed.

III.

Arkes has likewise spent a good deal of time relating the principles of the slavery controversy in American history to the principles of the abortion issue. He is quite clear that the same principles that freed the slave are those that should protect human life:

> In politics we are ever dealing with the righting of wrongs, the relief of injuries, the doing of justice – whether health care, the laying of taxes, or hazarding young men in war. Every one of these issues hinges on the prior question of just what constitutes the "person" who is the bearer of those interests and rights – and the object of our concern. The question of slavery was central in the

11 Hadley Arkes, "One Issue among Many?" *The Catholic Thing* (September 15, 2008), available at http://www.thecatholicthing.org/columns/2008/one-issue-among-many.html.

way that others were not because it touched the core of the question that *affected the rights of everyone else on every other issue.* And yet, 150 years later, a population showing far higher levels of formal education cannot quite grasp the same point when it comes to them as a matter of recognizing the human standing of our own offspring.[12]

This passage is more ironic than amusing. Those with formal education see less. They do not even see the "human standing" of their own "offspring."

In his essay "On Oratory," Cicero spoke of the requirements of a good rhetorician, of an orator who is able to persuade others. "Oratory is a much more considerable activity, and depends of a far wider range of different arts and branches of study, than people imagine,"[13] he wrote. In listening to or reading Hadley Arkes, one is struck with the range of his background. He is familiar with learned things, and he is also familiar with the non-learned language of ordinary people and common sense.

But Cicero notes the scarcity of good speakers. "There can only be one possible reason for the scarcity of speakers of any competence: the incredible vastness and difficulty of the subject." For "one has to acquire knowledge about a formidable quantity of different matters."[14] Cicero continues:

> To hold forth without this information will just mean a silly flow of windy verbiage. And then one has to be able to choose one's words well, and arrange them cleverly. It is also essential to have an intimate understanding of every emotion which nature has given to mankind: it is in the processes of calming or exciting the feelings of an audience that both the theory and practice of oratory find their fullest expression. Other requirements include a certain sparkle and wit, and the culture appropriate to an educated man, and a terse promptitude both in repartee and in attack. A

12 Ibid.
13 (trans. Michael Grant). Cicero, *On the Good Life* (New York: Penguin Books, 1971), 241.
14 Ibid., 241.

sensitive, civilized lightness of touch is also desirable. One's memory, too, must be capable of retaining a host of precedents, indeed the complete history of past things. Nor is it by any means advisable to be ignorant of the law and existing statutes.[15]

This lightness of touch, this sparkle, this thorough familiarity with the logic and history of issues – such are the talents displayed in almost everything Hadley Arkes touches.

In the introduction to his book *The Philosopher in the City*, Arkes tells of being at a conference on abortion and euthanasia. One of the biologists present, he recalls, expressed his doubt about the so-called "population problem." Arkes continued:

> He pointed out that if everyone in the world were somehow magically transported to Texas, there would be 1,500 square feet for every man, woman, and child in the whole world. It so happened that 1,500 square feet was the size of the lot on which the biologist's house stood in San Francisco, and with the population of the world concentrated in Texas, Texas would still have been less densely populated than San Francisco.[16]

Arkes cannot help but being amused at this statistic that so thoroughly deflates the over-population myths of our time.

But this statistic is not all. Arkes tells us that, after he considered the import of these numbers, "I rose to speak. I noted that I had always sought to avoid religious grounds for my arguments, but the projections for Texas had finally moved me to a recognition of personal faith. If all the people in the world really moved to Texas – if there was no one in Europe, no one in Asia, no one in the Middle East, and no one in Africa, I still *believed*: there would be 700,000 Democratic votes reported from Chicago."[17]

Much is to ponder in these delightful lines, above all Arkes' statement that he avoids "religious grounds" for his arguments. He does

---

15   Ibid., 241–242.
16   Hadley Arkes, *The Philosopher in the City* (Princeton, NJ: Princeton University Press, 1981), xiii.
17   Ibid., xiv.

avoid such grounds, I think, on what are themselves religious grounds. This is the religious position that reason is of itself valid, that the present attacks on life and human dignity are not religious in origin but scientific and philosophic–that is, rooted in bad science and bad philosophy. In other words, they are "arguments" that demand to be tested by logic and reason itself. What Arkes has discovered is that not only do those who "have the faith have the fun," to cite Belloc, but they also have the reason. They are increasingly the only ones.

Arkes concludes with this autobiographical "act of faith": "I have been transported, in my middle years, to a pastoral setting, but I remain a child of the city (where the dead man 'ate the last pizza'), and though there is much of late to challenge this faith, I still believe in the gods that watch over Chicago." These same gods, no doubt, have now sent Chicago to Washington where Hadley Arkes watches carefully the reasons given for issues beyond the president's "pay grade."

IV.

Immediately after the election of Barack Obama,[18] Hadley Arkes admits musing to himself. "I've been on the Internet," he tells us, "looking at real estate in . . . Malta. Just think, a four-bedroom townhouse, near the new marina, in Zabbar, $350,000 USD (asking). Hmm." The temptation to flee to another land where we were freer was widespread.

Arkes explains his thinking at the time: "It is not only that the outcome of our election portends a moral disaster at several levels. It is that the people around us, our fellow citizens, the people with whom we share control over our lives, have taken leave of their sober judgment, if they possessed any. For they seemed willing to drift happily into the camp of a candidate who is at odds with what most of them profess to favor."

It is the "moral disaster" that concerns Arkes, the outlines of which, perhaps more than anyone else, he has sketched for us. He has the

18 Hadley Arkes, "Wading Through the Debris, Clueless," *The Catholic Thing* (November 11, 2008), available at http://www.thecatholicthing.org/columns/2008/wading-through-the-debris-clueless.html.

capacity to leave us with epigrams and aphorisms that reach to the heart of our problems, epigrams and aphorisms such as: "There is something fearful in a family life whose founding doctrine is that no one may be bound ultimately when he chooses not to be bound."[19]

A country that chooses the laws and customs under which it lives cannot be surprised if someone offers to spell these laws and customs out over against a standard of what it is to be human. Our present ills are not "religious," but at bottom moral and intellectual in nature. Hadley Arkes is right to insist on this.

When the University of Notre Dame decided to honor Barack Obama with an honorary doctoral degree at its 2009 graduation, it gave as its reason that such an occasion would offer an opportunity for it to "present" the Catholic view to the new president.

In examining this proposal, Hadley Arkes began,[20] as he often does, by citing Immanuel Kant. Kant, he recalled, distinguished between "feelings of inarticulable affection" and "tendering respect." Respect means to "reverence" the law or principle "of which a person would be an example." The significance of that distinction, Arkes thought, "seems to have eluded the deep-dish minds among some professors and their wards at Notre Dame." Only an Arkes could point out to us the irony in the phrase "deep-dish minds." Such people cannot see that in honoring Obama "they are honoring the law of which he has made himself an example. They are honoring the principles that he has now marked off, inescapably, as the defining principles of his own character and the administration he directs. Mr. Obama is the first president to regard abortion not merely as a regrettable public choice, but as a public good to be promoted at every turn with the levers of law and public funding."

For his part, the President of Notre Dame claimed that he does not agree with Obama's policies but invited him there "to engage in conversation." What is important about Arkes is that he took this invitation seriously. He proposed a number of people, including himself, who

19 Arkes, *Philosopher in the City*, 409.
20 Hadley Arkes, "A Modest Proposal for Dialogue at Notre Dame," *The Catholic Thing* (March 30, 2009), available at http://www.thecatholicthing.org/columns/2009/a-modest-proposal-for-dialogue-at-notre-dame.html.

would be willing to engage the president in such a "conversation." "Yes," Arkes said, "I would not turn down the call myself, if asked." The president, Arkes pointed out, flew to Los Angeles to appear on "The Tonight Show" with Jay Leno, so there seems no reason why he could not converse at Notre Dame. "Let us take the official spokesmen at their word and hold them to it: Let us have that conversation and debate. On what tenable ground would they refuse?"

And that is where I should like to end with the mind and wit of Hadley Arkes. No president in his right mind would debate or converse with Hadley Arkes about the truth of life, family, and polity. What Hadley Arkes stands for in the public order is the "debate that never happened." And yet, it did happen in the writings and speeches of Hadley Arkes. There it is spelled out for us. If our actual kingdoms will not allow the standards of truth within their laws and customs, there needs to be, and is, a city in speech where we can see the truth that we deny or avoid.

This is what the writings of Hadley Arkes are about. They are about a people and their leaders who choose not to look at themselves. They cannot bear what Arkes calls the "logic" of their own morals. Hadley Arkes, fortunately for us, will not move from Amherst or Washington to a new townhouse above the marina in Zabbar, Malta. Nor can he be overly surprised if we kill our own kind because, so he says, understanding when human life begins is above our president's "pay grade."

Hadley Arkes knows human nature. He is from Chicago. He knows that the reason given for a murder in Chicago on a Saturday is that "*He ate the last pizza.*" He knows that such quaint, flimsy, but amusing reasoning is endemic to our whole intellectual and elite classes. Hadley Arkes is amused, and he is sad. What else can a good man be?

"But have you ever supposed . . . that men who could not render and exact an account of opinions in discussion would ever know anything of the things we say must be known?" These are the words of Plato. They are the spirit of Hadley Arkes. Briefly, the answer is, "No, if people do not discuss these fundamental issues, they will never know what they must know." Our public order deftly avoids this discussion. Hadley Arkes offers to engage it. We cannot be saved unless our minds are saved. It is for this reason that Hadley Arkes, with his wit and his oratory, happily exists among us.

II. Jurisprudence

Chapter 5:
The Morality of Positive Law
David F. Forte[1]

It was my second year of law teaching. I was Socrates – or at least I thought I was using his "method." My students stood as they answered my questions. I even called them by their last names.

"Mr. Carter." (Student rises.)

"So, just why did John Marshall dismiss Marbury's suit for his commission?"

"He found that the Court did not have jurisdiction?" (Student asks hopefully.)

"Is that a question or a statement?"

(Student forces an ingratiating chuckle.) "Marshall found that the Court did not have jurisdiction."

"Good. Why did the Court not have jurisdiction?"

"Because the law that gave the Court jurisdiction was unconstitutional."

"Right, Mr. Carter – one section of the law, of the Judiciary Act of 1789, was unconstitutional." (Student relaxes, hoping he can sit down.)

"But Mr. Carter, why is a law that is contrary to the Constitution invalid?"

1   I am grateful to my colleague, Professor Stephen Lazarus, for his advice on a draft of this work.

(Disappointed, student realizes he's not yet off the hook. Student pauses, considers.) "Well, I guess because the Constitution is higher."

"Higher?"

"Yes . . . a higher law."

"Really! Just what makes you think the Constitution is a law?" (Incipient panic sets in. Student's eyes flick side to side.) "Mr. Carter?" (Student stands mute.) I continue: "Well, let's start with the basics. What is a law? You're going to be a lawyer. Certainly you should be able to say what a law is. What is a law?"

(Student quiet, thinking.) "A law . . . is a rule. And . . . if you don't obey the rule, there's a penalty."

"Excellent! Mr. Carter, Are you a positivist?"

(Student smiles confidently.) "Well, I like to think that I look on the bright side of things."

By the end of the course, Mr. Carter, who had intuitively grasped Austin's notion of law,[2] still looked on the bright side of things. And well we should also, for Austin's positivism, which as Hadley Arkes has long argued as the equivalent of moral relativism, is not the positivism of the American legal system.

Legal positivism of the Austinian variety is the reputed antagonist of natural law. In the main, most versions of legal positivism describe law as a thing that, though abstract, is still subject to scientific analysis like any material thing. Within the legal positivist tradition, law may be based upon principles that are derived from power, or from consensus, or from some philosophical touchstone, such as utilitarianism, or pragmatism, or scientism, or equality. Law, *qua* law, however, does not, for the traditional positivist, derive its validity from some normative system outside of itself. There are good laws, and bad laws, but, analyzed in and of itself, law can be described and understood and its validity

2   John Austin, *Province of Jurisprudence Determined* (London: J. Murray, 1863).

tested outside of its substantive command. At bottom, legal positivism is nominalism applied to the formal (usually enacted) rules that regulate behavior in political communities.

For over two centuries, positivism has been ascendant among legal philosophers, confident that the ideas of natural law had no objective validity. A character in Stendahl declares, "There's no such thing as natural law. This expression is nothing more than a silly anachronism."[3] The "silly anachronism" was done away with in Fichte, Hegel, and Marx, in Bentham, Austin, and Holmes. Disparaged by utilitarians, historicists, pragmatists, sociological jurisprudes, and legal realists, natural law was generally regarded as, at best, an historical artifact, on view in some ancient texts or in Catholic seminaries.

It was not until the aftermath of World War II, in confronting the Holocaust, that natural law stirred again in the conscience of the philosopher and the judge. If the Holocaust were evil, pure and simple, then there must be a good, pure and simple. If we shrink from thinking that the Final Solution can ever have been a valid human law because its purpose was so utterly perverse, there must be a purposive standard by which we can know what laws are indeed legitimate or not. So thought the great German positivist, Gustave Radbruch, who after the war changed his views and argued that "there are, therefore, principles of law that are stronger than any statute, so that a law conflicting with these principles is devoid of validity. One calls these principles the natural law or the law of reason."[4]

And so the revival began, kindling in different places: Jacques Maritain in France; Russell Kirk in the United States; the Hart/Fuller debate across the Atlantic. By the 1980s, natural law had once again become a philosophical discipline. Dozens of books and hundreds of articles poured out. Natural law philosophers spoke to one another and argued with one another. Approaches to natural law theory developed in competition with one another. Henry Veatch revived an Aristotelian

---

3   Stendhal, *The Red and the Black*, trans. Horace Barnett Samuel (London; New York, NY: K. Paul, Trench, Trübner & Co., 1916), 517.

4   Gustav Radbruch, "Five Minutes of Legal Philosophy," in *Philosophy of Law*, ed. Joel Feinberg and Hyman Gross (Belmont, CA.: Wadsworth Pub. Co., 1991), 29.

approach to individual rights.[5] John Finnis developed something nearer to a phenomenological point of departure.[6] Russell Hittinger sought
to defend the Thomist tradition.[7] And Hadley Arkes grounded his
understanding of natural law in the moral rationalism of Immanuel
Kant.[8] Natural law theorists engaged in debates and explorations with
utilitarians, liberal theorists, natural rights thinkers, and communitari-
ans to the benefit and maturation of each other.

The argument of all natural lawyers is that legal positivism is inadequate to explain the normative validity of law. Natural lawyers do not
think themselves redundant when they ask, "Whence comes the lawful-
ness of law?" But most natural lawyers will nonetheless be careful to
distinguish legal positivism as a system from positive laws as facts –
facts that are themselves deserving of prudential or perhaps even moral
respect, provided that they are grounded, even in a derivative way, from
principles of natural law or "right reason." The thought of Professor
Hadley Arkes has itself travelled such a trajectory from his seminal
First Things, which argued for the validity of normative first principles
behind the law, to *Beyond the Constitution*, which sought to ground the
Constitution itself on a matrix of "higher" first principles, to his latest
opus, *Constitutional Illusions and Anchoring Truths*, which comes
round to asserting the necessity of respect for positive laws themselves.

But I wish to go a step further.

*The thesis of my argument here is that the contemporary debate
between natural lawyers and their positive law antagonists is based on
a false dichotomy, and that, with few exceptions, respect for the free-
standing validity of positive law as developed in the Anglo-American
tradition is a moral imperative for the true natural law adherent.*

I make this assertion against the backdrop of the continuing antagonism between natural law and positive law adherents. The contestants
are not limited to writers of legal philosophy. The supposed antipathy

---

5   Henry Veatch, *Human Rights. Fact or Fancy?* (Baton Rouge: Louisiana State
       University Press, 1985).

6   John Finnis, *Natural Law and Natural Rights* (Oxford: Clarendon Press, 1980).

7   Russell Hittinger, *The First Grace: Rediscovering the Natural Law in a Post-
       Christian World* (Wilmington, DE: ISI Books, 2003).

8   Hadley Arkes, *First Things* (Princeton, NJ: Princeton University Press, 1986).

of the two traditions has filtered into both the refined and the bowdler-ized discourse of men and women of practical affairs, judges and politi-cians, philosophers and religious revivalists. It has been so from the beginning of the republic.

In 1798, in the case of *Calder v. Bull*,[9] the opening salvo of the debate began in the United States Supreme Court. Justice Samuel Chase declared that "I cannot subscribe to the *omnipotence* of a *State Legislature*, or that it is *absolute and without controul*; although its authority should not be *expressly* restrained by the *Constitution, or fundamental law*, of the State . . . An ACT of the Legislature (for I cannot call it a law) contrary to the great first principles of the social compact cannot be considered a rightful exercise of legislative authority."[10] In reply, Justice James Iredell made it clear that he thought it strange to think first, that a judge could go outside of the Constitution to find rights not written there; second, that even if there were such rights, a judge could possess the authority to enforce these unwritten rights; and third, Iredell argued, it is in no wise certain what the principles of nat-ural law are and how they would be applied to particular cases. In sum, judges had neither the wit nor writ to decide cases based on natural law. Isn't it better, Iredell averred, to limit our uncertainty by focusing only on the written text of the Constitution?[11]

In 1843, Justice John McLean, an abolitionist (who would later dis-sent in the *Dred Scott Case*), was on circuit presiding over a civil dam-age suit against a man who had harbored an escaped slave. The case was *Jones v. Van Zandt*.[12] Now this was, or should have been, a truly hard case. Many northern abolitionist judges believed that slavery was con-trary to the natural law. They also knew that slavery was protected in positive legislation and, in some ways, by the Constitution itself. Hadley Arkes long ago compared the views of Justices Story and Marshall on this point.[13] In *Jones v. Van Zandt,* the defendant's attorney was Salmon Chase, future rival of Abraham Lincoln for the Republican nomination

9   3. U.S. 386 (1798).
10   Ibid., 387–88.
11   Ibid., 398–99.
12   13 F. Cas. 1040 (No. 7,502) (C.C.D. Ohio, 1843).
13   Arkes, *First Things*, 134–36.

for President, future Secretary of the Treasury under Lincoln, and future Chief Justice of the Supreme Court. Chase suggested to the court that natural law should be used to limit the sweep of the Fugitive Slave Law. McLean disagreed. He firmly charged the jury that conscience had no place in deciding the merits of the case. The only place for conscience, he told the jury, was to oblige oneself to obey the positive law.[14]

> In the course of this discussion much has been said of the laws of nature, of conscience, and the rights of conscience. This monitor, under great excitement, may mislead, and always does mislead, when it urges any one to violate the law. Paul acted in all good conscience, when he consented to the death of the first martyr; and, also, when he bore letters to Damascus, authorizing him to bring bound to Jerusalem all who called upon the name of Jesus. I have read to you the constitution and the act of congress. These bear the impress of the nation. The principles which they lay down and enforce have been sanctioned in the most solemn form known in our government. We are bound to sustain them. They form the only guides in the administration of justice in this case. I charge you, gentlemen, to guard yourselves against any improper influence. You are to know the parties only as litigants. With their former associations and views, disconnected with this controversy, you have nothing to do. It is your duty to follow the law, to act impartially and justly; and such, I doubt not, will be the result of your deliberations.[15]

In 1947, Justice Hugo Black could not contain himself when he saw Justice Felix Frankfurter – the disciple of the positivistic Justice Oliver Wendell Holmes, Jr. – seek to define fundamental rights according to the natural law tradition. In attacking the idea that the Due Process Clause of the Fourteenth Amendment "incorporates" some or all of the Bill of Rights and applies them to the States, Frankfurter declared that the tradition of natural law was a better guide to discerning the fundamental rights inherent in the idea of "due process."[16] For Justice Black,

---

14 Robert Cover, *Justice Accused* (New Haven, CT: Yale University Press, 1975), 173.
15 13 F. Cas., 1040, 1047–48.
16 *Adamson v. California*, 332 U.S. 46, 60 (1947).

such a course would "degrade" the Bill the Rights, and "appropriate for this Court a broad power which we are not authorized by the Constitution to exercise."[17]

Among conservative scholars, the opposition of Robert Bork and Justice Antonin Scalia to natural law has been vexing. In beginning his long and friendly colloquy with Hadley Arkes, Russell Hittinger, and William Bentley Ball, Bork asserted, "The formulation and expression of moral truths as positive law is, in our system of government, a system based on consent, a task confided to the people and their elected representatives. The judge, when he judges, must be, it is his sworn duty to be, a legal positivist."[18]

Similarly, Justice Antonin Scalia has opined, "Maybe my very stingy view, my very parsimonious view, of the role of natural law and Christianity in the governance of the state comes from the fact that I am a judge, and it is my duty to apply the law. And I do not feel empowered to revoke those laws that I do not consider good laws. If they are stupid laws, I apply them anyway, unless they go so contrary to my conscience that I must resign."[19]

The positions of Bork and Scalia recall the views of Justices Iredell, McLean, and Black. They also seem to echo the statement of Captain Vere at the trial of Billy Budd:

> How can we adjudge to summary and shameful death a fellow creature innocent before God, and whom we feel to be so? – Does that state it aright? You sign sad assent. Well, I too feel that, the full force of that. It is Nature. But do these buttons that we wear attest that our allegiance is to Nature? No, to the King."[20]

17   332 U.S., 70.
18   "Natural Law and the Constitution," in *First Things* (March 1992), reprinted *in A Time to Speak* (Wilmington, DE: ISI Books, 2008), 311. Arkes, Hittinger, and Ball answered Bork in "Natural Law and the Law: An Exchange," *First Things* (May 1992). The traditional critique of Bork's position was most recently articulated by Bradley C.S. Watson in "The Old Race of Judges," in *Claremont Review of Books* (Fall 2009).
19   U.S. Supreme Court Associate Justice Antonin Scalia, Rome Address at the Gregorian University (May 2, 1996), in ORIGINS: CNS Documentary Service, 26.6 (June 27, 1996): 89.
20   Herman Melville, *Billy Budd* (New York, NY: Aerie Books Ltd., 1988), 84.

But as I hope to show, there is more morality to Bork's and Scalia's position than seems to be with Vere.[21]

We see that even among those who would defend the original content and understanding of the Constitution against modern reinterpretations, or rather, departures from it, there is the fear that looking for legal norms in natural law would unground the judge from his duty to the Constitution, just as much as contemporary autonomy theories do. Thus do Robert Bork and Antonin Scalia take the side of Iredell against Chase.

The debate over the relevance of natural law to the judicial craft has not been limited to judges and political theorists. In 1991, then-Senator Joseph Biden was shocked to hear that Clarence Thomas had said that he considered natural law to be a basis for interpreting the Constitution. In a tangled opening statement at Thomas's confirmation hearing, the Senator opined that there were different types of natural law according to the political content of each. Some natural law was good, and some was bad, he declared. Bad natural law allows for economic liberty against the regulatory power of the state. Good natural law allows for reproductive freedom and sexual privacy. The kind of natural law Clarence Thomas is talking about, Biden implied, would be the kind that allows "the freedom of a factory owner to lock his employees into a building, where 25 of them perished in a fire."[22]

I do not here wish to reprise the rich debate among scholars regarding the positions of Justices Chase, Iredell, Frankfurter, Black, and Scalia and of Judges Bork or review the skepticism of Judge Richard Posner,[23] let alone the not-so-rich but revealing statements of then Senator Joseph Biden. Rather, I shall turn now to my central argument:

---

21 For present purposes, I put aside the continuing debate over the validity of Vere's position. See Richard H. Weisberg, *The Failure of the Word* (New Haven, CT: Yale University Press, 1984) and the debate over *Billy Budd* in *Cardozo Law Review* 26 (2005): 2223–46.

22 Opening Statement of Senator Joseph Biden on the confirmation of Clarence Thomas to the United States Supreme Court, at www.gpoaccess.gov/ congress/senate/judiciary/sh102–1084pt1/6–21.pdf.

23 See Richard A Posner, *The Problematics of Moral and Legal Theory* (Cambridge, MA: Belknap Press of Harvard University Press, 1999) and *How Judges Think* (Cambridge, MA: Harvard University Press, 2008).

the moral *centrality* of positive law to a natural law scheme of practical jurisprudence. Be it noted once again that the positive law I speak of is not the one expounded by the philosopher John Austin, but rather it is the positive law built and practiced over the centuries by the judges of the common law system.

Let us begin with a working definition of natural law so that we have an appropriate foil against which we can contrast the positive law I speak of.

Why is natural law *natural*, and why is natural law *law*? To begin, we may say that:

1. Nature is the reason why something is the way it is. For example, we can discover and define what the nature is of a manatee and by that determine and define why it is different from other water mammals.
2. Laws are rules of behavior, some predictive, as in the phases of the moon, some subject to voluntary actions, as in moral laws or moral rules of behavior. My heart beats to a predictable pattern, but I can choose to lie or choose to follow the moral rule of truth-telling.

We normally use the phrase "natural laws" to refer to the patterns of behavior of material bodies and of animals. "Natural Law," on the other hand, is normally reserved for the moral rules of behavior deriving from the nature of man. The rules apply to each individual in his relation to others and himself. Some rules of natural law become translated into refined schemes of positive law. For example, the moral rule – do not intentionally take the life of another human person – becomes the basis of the various levels of the criminal law of homicide. On the other hand, some natural law rules remain, for the most part, moral. The moral rule – do not deceive another person to his disadvantage – can be the basis of civil and criminal rules relating to fraud, but most lying remains outside of the positive law's cognizance. In fact, most positive laws are simply prudential or practical, and are not derived from natural law at all, or very indirectly. Beyond the underlying principle of taking care not to harm others, the question of whether there should be a speed limit on interstate highways and what it should be is a prudential question. Natural law is not seriously part of the particularities of the issue. As Aquinas puts it,

"For positive right has no place except where *it matters not,* according to the natural right, *whether a thing be done in one way or in another.*"[24]

There are many traditions of natural law: the Aristotelian, Stoic, Thomistic, neo-scholastic, Grotian, Kantian, phenomenological. But for our purposes here, let us take a modern formulation as an example, that of John Finnis, one that has been accepted or found harmonious with other contemporary natural lawyers.[25] Finnis, as do many other natural law theorists, begins (after establishing his epistemological methodology) by ascertaining what are the objective goods to human nature. When these goods are realized, a person flourishes in his or in her humanity. These are irreducible goods, such as life, knowledge, play, aesthetics, friendship, spirituality, and craft. Each of these goods is a goods-in-itself, not a mere instrumental good. Some, of course, can be both. I can listen to Mozart's Jupiter symphony because of its beauty, pure and simple (a good in itself), or I can listen to it to prepare for my music appreciation exam (an instrumental good).

The key to modern natural law theory is that *each person participates in these goods in a radically individualistic way.* Each person, by an experiential and reflective choice, mixes these goods in a way that is peculiar to that person, and that will not be and cannot be replicated in any other person at any other time. In a society that is based on natural law, we are confronted more with a choice among goods, and not simply choices between good and evil. This leads us to our first legal principle based on natural law. *A society based on natural law must be a free society.* We need the opportunities and the capacities to engage in the living of these goods, that is to say, we require a set of fundamental legal rights. By anchoring rights in the matrix of the fundamental goods of the human person, they become indefeasible and inalienable, as the Declaration of Independence proclaimed. A good society and a good government, therefore, foster and protect the individual in his enjoyment of certain fundamental legal rights.

Because of the radically individual way we participate in these

---

24 *Summa Theologiae*, Pt. 11–11 Q. 60 Art. 5, *Reply Obj.*1.
25 The following summary is taken from Finnis's seminal work, *Natural Law and Natural Rights*.

goods, a government consonant with the values of natural law must of needs leave a wide range of freedom to the individual, so that he can learn, form friendships, develop relationships, find (or not find) God. Government is *necessarily* limited. Beyond guaranteeing the exercise of the inalienable rights of individuals, government must leave a wide social space free for the individual and for human associations to operate, which means, in the vocabulary of natural lawyers, the polity must be based practically on the principle of subsidiarity, wherein private and semi-public civic associations thrive. The conclusion, then, is patent. *The first enemy of a natural law society is tyranny.* It is instructive that every tyranny in history justifies itself by claiming that they are using their powers to "do good" to the people. But under natural law, that is a contradiction in terms. Only the individual can "do good" by exercising his liberty to choose among the panoply of human goods. The role of government is to serve the capacity of the individual to "do good," not to do it for him.

Any appropriate natural law polity is necessarily – and properly – subject to the contingencies of its history and its culture. Such was the teaching of Edmund Burke. A natural law society can take many forms, but a natural law society anywhere in whatever form still fulfills the fundamentals of the human spirit. As Aristotle put it, "Laws that are not natural but man-made are not the same everywhere, because forms of government are not the same either; but everywhere there is only one natural form of government, namely that which is best."[26] What is the "one natural form of government" that is everywhere "the best"? Under modern natural law theory it is a government that fears tyranny and that allows for the full play of the attributes of human flourishing, or at least it should, if properly run.[27]

Turning now to the American form of what is the "best" polity, we confront the Constitution. The Madisonian structure of the separation of powers and of federalism was created by men who feared tyranny

---

26 Aristotle, *The Ethics of Aristotle: The Nicomachean Ethics*, trans. J.A.K. Thomson (New York, NY: Penguin, 1976).

27 See a more libertarian version of the classic natural law theory in Douglas J. den Uyl and Douglas B. Rasmussen, "Ethical Individualism, Natural Law, and the Primacy of Natural Rights," in *Social Philosophy and Policy* 18.1 (2001): 34–69.

and who were conscious of the tradition of natural law, albeit in a derivative way. The Founders were aware, and more or less conscious, of a set of "first principles," as Hadley Arkes would put it, of which the Constitution was the culturally defined positive law emanation.

Not contradictorily, the Founders desired a government that would be "energetic" in its essentials. Within the limits placed on the government to prevent tyranny, a limited government can nevertheless foster and protect the natural law goods of individuals by creating a legal and economic infrastructure by which these goods can flourish. The entire Federalist papers can be summed up in that Madisonian model: prevent tyranny and allow government to create an infrastructure for the individual pursuit of natural law goods.

Among the moral obligations of government is to provide for the common defense, to establish justice among individuals, to maintain a stable currency and promote economic conditions that will allow people to learn, to pursue knowledge, to seek the sacred, to form friendships, in other words, "to promote the General Welfare" (the common good). These are the practical moral requirements of a polity. The preamble to the United States Constitution can be seen as a natural law aspirational command to government, or more properly, to those persons who wield the power of government.

Notice that natural law is not some ceiling put over society above which the state cannot go. It is no brooding omnipresence in the sky. Rather it is what invigorates the whole society *through the positive law*.

This finally brings us to the judge and to his obligations under natural law and positive law.

It is no accident that in the debate over the relevance of natural law to judicial decision-making, the judges, for the most part, are on one side, and the legal theorists are on the other. Where legal theorists may find themselves morally anchored in the principles of the natural law, judges find themselves morally anchored in the positive law. It is important to repeat that point. Judges, like Bork, find themselves *morally* obligated to follow the positive law. They, as Cicero taught, find themselves limited and constrained by the moral duties of their office. In their morally limited function, they actualize one of the primary requirements of natural law, namely that the people must be protected from tyranny.

The positive law for judges is not just a set of enacted laws that need to be applied consistently and coherently. In the Anglo-American system, positive law defines the moral limits of the judicial craft. Everywhere he turns, the judge applies his reasoned evaluation to the positive law. There is an existential substance and reality to the positive law, which is the gravamen of the judge's daily life, in a way that can make natural law look to him as diffuse, attenuated and incapable of being easily redacted into his daily wont.

What then is the moral matrix of positive law in which the judge operates?

There is, to begin, the *positive law of statutes*, of administrative regulations, and of executive orders. In quoting Augustine, Aquinas writes, "*In these earthly laws, though men judge about them when they are making them, when once they are established and passed, the judges may judge no longer of them, but according to them.*"[28] By respecting the authority of the legislature and the executive, the courts affirm the political legitimacy of those branches that have a closer accountability to the people. Courts that are faithful to the positive law of statutes thereby strengthen the legitimacy of the polity.

It is in effectuating the validity of the positive law of statutes that the courts have developed sophisticated methods of statutory interpretation, which have evolved into a set of detailed and refined methods for ascertaining the true meaning of the text.[29] Justice Scalia has been particularly outspoken in the need for judges to abide by the rules of statutory interpretation.[30] Judges, in the main, abide by these rules and provide an essential link between the promulgation of the law in its true and intended effect upon human behavior.

Both Congress and the Executive develop laws and regulations against the backdrop of the judicial rules of statutory interpretation. By

28 *Summa Theologiae*, Pt. 11–11, Q. 60, Art 5.
29 See the illuminating summary of the rules of statutory interpretation in *Statutory Interpretation: General Principles and Recent Trends*, Congressional Research Service (2008).
30 *United Savings Ass'n v. Timbers of Inwood Forest Associates*, 484 U.S. 365, 371 (1988).

Executive Order, for example, the President has directed federal agencies to adopt methods in formulating regulations that are complementary to the judicial rules of interpretation.[31] Congressional staffers adjust the text of laws to make them coherent and harmonious with the vast panoply of extant federal legislation. More controversially, committee reports, Congressional findings, speeches on the floor of Congress, and the development of "legislative history," as well as the interpretive gloss given by the executive signing statements, provide additional direction. Justice Scalia argues against reliance upon legislative history, not because he is opposed to ascertaining the true intent of the law, but because he believes that much "legislative history" today is contrived and does not reflect the true meaning of the words in the statute. But the debate over the relevance and appropriateness of "legislative history" only makes sense against the fundamental premise that the judge's duty is to interpret, understand, and apply faithfully the meaning of the positive law of statutes. Thus, by adherence to the rules of the statutory interpretation, courts become habituated to be constrained to affirm the intent and will of the legislature, and not – if the judge applies the rules fairly and honestly – the judge's own policy preferences.

A second element comprising the moral matrix of positive law is *the law of the court*, or the rules of precedent or *stare decisis*. Precedent operates as a form of a judicially created statute, which, like legislative statutes, is binding but which still must be interpreted. Judicial interpretations of statutes can be corrected or modified by subsequent legislation. Similarly, rules enunciated in cases can be re-interpreted, narrowed, expanded or, in rarer cases, overruled (repealed) by a later court. There is, to be sure, a contemporary lively debate over whether incorrect interpretations of the Constitution should be maintained under the rule of *stare decisis*. Whatever the correct resolution of that conflict should be in particular cases, it is nonetheless telling that the debate would have no traction at all if precedent did not have a binding function on courts.

There is an additional parallel between the law of statutes and the

31   61 Federal Register 4729 (Feb. 5, 1996), *reprinted in* 28 U.S.C. §519.

law of precedents: both direct a judge's attention to what has gone before. Both testify to the fact that the law that comes to the judge is *de lege lata*, something already laid down, as opposed to *de lege ferenda*, law as it ought to be. Thus do both the law of statutes and the law of the court channel the judge away from subjective preferences. We should mention here that allied and part of the law of the court is the law of judicial system, by which lower courts follow the rules laid down by superior courts within their jurisdiction. The system provides consistency and coherence in the law throughout the country in its thousands of applications.

A third element is *the law of process*, which limits what a court can hear, what evidence may be admitted, and how a court may dispense legal justice. As every law student learns – and what every lawyer and judge knows – courts may not choose what issues to decide. They are limited to cases, which means that there must be a plaintiff (or petitioner), a defendant (or respondent) and a legal cause of action. The parties must have standing, that is,

First, the plaintiff must have suffered an "injury in fact" – an invasion of a legally protected interest which is (a) concrete and particularized, and (b) "actual or imminent, not 'conjectural' or 'hypothetical.'" Second, there must be a causal connection between the injury and the conduct complained of – the injury has to be "fairly . . . trace[able] to the challenged action of the defendant, and not . . . th[e] result [of] the independent action of some third party not before the court." Third, it must be "likely," as opposed to merely "speculative," that the injury will be "redressed by a favorable decision."[32]

The cause of action must be one that sounds in law, the positive law. The rights claimed are those that are asserted already to exist. There must be a genuine controversy, where the parties have opposing claims in an actual dispute. Collusive lawsuits are not to be permitted for compromise and consensus are normally to be found in the legislative process, not the judicial.

The law of process requires that the suit must be ripe for judicial

---

32   *Lujan v. Defenders of Wildlife*, 112 S. Ct. 2130, 2136 (1992).

action: all administrative remedies must have been exhausted, the suit must not rest *upon contingent future events that may not occur as anticipated*,[33] and the claim must be judicially resolvable. If the claim has been settled, or cannot be resolved, or has been given to another governmental entity to decide, it becomes moot, and is dismissed. In addition, the positive law of process includes all the requirements of pleadings, due notice, evidentiary rules, procedural rules of the particular court, and motion practice under which the judicial dispute is heard and resolved.

A fourth element of the law that judges deal with is *the positive law of the subject,* or of legal doctrine. Every legal dispute is brought in one or more subject areas, each of which has its own complex concepts, standards, and history. Known as "doctrine" in legal studies, each subject has a coherent and definable content, whether it be contract law, tort law, anti-trust law, tax law, bankruptcy law, divorce law, corporation law, or any of the other myriad substantive subjects taught at law school and continued on in the practice of lawyers. The vast detail, the motivating principles in every area provides a positive law of direct relevance to the resolution of each particular legal dispute.

There is, in addition, *the positive law of the case*, or *res judicata*. Once a case has been fully and completed decided, no court may revise or reopen the litigation. Although the legislature may change the underlying law and affect the legal rights of the parties even in an ongoing case, once the dispute has been resolved judicially, not even a legislative act can change the rights and duties of the parties decisively determined by the court.[34] As defined by the Supreme Court,

> The judgment, if rendered upon the merits, constitutes an absolute bar to a subsequent action. It is finality as to the claim or demand in controversy, concluding parties and those in privity with them, not only as to every matter which was offered and received to sustain or defeat the claim or demand, but as to any other admissible matter which might have been offered for that purpose.[35]

Like the other elements that make up the field of positive law, in

33   *Texas v. United States*, 523 U.S. 296, 300 (1998).
34   *Plaut v. Spendthrift Farm*, 514 U.S. 211 (1995).
35   *Cromwell v. County of Sac*, 94 U.S. 351, 352 (1876).

America, the rules delineating the reach of "claim preclusion" or *res judicata* are extensive, so much so that they take up over 170 pages in Moore's Federal Practice.[36] It was Abraham Lincoln's respect for the positive law of *res judicata* that led him in his criticism of the decision in *The Dred Scott Case* nonetheless to declare, "[N]or do I deny that such decisions must be binding in any case upon the parties to a suit as to the object of that suit."[37]

The judge who respects the positive law is also bound by *the positive law of the judge*, or, judicial ethics. The appropriate behavior of judges has been part of Western legal history for centuries.[38] In the United States, the American Bar Association first adopted Canons of Judicial Ethics in 1924. In 1972, the Canons were revised and redacted into a Code of Judicial Conduct that served as the basis for nearly all state codes of judicial conduct.[39] The Code covers such areas of judicial conduct as compliance with the law, diligence and impartiality, conflict of interest, and electoral activities. In addition, federal statutes cover disqualification and recusal of judges.[40]

Besides the positive law of statutes, of the court, of process, of the case, and of the judge, there are more global positive law elements to which a judge is morally beholden. The foremost can be termed the *positive law of law*, or more particularly, the principle of legality. It is here where the contribution of legal positivists (and their opponents) has assisted in determining what makes a law, *in its nature*, law. In Anglo-American law, the principle of legality is first evinced in the Magna Carta, which subsequently became part of the law of due process in America, or natural justice in England:

> No free man shall be seized or imprisoned, or stripped of his rights

---

36   18 *Moore's Federal Practice* 3d, Section 131.
37   Abraham Lincoln, First Inaugural Address (4 March, 1861).
38   See Aquinas's treatment in "Whether it is Lawful to Judge," *Summa Theologiae*, Pt. 11–11 Q. 60 Art. 2.
39   The most recent revision took place in 2007. See Stephen Gillers, Roy D. Simon, and Andrew M. Perlman, *Regulation of Lawyers: Statutes and Standards* (New York, NY: Aspen, 2010). Lawyers, of course, are also bound by state rules of professional conduct.
40   Ibid., at 715.

or possessions, or outlawed or exiled, or deprived of his standing
in any other way, nor will we proceed with force against him, or
send others to do so, except by the lawful judgement of his equals
or by the law of the land[41]

In the twentieth century, the principle of legality was illuminated in the
famous Hart/Fuller debate: H.L.A. Hart's notion of "Rules of
Recognition," and Fuller's rejoinder, best developed in his *Morality of
Law*.[42] Although Fuller referred to his theory as "internal natural law,"
his view is more of a delineation of the nature of positive law, qua law,
and the outer moral limits of what a judge can enforce as true positive
law. For positive law to be legal, argues Fuller, it needs to have certain
internal attributes: the rules must be general, publicly promulgated,
prospective, clear and understandable, consistent, capable of being
complied with, relatively stable, and administered faithfully. The Fuller
rules fall into the Anglo/American notion of the principle of legality
under which laws are not accorded recognition if they are vague,
absurd, impossible to administer, or invalid from desuetude.

The last global element that infuses the moral fabric of positive law
is *the law of reason*, or more exactly, *the law of reasons*. The Anglo-
American legal system's hallmark is the moral accountability of the
judge for his decision, particularly at the appellate level. He must give
reasons, publicly stated, justifying his decision, open for criticism and
rational impeachment. It is not enough for the judge to follow the various elements of the positive law, as outlined above. He must justify to
the people and the polity that he has been faithful to the positive law.
Not only, therefore, is the judge bounded by the moral constraints of the
positive law, he must be transparent in doing so.[43]

If faithfully adhered to, the judge who abides by the positive law

---

41   *Magna Carta*, Art. 39 (1215).
42   H.L.A. Hart, *The Concept of Law* (Oxford: Clarendon Press, 1961); Lon L. Fuller,
      The Morality of Law (New Haven, CT: Yale University Press, 1964). The debate
      initially took place in *Harvard Law Review* 71 (1958).
43   Apparently, the judicial opinion arose in the early 16th century in response to the
      development of the pleadings of lawyers before the bar on points of law. See
      Matthew Frank's review of Neil Duxbury, *The Nature and Authority of Precedent*,
      at www.bsos.umd.edu/gvpt/lpbr/subpages/reviews/duxbury1208.htm.

performs a rationally moral task without the need to refer to natural law principles that lie at the base of law's function, and, in many cases, of law's substance. The positive law of statutes, of the court (*stare decisis*), of the case (*res judicata*), of process, of the judge (judicial and legal ethics), of the subject (legal doctrine), of law itself (the principle of legality), and of reason provide the moral matrix by which a judge can ply his craft in consonance with natural law without needing to give it formal judicial notice.

All of the above impels a judge in the American legal system to adhere to *the law of the Constitution*, which provides the moral basis for originalism. The Constitution, as noted above, is the "culturally defined positive law emanation" of the principles of natural law – even with the embarrassing and even then admitted contradiction of slavery. If we take, for example, Justice Chase's plea for judges to acknowledge and enforce precepts of natural law, we find that each of his examples already sounds in the positive law of the Constitution.

"A few instances will suffice to explain what I mean," Chase wrote. "A law that punished a citizen for an *innocent action*, or, in other words, for an act, which when done, was in violation of no *existing* law" (N.B. in fact prohibited by the ex post facto clauses in Art. I, Sections 9 & 10); "a law that destroys, or impairs, the *lawful private* contracts of citizens" (N.B. prohibited by the impairment of contracts clause in Article I, section 10); "a law that makes a man *a Judge in his own cause*" (N.B. prohibited by the due process clause of Amendments 5 & 14); "or a law that takes *property* from A and gives it to B" (N.B. prohibited by the takings clause of Amendment 5). "It is against all reason and justice, for a people to entrust a Legislature with such powers; and, therefore, it cannot be presumed that they have done it."[44] (N.B. a principle of statutory interpretation that courts will always interpret a statute to be constitutional if it can plausibly be done.)[45]

It is true that Justice Chase goes on to aver that "to maintain that our Federal, or State, Legislature possesses *such powers*, if they had not been *expressly* restrained, would, in my opinion, be *a political heresy*,

---

44 3. U.S. 386, 388 (1798).
45 See, e.g., *United States v. Salerno*, 481 U.S. 739 (1987).

altogether inadmissible in our *free republican governments*."[46] But those fundamental principles are in fact instantiated in the positive law of the Constitution, and thus a judge who insists on adhering to the positive law of the Constitution is conforming himself to the natural law in the very act of following the moral commands of the positive law.

Some years ago, I too entered the lists against Judge Bork's positivism.[47] I argued that it was the practice of positivism that had "led to the most massive and unapologetic assertion of judicial power in our history." Obviously, I was defining positivism in Austinian terms. But perhaps because of my fleeting experience on the bench as an acting judge in my municipality, or perhaps because of reading Cicero again, I have come to modify my views. The problem with the legal realists and their disciples who wrote opinions such as *Roe v. Wade* is that they, in fact, did not follow the *positive law*. In that case, Justice Blackmun violated *the law of the court* by ignoring the tradition of cases opposed to such an innovative "right." He violated *the principle of legality* by proposing a rule that had little internal consistency. He violated *the law of reason*, for the opinion was simply a dictate declaring a result that had no colorable reasoning behind it with a flippant disregard of the norms of justification and transparency. Blackmun violated the positive *law of the Constitution*, for there was no privacy right encompassing abortion in the original understanding of liberty or in any reasonable of application of the original understanding.

Roe v. Wade is not censurable because it violates natural law – it does. Rather, it is censurable because Justice Blackmun violated the most fundamental moral norms of the positive law, prompting the famous observation of John Ely, "It is . . . a very bad decision . . . because it is bad constitutional law, or rather because it is *not* constitutional law and gives almost no sense of an obligation to try to be."[48]

Granted, slavery stood as a contradiction to natural law and the nat-

---

46   3. U.S. 386, 389 (1798).

47   David Forte, "Natural Law and the Rule of Law, On Principle," Ashbrook Center (April 1996). An expanded argument was in "Natural Law and the Limits to Judicial Review," in *Catholic Social Science Review* 1 (1996): 42.

48   John Hart Ely, "The Wages of Crying Wolf: A Comment on *Roe v. Wade*," in *Yale Law Journal* 82 (1973): 920, 947.

ural law principles that lay behind the Constitution. That painful dilemma remained for judges and others of good will until the end of the Civil War. But *Dred Scott, Roe v. Wade,* and the recent judicial usurpations of the legislature in attempting to establish same-sex marriage as a right are primarily violations of the commands of the positive law to which judges are morally beholden by virtue of their office.

It is true that in some sense, Taney, Blackmun, and the local courts declaring same-sex marriage a right all acted in an Austinian mode, but Austinian positivism is not American legal positivism. If those judges, as Robert Bork has argued, had been faithful to the moral commands of the American scheme of legal positivism, they would not have committed such egregious distortions of the Constitution, and incidentally – and Judge Bork would emphasize that it was indeed "incidental" – of the natural law as well.

Chapter 6:
Statecraft as Soulcraft:
The Case for Morals Legislation
Micah Watson

There are fundamental truths that lie at the bottom, the basis upon which a great many others rest, and in which they have their consistency.

These are teeming truths, rich in store, with which they furnish the mind, and, like the lights of heaven, are not only beautiful and entertaining in themselves, but give light and evidence to other things that without them could not be seen or known.

- John Locke, On the Conduct of the Understanding[1]

Prelude

The summer of 2009 witnessed an unusual standoff between the state of California and Los Angeles County and one of the Golden State's most profitable and popular businesses. As detailed by *The Los Angeles Times*, California's Division of Occupational Safety and Health and the Los Angeles County health department encountered resistance in their attempt to investigate an outbreak of sixteen cases of HIV among Southern California's estimated 1,200 pornographic "performers."[2] As is the case with many businesses, pornographers – whose industry is estimated to yield twelve billion dollars a year in the state of California

---

1 John Locke, *Some Thoughts Concerning Education* and *Of the Conduct of the Understanding*, ed. Ruth W. Grant and Nathan Tarcov (Indianapolis, Indiana: Hackett Publishing Co., 1996), 222.

2 Kimi Yoshino and Rong-Gon Lin II, "More Porn HIV Cases Disclosed," *The Los Angeles Times*, June 14, 2009, A4, www.latimes.com/news/local/la-me-porn-hiv12–2009jun12,0,3569962.story, accessed online June 13, 2009.

– prefer to regulate themselves and attempt to do so through a private institution, the Adult Industry Medical Healthcare Foundation (AIM). Their interest in remaining as unregulated as they can is rather prosaic and does not require much comment; their goal is to provide the least inhibited "product" possible without attracting the governmental scrutiny that shut down production for a month due to a similar situation in 2004.

The interest from the regulatory agencies of the local and state governments, however, raises some very interesting questions. State officials expressed frustration with the pornography industry's citation of privacy concerns in rejecting the state's inquiries about which actors in particular had acquired HIV. Their interest was in preventing a health epidemic, and the industry's reluctance seemed to them obstructionist.

This may seem obvious enough to the common observer. Yet there is a sense in which one might question the rationale of state officials to intervene, given that the industry in question involves the behavior of consenting adults presumably cognizant of the health risks of their profession. Why cannot free citizens, acting by their own lights and under no compulsion, choose to engage in medically risky behavior in order to earn a living? By what right can the public officials of the county of Los Angeles and the state of California seek to restrict this flourishing business, even if it is a curious type of business that combines transactions of a commercial and sexual nature?

The answer seems to be two-fold. First, the consequences of contracting HIV are known by all to be potentially devastating to the individual and thus to be avoided. Granted, this judgment depends upon a shared conception of what it means to be physically healthy, but this conception is still shared by a robust proportion of California's citizenry and established by the accepted authority of medical science. Nevertheless, one might respond, the chances of contracting HIV by working in the adult film industry are best considered by the individuals who will bear the consequences of the possible rewards and costs of such a course of action. True, the possible onset of AIDS as a result of an HIV contraction is an undesirable outcome, but so is the possibility of Parkinson's for the boxer, concussion-related brain damage for the football player, and lung disease for the coal miner.

What sets off this particular industry from these others, and is the second part of the answer, is the risk of passing on this particular condition and creating a public health epidemic. In this sense, pornographic actors are viewed as similar to nurses and other health workers, whose exposure to contagion is understood to justify governmental oversight. Thus officials from the State of California, relying on the traditionally understood police powers to protect public health, safety, and morals, considered themselves to be rightfully exercising their mandate on behalf of the public.

Even so, what might strike one as odd in the phrase "public health, safety, and morals" is its concluding word. Including "morals" among the reasons for which the state might regulate the behavior of its citizens and their businesses seems today rather quaint. Yet it was not too terribly long ago that state officials believed themselves competent not only to judge what was detrimental to the physical health of its citizens but also to what corrupted their moral health and well-being. Like the ravages of a physical disease, ordinary citizens and their officials could point to good reasons to think that pornography not only damaged the producers, "actors," and consumers, but also those with whom they shared their communities. Furthermore, the authority constituted by the consent of the citizens – the state – was understood to be justified in principle to assist people in protecting themselves and their neighbors from destructive behavior.

We could track the transformation of this understanding through a somber review of California's legislative and judicial history. Yet we can find a more direct and perhaps more telling illustration of just how the moral and legal climate has changed with an example from popular culture. We find this example by briefly visiting the detective story set in California and masterfully told by Raymond Chandler in *The Big Sleep* (1939) and portrayed in the 1946 film of the same name, with Humphrey Bogart as hard-boiled detective Philip Marlowe and Lauren Bacall as spoiled socialite Vivian Sternwood.

Consider the plot of the film and the book. A world-weary and almost cynical detective, Marlowe, is called in to assist with the blackmail of an elderly patriarch of a very wealthy family, General Sternwood. Sternwood has two beautiful and rather wild daughters. In his investigation Marlowe discovers that the blackmail revolves around nude pictures taken of the younger daughter, Carmen. The pornographer who took the pictures, Geiger, runs his business in the back of an antique bookstore, and the men who purchase his wares must surreptitiously conduct their business in a password-protected backroom. A young man who has fallen in love with Carmen confronts and kills the pornographer in an attempt to defend her honor, and the remainder of the movie depicts Marlowe pursuing the twists and turns as he and the cops attempt to figure things out while keeping the Sternwoods from experiencing the public humiliation that would ensue if the daughter's escapades came to light.

The worries of the characters in the film seem rather innocent in retrospect. The entire plot of the film turns on the attempt to shield the younger daughter from her own self-destructive behavior, and the murder of the pornographer arises from one man's unfortunate attempt to protect her virtue. Remaking this classic film for a contemporary audience would be a challenge indeed.

In the 1930s and '40s it was taken for granted that such bookstores were not only seedy, but also illegal. Sure, one knew that such things went on, but one had to go behind closed doors to indulge in it. The pornographer Geiger needed the protection of a gangster and hid his wares behind a front business. Because of the standing law, his "business" was restricted to back alleys and clandestine transactions.

This fictional account reflected the reality of morals legislation in an earlier and more genteel era. The contrast with the contemporary scene is revealing. Then young women and their well-to-do families could be ruined by pornography. Now young women from wealthy families become positively famous by creating pornography. Then young men defended their beloved's honor by assaulting those who would exploit them; now young men cash in on the earnings made by the exploitation. Most importantly for our topic, then the law forced pornographers to ply their wares surreptitiously, without the public approval of the laws and always under the threat of being discovered and possibly prosecuted. Now the law protects the "free speech" of pornographers, provides them official avenues for lobbying politicians, and offers the defense of "privacy" such that state officials have trouble interfering with the "industry" even for the purpose of preventing a serious health epidemic. The shift in mores cannot be understood apart from a shift in the law, which underscores the transformative and pedagogical role of the law.

This is exactly the sort of situation that our friend, colleague, and teacher Professor Hadley Arkes might use to illustrate the inescapable connection between the logic of morals and the logic of law. In this chapter I will use this Californian example as a jumping-off point to sketch out in three parts a conservative case for morals legislation, with frequent recourse to Arkes's own inimitable articulation of the first principles that are befitting human beings as rational creatures with moral natures. The first part concerns the nature of human beings as such, and what characteristics they possess such that the state has a rightful role in intervening in their lives by marking off some choices as legitimate and others as wrongful and thus removed from the domain of rightful choice. In part two, I consider certain basic truths about human nature and articulate the conception of the state that follows from these truths. Part three responds to some common objections about the role that the properly constituted state should play in the promotion of excellence among its citizenry.

The Nature of Human Beings

The conservative case for morals legislation rests upon a conception of the human being as a rational, relational, and moral creature. Arkes is fond of paraphrasing Samuel Johnson in saying that we are geometricians by accident, but moralists by nature.[3] Like other creatures, we live socially, depending on one another and living communally. But unlike other creatures, human beings use reason to order their lives and interact with one another. Further still, this use of reason is not merely a function of calculation, like that of lab mice learning how to navigate a maze to satisfy their appetites. Such calculation is useful and necessary, even for humans, but human beings go further in our interactions:

---

3   Samuel Johnson, *The lives of the most eminent English poets. With critical observations on their works. By Samuel Johnson. A new edition corrected. In four volumes. . . .* Vol. 1 (London: 1794), 133.

considering what appetites are appropriate, if they ought to be satisfied and to what extent, and how we should relate to other reasoning beings in going about pursuing a life well-lived. In other words, human beings are moral creatures who cooperate to pursue the good life, lived well together.

This truth about human nature is properly described as a basic or self-evident truth, as seen in Thomas Aquinas's formulation of the first principle of practical reason: do good and avoid evil.[4] "Self-evident," in this sense, does not mean obvious to all, as many contemporary college students initially think when first confronted with the idea. A self-evident or basic principle is one that does not depend on a more fundamental principle for its validity. When it comes to apprehending a basic truth one either "sees" it, or one does not. If a young student does not understand the transitive principle in mathematics – that if A=B and B=C, then A=C – there is no more fundamental truth that will lead our student to take a further step and understand the principle. The same is true for the notion that human beings are moral creatures who are to pursue good and avoid evil.[5]

To this a skeptic might ask: Does this idea of self-evidence not leave the defender of a normative human nature without resources for putting forth his case? Not in the least. For certain expectations follow if this basic truth about human beings holds true. Though one cannot argue *to* the first principle of practical reason, one can find ample evidence of its existence. For instance, we might expect that if human beings were endowed with a moral nature they could not help but appeal to moral norms. If human beings everywhere and at all times have spoken not only with "is" but also with "ought" in their syntax, then that would be a powerful clue as to the sort of creatures they are. And, of course, humans do speak in the language of "ought" as well as "is."

---

4   Thomas Aquinas, *Summa Theologiae*, 1–2, Question 94, Article 2. This is not to take a side on the intramural debate among some natural lawyers about just what exactly Thomas meant by "good" and "evil" in this formulation.

5   To be sure, this is a normative first truth, not a descriptive claim about how human beings actually behave. If human beings naturally pursued good and avoided evil there would be no need to encourage them to do so, not to mention the world would be quite a different sort of place.

To be sure, one does run across a relative few people who deny that men and women are moral beings, or that the moral law has any validity apart from what any particular individual might subjectively choose to accept in it. These skeptics may be relativistic in theory, but are in all likelihood moral realists in practice. This can be ascertained by a question. One might ask, "At this moment, somewhere in the world, are there some people performing actions upon other people that you think are wrong and should be stopped, by force if necessary, even if the instigators understand their actions to be morally justified?"[6]

A negative answer to this question reveals a particular sort of ignorance (or self-delusion) that does not bode well for the character or awareness of any who would make it. The vast majority, however, will answer in the affirmative and betray an implicit commitment to the logic of morals in practice, if not in theory. Their answer opens them up to the question of what would it mean for an action to be truly morally justified. This question in our hypothetical conversation illustrates the rational character of human beings. For not only do men and women congregate together and so evidence their social nature, and not only do they speak in moral terms, but they demand, and offer, reasons and explanations for moral propositions and moral, and immoral, behavior. Even the most hardened skeptic tends to back himself into the logic of morals, and the moral nature of human beings, eventually.

Why would we propose interference with the architect of genocide in a foreign country, or intervene with an indigenous tribe's practice of female infanticide? We oppose such practices because we have good reason to know such actions are grievously wrong, and thus we are obligated to act where we can.[7] Describing genocide, racial discrimination, and infanticide as morally wrong is a fundamentally different claim than describing these evils as things which we happen to dislike. To echo Arkes's formulation in *First Things*, we understand those acts to be wrong in principle and thus not admitting to degrees of intensity nor of particularity of location or history.[8] If genocide is morally wrong,

6   I owe the basic idea of this question, if not the exact wording, to Tim Keller.
7   The third part of the chapter considers the question of how prudence plays a role in how we go about acting on grievous wrongs.
8   Hadley Arkes, *First Things* (Princeton, NJ: Princeton University Press, 1986), 167.

then a little bit of genocide is not a little bit better; if racial discrimination is wrong in the United States in the 1980s, then it is also wrong in Slovenia in the 2010s. Moreover, we find ourselves repeatedly returning to the discourse of rational moral explanation when challenged by others about our moral judgments. Rational moral creatures offer, demand, and deserve to be offered reasons regarding moral conduct.

I have suggested in this first section that human beings are relational, moral, and rational, and certain observable consequences follow from these truths. It must be admitted that the observation of moral discourse throughout every human society does not establish the truth of any basic moral principle because "basic" means such principles are self-standing and cannot be derived from observation, even if that observation seems universal. Yet such evidence can help one reflect and come to "see" the truths about human nature about which any moral understanding must take account.

Yet there is one more truth about human nature that is as sure as the reality of a moral law. This truth has two sides to it. The first is that human beings are to some extent free creatures, and this freedom has moral implications. Unlike the law of gravity, human beings can break the moral law, and they do. To borrow an example from C.S. Lewis, we blame the man who tries to trip us and does not succeed. We don't blame the man who accidently trips us, even though the second may actually harm us and the first has not.[9] Moral approbation requires moral freedom, and we can condemn immoral actions only because we believe, implicitly or explicitly, that human beings have this freedom.

The other side of this truth is not expounded upon or made as explicit in Arkes's work, but it is implicit throughout. This truth is that as surely as there is a moral law built in to human nature, there is also a resistance and rebellion against that law and the norms that flow from it. This is not the place to delve into the debate over whether this rebellion stems from humanity's ignorance, as elements of the Greek tradition have it, or from men and women's consciously chosen disobedience, as explained by the Judeo-Christian doctrine of sin and the Fall and famously illustrated in Augustine's episode with the stolen

9   C.S. Lewis, *Mere Christianity* (New York, NY: MacMillan, 1943), 28.

pears.[10] What is crucial is to keep alongside our conception of human nature as relational, rational, and moral is that competing human dynamic that results in damaged and hurtful relationships, irrationality, and immorality. Only with these truths about human nature in mind can we move on to consider the logic of law as it applies to human nature.

Governing Authority given Human Nature

While often made half-jokingly, the common refrain in response to a perceived outrage, "There oughta be a law!" is a revealing turn of phrase. As Aristotle explains in his *Politics*, humans are between the beasts and the gods, and the proper arrangement for such creatures is the political community.[11] Unlike human beings who reason morally, beasts have no capacity for morals nor for the giving and understanding of reasons. They need direction and rule, but unlike human beings are not equipped to provide it or consent to it. Gods, by definition, do not need to be governed by laws even though they understand the good. Presumably self-sufficient, gods do not need the help of the community and its laws to achieve their perfection.

Human beings have both the capacity to act like animals in the negative sense, as reflected in our common discourse ("he's acting like a pig!"), and the god-like ability to employ reason and thus pursue the good. We see both dynamics accounted for in the community or the polis in that it is governed not only by a common commitment to the good, but also by laws employed to enforce the good. The laws are necessary precisely because human beings, unlike gods, are not perfect and thus will not always choose the good.

It is a further mark of the polis that the "good" here in question is not merely the product of passing fads or idiosyncratic preferences. When something is wrong, it is not wrong merely because it offends someone's personal taste. The governing authority's power to pass and enforce laws depends on the beastly side of human nature as well as the

10   Augustine, *The Works of Saint Augustine*, ed. Boniface Ramsey, Vol. 1 (Hyde Park, NY: New City Press, 1990–), 68–74.

11   Aristotle, *The Complete Works of Aristotle*, ed. Jonathan Barnes. Vol. 2 (Princeton, NJ: Princeton University Press, 1984), 1988.

core belief that some wrongs are so fundamental that they demand a robust and coercive response. If there are truly deeds that are morally wrong, then it follows that there must be an authority established to command such deeds be avoided and to punish the transgressors when they are committed. Arkes's teaching on this point is instructive: if it is wrong to torture other human beings, then we do not content ourselves with mere tax incentives to encourage citizens to stop. We know that the wrong of torture requires that this choice be removed altogether from the domain of what is acceptable. You can enjoy the symphony, a NASCAR race, or the latest offering at the movies, but the logic of morals and law removes the option of torturing your neighbor for your weekend's entertainment – even if your neighbor annoys you.

If this is the case, then it raises the question of what should characterize this authority that acts to enforce the moral law. Again, the connection between the morality of human nature and the logic of law is salient. If human beings are neither beasts nor gods, then we are equal in the sense that no man or woman is by nature fit to rule over another human being as animals are ruled by humans. Thus, while human community is natural, coercive authority must be established by consent; it is conventional. Moreover, because human beings are rational and expect and deserve to be given reasons for actions that restrict their freedom, governments should be designed so as to best promote the giving and understanding of reasons.

Given these factors, a government befitting human nature will be marked by consent, and this consent can best be established by free elections in which candidates for office compete by offering reasons to those whom they would serve in promoting the common good. This conception, when manifested in republican constitutional government, combines the natural sociability of Aristotle's polis with elements of the contract theory of the early modern political theorists. At the same time, it rejects Aristotle's conception of natural slavery while simultaneously rejecting the notion of atomistic, unsociable, and miserable creatures who come together in Hobbes's state of nature/war to form the Leviathan.

One negative characteristic of a properly constituted governing authority should be clear from the outset. No such authority can in any way be understood to be morally neutral. That some think such a chimerical understanding is possible is reflected in the unfortunate (but popular) phrase, "you cannot legislate morality."

What this utterance has to mean for the speaker is something more like "you shouldn't legislate that sort of morality because it doesn't agree with my preferences," because in fact the opposite is true. You cannot *not* legislate morality. Every law and regulation that is proposed, passed, and enforced has inherent in it some idea of the good that it is meant to promote or preserve. It is of course true that some laws will be better conceived than others, and many may fail entirely to achieve their purpose. But that they have a purpose, and that that purpose includes at least an implicit moral element, is incontrovertible. One need only ask of any law or even action of government, "What is the law for?" The answer at some point will include a conception of what is good for the community in which the law holds. The inversion of the question makes the point even more clearly. What would provide a rationale for a law or governmental action apart from a moral purpose?

It is certainly the case that the governing authority will mark off some choices as falling within the discretion of a polity's citizens. Not every decision has profound moral consequences. But drawing the line between morally innocent choices and morally culpable choices does evince a moral understanding. Abraham Lincoln made this clear in his debates with Stephen Douglas.[12] Lincoln noted that Douglas's professed ambivalence about whether states voted for or against slavery showed that he did not think slavery belonged in that category of actions that are truly morally wrong.[13] The logic of morals means that there can be no principled right to a wrong, and built into the notion

---

12   See *The Collected Works of Abraham Lincoln*, ed. Roy P. Basler (New Brunswick, NJ: Rutgers University Press, 1953), vol. III, 256–57, and Arkes, *First Things*, 24–25.

13   The contemporary issue in which we see this difference at work is abortion. Advocates of the "Against abortion? Don't have one" line of thinking are unwitting inheritors of Douglas's approach. The pro-life analogy linking slavery to abortion makes this clear by inserting slavery into the abortion question: "Against slavery? Don't own one." Both lines of thinking express a moral position the advocates of which would enforce with the power and authority of the state.

of wrong is the corresponding truth that an authority is right in principle to punish perpetrators of the wrong. The idea that government can act as a neutral arbitrator between competing notions of the good life is ultimately incoherent because the idea itself promotes an underlying conception that this arrangement will lead to the best state of affairs.[14]

There is no escaping the connection between the logic of morals and the logic of law, and yet the contrary position does not lack for eminent and influential spokesmen.[15] Perhaps the most famous attempt to sever the connection between law and morals was made by Oliver Wendell Holmes in his 1897 address at the graduation of Boston University Law School, "The Path of the Law."[16]

Holmes's argument is an ideal foil for the propositions about morals and law put forth by Arkes and others.[17] His primary target in this address is the very connection between the two, which he charges with spreading confusion:

The confusion with which I am dealing besets confessedly legal conceptions. Take the fundamental question, What constitutes the law? You will find some text writers telling you that it is something different from what is decided by the courts of Massachusetts or England, that it is a system of reason, that it is a deduction from principles of ethics or admitted axioms or what not, which may or may not coincide with the decisions. But if we take the view of our friend the bad man we shall find that he does not care two straws for the axioms or deductions, but that he does want to know what the Massachusetts or English courts are likely to do in fact. I am much of this mind. The prophecies of what the

---

14 And an explanation of what "best" means must at some point revert back to a moral conception.

15 As Arkes said about his own work and the work of Robert P. George at a conference honoring the latter's *Making Men Moral*, it has been part of a "movement to restore the understanding of that classic connection between morality and law, and in that project I've found my own place over the years and we have steady work." Hadley Arkes, address at the Making Men Moral conference, Union University (February 27, 2009).

16 Oliver Wendell Holmes, "The Path of the Law," *Harvard Law Review* 10 (1897).

17 Not surprisingly, Holmes often makes an appearance in Arkes's works, e.g., Arkes, *Natural Rights & the Right to Choose* (Cambridge: Cambridge University Press, 2002), 50–51.

courts will do in fact, and nothing more pretentious, are what I mean by
the law.[18]

Holmes's solution that might clear up this confusion is to completely eviscerate moral considerations from our understanding of law. "For
my own part," he said, "I often doubt whether it would not be a gain if
every word of moral significance could be banished from the law altogether, and other words adopted which should convey legal ideas uncol-
ored by anything outside the law."[19]

It might be a bit too simple to inquire as to what Holmes means by
"a gain," and others have aptly responded to his overall argument and
subsequent record as a justice and legal thinker. Yet there is something
remarkable in his formulation – something that, somewhat ironically,
makes the case for the connection between morals and law in precisely
the way Arkes would teach us to expect. For Arkes remarks that those
who deny the import of the moral law, either in its entirety or in its connection to law, will inevitably back themselves into the language of
morals and law.[20] Such is the case with Holmes.

For what is it that Holmes is attempting to convey to his audience
if not the means by which we can truly understand what the law is, and
what judges and courts do? His immediate audience consisted of those
young graduates about to make their way into the world through the
actual practice of law, and his extended audience through publication
was larger and more influential yet. What conceptual key does Holmes
suggest to us to truly understand what the law is? He opines:

> If you want to know the law and nothing else, you must look at it
> as a bad man, who cares only for the material consequences which
> such knowledge enables him to predict, not as a good one, who
> finds his reasons for conduct, whether inside the law or outside of
> it, in the vaguer sanctions of conscience.

---

18 Ibid., 460–461.
19 Ibid., 464. For an interpretation that understands Holmes to be overstating his case
    for the purpose of provocation, see Robert P. George, "What is Law? A Century
    of Arguments" in *The Clash of Orthodoxies: Law, Religion, and Morality in Crisis*
    (Wilmington, DE: ISI Books), 2001, 211–215.
20 For example, Arkes teases out this dynamic with regard to George McGovern in
    First Things, 271–74.

The key to understanding the law is to look at the law as the bad man does. But Holmes cannot mean that we entirely enter into the bad man's mind-set, because per his definition the bad man is not interested, as we are, in understanding, but only in material consequences. The bad man is not interested in morality, but we who sit on the outside looking in must, just as a conceptual matter, keep morality in mind if only to guard against its invasive language and history from invading our understanding of the law.

But this raises a question. How, might we ask, are we to truly understand what it means to be a "bad man" and what it means to be a "good one"? Is it not telling that Holmes's very attempt to expurgate morality from the law itself depends on making a moral distinction? If Holmes is using the terms "good" and "bad" merely as descriptive statements about how some men see themselves (the bad men looking to keep out of trouble, and the good men thinking that they are beholden to some external morality), then he is doing more than attempting to separate morality and law; he seems to be denying morality altogether. This is an unlikely interpretation.[21]

But if Holmes is using the normative words as truly normative, then he cannot help but back himself into the logic of morals by requiring us to make a judgment about good and bad men. That is, he requires us not merely to make moral judgments distinguishing between "goodness" and "badness" (and thus better and worse, right and wrong) but also to associate "badness" with those who do not see a link between morals and law. Whatever his intentions might have been, Holmes winds up illustrating the link between the logic of morals and the logic of law.

To legislate, then, is to legislate morality. One can no more avoid legislating morality than one can speak without syntax. One cannot

---

21   Holmes, "The Path of the Law," 459:

"I take it for granted that no hearer of mine will misinterpret what I have to say as the language of cynicism. The law is the witness and external deposit of our moral life. Its history is the history of the moral development of the race. The practice of it, in spite of popular jests, tends to make good citizens and good men. When I emphasize the difference between law and morals I do so with reference to a single end, that of learning and understanding the law. For that purpose you must definitely master its specific marks, and it is for that that I ask you for the moment to imagine yourselves indifferent to other and greater things."

sever morality from the law. Even partisans of the most spartan libertarian conception of the state would themselves employ state power to
enforce their vision of the common good, if only in preventing competing and more expansive political ideologies from taking hold. Given
this understanding, the term "morals legislation" is, strictly speaking,
repetitive or redundant. The real question is not whether the political
community will legislate morality; the question is which vision of
morality will be enforced and by what sort of government.

Common Objections

Thus far I have described a concept of human nature that sees human
beings as relational, rational, and moral, and yet prone to breaking the
moral law. Because human beings are social, they will live in communities directed toward a vision of the good life. Because human beings
are fallen, to borrow the Judeo-Christian term, an authority is needed
to promote that understanding of the good life and punish actions that
transgress moral boundaries. Moreover, given human equality – no
human being is appointed by nature to rule over another – a necessary
component of a government's legitimacy is that it is established by the
consent of the governed. As men and women offer, expect, and deserve
reasons for actions impacting their lives, such consent is best determined by elections in which candidates for office can compete for support by offering reasons for why they would be best suited to promote
and preserve the common good.

Such a brief sketch cannot help but invite several questions. It is
beyond the purview of such a chapter to complete the line of reasoning
between the general principles expounded above and particular examples of morals legislation such as, say, laws restricting the production
and dissemination of pornography. Nevertheless, considering some
common objections and questions can fill out a broader picture than
afforded by the general outlines already described. The first question
revolve around a basic skeptical approach toward authority, colloquial-
ly known as the "Sez who?" question.[22]

---

22   See Arthur Leff, "Unspeakable Ethics, Unnatural Law," *Duke Law Journal* 1229
     (1979).

"Who are you to justify limiting my freedom?"

We have already answered this objection in part by considering that any conception of ordering our lives together will necessarily include the possibility of interference from outside the atomistic individual. Interference is a given; the question is by what sort and with what justification. This question can be understood in two ways.

First, behind this question might be the stance that there is in principle no justification for anyone else to interfere with one's choices, whether those choices include vacationing at the beach or defrauding seniors out of their Social Security. Besides being a rather remarkably stark assertion of a mysterious self-standing right, this position cannot hold its own weight, since the negative formulation that "no one can tell me what to do regarding my choices" also entails the positive right asserted that "I can do whatever I want without repercussions from others." But when countered with "Why do you alone have this right and not others?" this position falls apart. It makes an exclusive moral claim – you should not interfere with my choices – without explaining why the claimant is somehow different from his neighbors.[23]

But this is not likely to be what someone means by this objection, and the second reason this question might be asked is much more common and understandable. Someone asking "who are you to justify limiting my freedom?" might really be asking: "given that human beings are free creatures, what justifies the state interfering with how I live my life?" Notice that this question illustrates that human beings demand, and deserve, reasons.

In a well-functioning state in which officials take office with the consent of the governed through free elections, the answer to this question is fairly straightforward. When officials of the state pass and enforce legislation that interferes with how any particular citizen would otherwise conduct his life, their warrant is that such officials properly exercise their power because it has been authorized by a majority of this particular citizen's neighbors. Every citizen has consented to the system by which the law is implemented, even if not to the particular code in question.[24]

---

23 And it is obvious that two people cannot simultaneously have this right.

24 This is the deal we make so long as we trust that the system is basically decent,

That this is in principle correct is not threatened by inappropriate or misguided applications of the principle. Legislators and executives will, of course, make mistakes. They will misidentify moral ends or badly botch the political means by which to promote morally correct goals. The episode of Prohibition early in the last century is a prominent example. Temperance advocates and the politicians they sponsored and influenced had good reason to think the excessive use of alcohol was an epidemic leading to a great deal of human misery and injustice. Some of their goals were undoubtedly worthy; in retrospect their means were not effective. Temperance proponents misjudged not only the efficacy of the government to impose and enforce a ban on alcohol production and consumption; they badly misunderstood the character of citizens who resented a totalizing solution to a problem that admitted of degrees and proportion. It is inevitable that attempts to govern for the common good will sometimes result in overreaching, poor judgment, and clumsy governance.

To hold this as an objection to morals legislation, however, would be to object to any human endeavor and any form of government. An objection that slays all conceptions of government is not so much an objection as it is an indication of a perennial political reality and problem. The alternative to a government that misapplies its power to a vision of the common good does not exist. The virtue of constitutional republican government is that such mistakes can be remedied either by the very same legislature, or by a newly constituted legislature created by an intervening election. The more such elections are marked by competing candidates offering rational citizens reasons for repeal or passage of this or that law, the better.

One final consideration regarding the question about limiting freedom is that the objection has been construed so as to associate the word

and it also shows another facet as to why reason-giving is so important. It is one thing to lose on an issue in which you can hear and understand your political opponents' position and reasons. You've attempted to win the public over and failed. Perhaps your position itself needs to be tinkered with or thrown out, or perhaps the means of delivering your message must be improved. Regardless, even in losing this is much to be preferred to a contest in which your position has lost and you have not had a chance to offer your reasons, nor engaged with the other side. Perceived arbitrariness destroys trust.

"freedom" entirely with the individual and not at all with the community passing laws to restrict some behavior or another. But if freedom is claimed by the individual wanting to indulge in a particular behavior, then surely freedom may also be claimed by a community – a larger group of individuals – to be free from what they perceive to be the ills that accompany the behavior in question.

If we return to the example with which this chapter opened, some individuals want to engage in the production and consumption of pornography. Other individuals believe that pornography is so harmful that some steps should be taken by the government to discourage it and make it more difficult to indulge in. The latter believe that the harms are not confined to the hermetically sealed private lives of the consumers and regard pornography as a public matter.[25] The former do not think it is harmful, or if it is, they do not think it is the purview of government to decide such matters. Opponents of pornography want the freedom to live in a relatively porn-free community. Pornography consumers want the freedom to freely engage in it. How to resolve such a standoff?

Is not the answer that each side's adherents put forth their view of human flourishing and compete for the support of their fellow citizens? Either way, a moral vision will be promoted and enforced by the governing authorities. Either way, some citizens' freedom will be restricted. Better to let that vision be aired out before an audience of rational, relational, and moral citizens and decided on the merits of what pornography is and what it does to human flourishing than to arbitrarily rule out of bounds one approach because it restricts human freedom. Every approach to any controversial topic will restrict someone's version of human freedom, just as it will allow and encourage other versions. Elections and referenda will be held, laws passed and enforced, results weighed, and another round of electoral contests will ensue.

This is, at least, the procedural answer to how such a standoff should be resolved. It respects the audience of such a debate as reasoning creatures capable of moral understanding. That said, describing this

---

25   Even if the harms were confined to the users only, that would provide only a prudential, not a principled, reason for the state to forbear from acting.

as a contest of moral visions should not be thought to imply relativity between such visions.[26] As already intimated, conservatives have good reasons to present in public about the harms of pornography and the case for its restriction.[27] As such, conservatives should make their case winsomely and confident that they have the correct understanding of the issue, undeterred by the specious charge that "freedom" is found on only one side of the debate.

"Isn't the American experiment an experiment in limited government? Doesn't the conception you've described open the door to an omnicompetent state overseeing each and every aspect of our lives?"

One of the very reasons that I have offered to justify morals legislation is that human beings rebel against the moral law and treat each other poorly. Madison's observation about men and angels and the need for government comes to mind.[28] As noted, this characteristic of human behavior may result from ignorance of the moral law or an unwillingness to carry it out even if it is understood.[29] This very observation about human nature, however, leads to a rather powerful objection to legislation designed to help make men and women moral.

Someone taking this position might say something like the following:

"I grant that there are some acts so abominable that there must be an authority to forbid such acts and punish perpetrators of them.

26 Arkes employs a similar strategy in his proposed speech for President George W. Bush in *Natural Rights and the Right to Choose*, 92–94. Here he crafts a speech that recognizes the deep divisions surrounding abortion, yet makes the case for a conversation to take place about the modest proposals for agreement. Such an approach recognizes the necessity of engaging the culture we inhabit, complete with incommensurable moral visions, without in any way implying that the various positions are equally valid or deserving of governmental endorsement.

27 See Mary Anne Layden and Mary Eberstadt, *The Social Costs of Pornography: A Statement of Findings and Recommendations* (Princeton, NJ: The Witherspoon Institute, 2010).

28 "If men were angels, no government would be necessary." Alexander Hamilton, John Jay, and James Madison, *The Federalist: The Gideon Edition*, ed. George W. Cary and James McClellan (Indianapolis, IN: Liberty Fund, 2001), 269.

29 We find this continuum in the Christian tradition between those who think the Fall has damaged man's ability to know the good apart from divine revelation and those who think it has more damaged his ability to carry it out.

Clearly there is a proper place for government to keep the peace both domestic and foreign. But restraining evil is a much different task than promoting the good. The very same flawed human nature that necessitates government leads me to be wary of that same government, populated by men and women with a flawed human nature. Better to conceive of government as a necessary evil with a very limited purview and leave the task of cultivating virtue to other entities like the church, synagogue, and family. I simply don't trust governmental officials to know the good and to carry it out as they should."

It must be admitted that this objection is a powerful one. If the conservative case for morals legislation required the state to be the only or even the primary producer of moral virtue, then it would likely be a fatal objection. Fortunately, however, this is not the case. A healthy dose of skepticism about the abilities of government at all levels is a crucial component of any feasible conception about politics.

Yet recognition of government's limits is compatible with a commitment to the logic of morals and the logic of law. This is because of the crucial distinction between principled moral ends and prudential means to achieve these ends. We can affirm truths about justice and human life without thereby committing ourselves to an overly sanguine confidence in governmental efficacy. About moral principles we should not be bashful about standing behind claims to moral certainty. Human dignity exists and should not be violated. Genocide and rape are not merely the result of preferences others happen to have but tear apart a moral reality whether or not their perpetrators admit as such. Mistreating or killing others because of non-moral characteristics, such as stage of development (in abortion) or skin color (in racial slavery), is wrong – even if a given society has not widely recognized the wrong. On these and other principles conservatives should stand firm and make our case in the public square as to why.

The difficulty comes in how to go about remedying and preventing these wrongs. Given the truth of human equality, how should a representative to the Constitutional Convention have voted given the Constitution's begrudging allowance of the continuation of slavery in the new nation? Would that principle of justice have been better served by supporting an imperfect political order that may hold within it the seeds of slavery's eventual demise? Or would a more abolitionist stance have better served human equality, even if it meant the partition of the early states into a few free New England states and several Southern slave states?

The goal or end in either course is to secure the principle of human equality. Yet we must acknowledge that how best to achieve that principle could not have been nearly as clear in the moment as it now appears to us in retrospect. This is both what makes prudence so necessary even as it is rather frustrating. It is necessary because human behavior is too variegated to accurately predict. It is frustrating because we cannot write a how-to manual with neat bullet-points detailing what prudence requires in advance.[30] Prudence in the statesman is the art of assessing each particular situation and applying timeless moral principles to contingent historical realities. It is only after the fact that we can collectively look back and recognize the prudential genius of a Lincoln or a Washington.

We can therefore qualify and adopt this objection as part of the conservative case for morals legislation. If, as we noted earlier, there can be no right to a wrong, then Arkes would invoke Lincoln in reminding us that there is in principle no category of wrongdoing sealed off from the authority of the state. Nevertheless, given the humanity of those who wield power, even in the best of polities and with the consent of the governed, there will always be strong prudential grounds for limiting the reach and power of the state.[31]

"Does the state occupy the primary role for promoting virtue among its citizens?"

Any proper government is established by consent and so must be seen as a creature of its citizens. It is conventional even if the morals it

---

30   As Aristotle reminds us in his *Nicomachean Ethics*, 1094b12. See Aristotle, *Complete Works,* 1730.

31   This is a topic for another essay. That it is difficult to retain the state's power to effectively promote the good is well put by Madison in Federalist 51:

In framing a government which is to be administered by men over men, the great difficulty lies in this: you must first enable the government to control the governed; and in the next place oblige it to control itself. A dependence on the people is, no doubt, the primary control on the government; but experience has taught mankind the necessity of auxiliary precautions.

protects and promotes are not. There is nothing in this formulation thus far that requires the state to have the only or even primary role in making men and women moral. The state comes into existence amid already existing institutions such as the family and the church. A well-functioning state also allows other intermediary institutions to flourish: charitable organizations, bowling leagues, neighborhood groups, and professional organizations.

In between an anemic state that cannot provide security nor promote a healthy conception of the good life, and an overbearing state that creates more evils than it stamps out, is a robust government active enough to promote moral goodness while modest and wise enough to know its limits. While there is no exact blueprint to achieving this balance, two considerations may help. The first is that the state, while crucial, is only one actor among many charged with inculcating moral virtue. The second is that the very nature of moral improvement requires a voluntary disposition and thus a government's role as teacher and enforcer will be largely negative.

A well-functioning state works in tandem with these other entities to create an environment conducive to human flourishing. While the family is prior to the state, its health depends on the protection and definitional power of the state.[32] There is no such entity as a private marriage, and the well-being and upbringing of children is a matter of public concern. Once again we see the logic of morals and the logic of law apply even in the most intimate matters concerning the family, for we rightly distinguish between the rightful privacy of a family engaged in an evening of Monopoly from the wrongful privacy of a family marked by child abuse and neglect, and we invoke the power of the state to intervene in the latter case.

Nevertheless, the family can also teach in ways that a government cannot. A government can teach in marking off some actions as wrongful and others discretionary, but a government cannot weave into a child the virtues and character that will lead that child to become an adult

---

32 As marriage is a legal institution, and the state's laws cannot help but teach, what the state *defines* marriage to be will have a profound influence on how a culture understands, and values, "marriage."

willing to do the right thing even when the prospects of punitive consequences are unlikely to nonexistent. These are lessons better taught by a mother and father presiding over a quarrel between brothers and sisters, perhaps augmented by the wise counsel of a pastor, priest or rabbi at worship, and hopefully mirrored, to some extent, in the neighborhood. It may sound rather prosaic, but governments cannot be the primary instructor of moral virtue because governments cannot love.

And this leads to the second consideration that will help us maintain a balanced view of government. As Arkes reminds us in quoting the English journalist and Christian provocateur, G.K. Chesterton, there are some things we want people to do by their own choice and by their own power, even if they do it badly.[33] Chesterton pointed to blowing one's nose, writing love letters, and practicing self-government.

Something similar is true of developing moral character; we cannot become more moral by isolating ourselves as rugged individualists and finding our own way. We are, after all, relational creatures meant to pursue the good life in community. Yet there is a voluntary aspect of moral growth that is crucial. Forced apologies might be appropriate in training children, but no one would mistake them for real apologies. Moral deeds done only out of compulsion or the fear of punishment are not enough.

We want our elected officials to create laws and punishments such that Holmes's bad man will find them weighing on him when he has in mind some shady transaction or wrongful deed. But we do not aspire to produce a nation full of bad men. Rather, we hope that whatever motivation the stick may provide it will not be the primary motivation for the majority of our fellow citizens. We hope, rightly so, that we will choose the good not merely because we fear being punished but for the sake of the good and its realization in ourselves and our neighbors. A prudentially wise government will leave room for her citizens to do this – to pursue good and avoid evil – while still marking off some boundaries that cannot be transgressed. Within these boundaries it lies to those other entities – families, friends, schools, churches, clubs, etc. – to positively inculcate the moral virtue needed for human beings to live well.

33   G.K. Chesterton, *Orthodoxy* (Charleston, SC: BiblioBazaar, LLC, 2009), 68.

Conclusion: What is the point of it all?

The conservative case for morals legislation assumes certain truths about human nature and draws various conclusions about the proper role of government. Human beings are remarkable creatures who reason with one another about the best way to live together. At the same time they can treat each other abominably and so they consent to an authority by which the boundaries of right and wrong are laid out and enforced.

We might return to Holmes's good and bad man in concluding. If government exists to promote and protect the common good, and is established by consent, then morals legislation consists of individuals promoting their freedom to live well by restricting their freedom to behave badly. Holmes is right to draw our attention to our need to understand the logic of morals in order to properly conceive of the law, but he is wrong to draw such a distinction between the good and the bad man.

For the true condition of human nature is that we find within ourselves inclinations both to the good and to the bad. The young college co-ed is completely persuaded of the wrong of abortion when the sun is shining and she sits in a college classroom. The newlywed groom does not doubt the evils of adultery or pornography shortly after taking his vows. The respected accountant would never dream of cutting corners when his business is in the black and all is well. Yet those moral convictions will be put to the test when the young woman finds herself unmarried, pregnant, and abandoned, with her bright future in doubt, or the husband is no longer newlywed but rather lonely while serving overseas far away from his wife, or the accountant's business has taken a turn for the worse and he faces unexpected medical bills. Even ethics professors, politicians, and lawmakers face this undulation between moral certainty and moral temptation. What is at stake in these situations is not the truth of the principles themselves, but the strength of our character needed to abide by them.

What the law does in these instances is provide an additional reminder and motivation so the person in difficult circumstances is reminded of the reasoned judgment made by the same person earlier.

Good morals legislation occurs when a group of people exercise their freedom to bind themselves to a moral vision so important that they will restrict their own future behavior. It is members of a sober community considering how best to restrain themselves in those not-so-sober moments. It comprises a necessary, though not sufficient, component of the pursuit of human flourishing. There is no escaping the law's role as a teacher of what is good and what is bad, what is conducive to human well-being and what harms it. The law will teach its lessons, one way or another, and society will bear the fruits of the law's pedagogy.

Chapter 7:
Natural Law and
Contemporary Liberalism
Christopher Wolfe

The American Founders clearly embraced a conception of natural law. In my view, this was largely a conception of natural law drawn from John Locke[1] rather than from the classical natural law doctrine of St. Thomas Aquinas – because it focused primarily on life, liberty, and property rather than a fuller range of human goods (including intellectual and moral virtue). At the same time, the strength of Christianity in early America and the variety of sources of the English common law[2] suggest that some elements of the more classical form of natural law were part of the mix.

But what has happened to natural law in American political thought since the Founding, and, in particular, what is its status today? There is no question that classical Thomistic natural law is not a major factor in much of academic jurisprudence and contemporary American public discourse, though occasionally it may be referred to in passing. (For example, in 1987 then-Senator Joseph Biden assailed Supreme Court nominee Robert Bork for not embracing natural law, and then in 1991

1   Though, of course, there are extensive debates about exactly what Locke's natural law was. For contrasting views, see Thomas West's Witherspoon Lecture, at http://www.frc.org/get.cfm?i=WT01F1, and Michael Zuckert's *Launching Liberalism* (University Press of Kansas, 2002).
2   On the importance of Christianity providing a moral framework for political freedom, see Alexis de Tocqueville, *Democracy in America*, eds. Harvey Mansfield and Delba Winthrop (University of Chicago Press, 2002). On the roots of the common law in pre-Enlightenment philosophy, see, for example James Gordley's *The Philosophical Origins of Modern Contract Doctrine* (Oxford University Press, 1993).

he criticized nominee Clarence Thomas for accepting it.) Even Lockean natural law is much less influential in our society than it was, say, fifty years ago, before the Declaration of Independence had come to be described by some as merely a propertied white man's document. The grounding of human rights in "Nature and Nature's God," which was axiomatic for the founders, is highly controversial today.

Some may argue, however, that one finds "natural law" thinking is alive and well in the works of two of the leading lights of American public philosophy, John Rawls and Ronald Dworkin. Although there is a sense in which this assessment of these influential liberal thinkers is correct, it seems to me that their views are too thin to be properly classified as examples of natural law thinking. In order to make that argument, it is necessary that I first clarify the meaning of natural law. Following that clarification, I take up the question of whether Rawls and Dworkin are natural law thinkers. I conclude by suggesting that their political philosophies may be incapable of sustaining over the long term the values of liberal democracy against both internal and external threats.

"Levels" of Natural Law

Discussions of natural law are complicated by the fact that the term has been around for a long time, and has been used in very different ways. We may start by identifying the most common ways in which it has been used.

Natural Law as Objective Value

The first and most abstract notion of natural law is implicit in what is perhaps the most basic intuition giving rise to natural law — namely, the sense that there must be some general (or even "objective") standard in light of which it is possible to judge human laws or conventions. One classic instance of this idea is found in Sophocles' *Antigone*, in which a sister disobeys a city's law by burying her treasonous brother, and claims a justification in higher law for doing so. The understanding of natural law at this level of generality, however, is very abstract and formalistic. It is so general that almost any thinker would fall in this category, except for those who think that there are *no* norms or standards independent of human will that govern human action. Russell Hittinger makes this point well in his broad-ranging and insightful article, "Liberalism and the American Natural Law Tradition."[3] There, he notes that some contemporary uses of "natural law" identify it with the position that "values are woven into the fabric of the world" and thus "value judgments and the moral prescriptions derived from them are not regarded as merely subjective statements of approval or disapproval; nor is the binding quality of the judgment about objective goods simply a function of the standards which we invent."[4] In this view, virtually "any account of morality – whether personal, moral, or political – that grounds at least some reasons for action in objective values, or at the very least, anthropological values" qualifies as natural law. "Natural law, then turns out to be any understanding of the relationship between law and morals which is neither positivistic nor nihilistic" and "formulated at this level of generality, natural law theory of one sort or another represents the great tradition of the West."[5] Hittinger goes on to point out that this definition of natural law includes many thinkers who would never have used the term in regard to their own work and who have been ambivalent, or hostile, to the "epistemological ideal of attunement to an evident order of being"[6]: for example, Immanuel Kant and his descendants, including John Rawls and Alan Gewirth, and

---

3   Russell Hittinger, "Liberalism and the American Natural Law Tradition," *Wake Forest Law Review* 25 (1990).

4   Ibid., 466.

5   Hittinger cites a classic discussion of "higher law" by Edward Corwin, an influential constitutional scholar in the first half of the twentieth century:

There are, it is predicated, certain principles of right and justice which are entitled to prevail of their own intrinsic excellence, altogether regardless of the attitude of those who wield the physical resources of the community. Such principles were made by no human hands; indeed, if they did not antedate deity itself, they still express its nature as to bind and control it. They are external to all Will as such and interpenetrate all Reason as such. They are eternal and immutable. In relation to such principles, human laws are, when entitled to obedience save as to matters indifferent, merely a record or transcript, and their enactment an act not of will or power but one of discovery and declaration.

Ibid., 466–67.

6   Ibid., 479, quoting D. A. J. Richards, *Toleration and the Constitution* (New York: Oxford University Press, 1986), 80.

contemporary legal thinkers such as H.L.A. Hart, Lon Fuller, Lawrence Tribe, Ronald Dworkin, David A.J. Richards, and various Supreme Court justices.

This definition of natural law is interesting because it identifies and emphasizes a common feature that a wide variety of opposing thinkers hold in common – the principle of objective value. For the same reason, however – that is, its lumping of so many different thinkers into the same category – its usefulness is limited.

Natural Law Rooted in Human Nature

A second form of natural law, still at a very high level of generality, is the idea that there is a stable human nature that sets limits to how men should act in order to maximize the conditions for achieving a satisfactory existence. This approach is shared by important historical representatives of ancient philosophy ("natural right"), medieval philosophy ("natural law"), and early modern liberal political philosophy ("natural rights").[7]

In his *Natural Law in Political Thought*, Paul Sigmund observes that there is much apparent variety in the content that different thinkers ascribe to natural law; "they have equated the natural with the rational; the divine; the distinctively human; the normally operating; the frequently recurring; the primitive; the elements not subject to human artifice or control; the self-evident; and the nonhistorical." But despite that apparent variety, he says,

> there seems to be a central assertion expressed or implied in most theories of natural law. This is the belief that there exists in nature and/or human nature a rational order which can provide intelligible value-statements independently of human will, that are universal in application, unchangeable in their ultimate content, and morally obligatory on mankind. . . . In all its diverse forms, the theory of natural law represents a common affirmation about the possibility of arriving at objective standards, and a common

7   The distinction between natural right, natural law, and natural rights is central to the work of Leo Strauss. See, for example, *Natural Right and History* (University of Chicago Press, 1953).

procedure for doing so – looking for a purposive order in nature and man.[8]

Given the diversity of conceptions of "nature" in this account, very different philosophies may count as "natural law," which explains why it can include Plato and Aristotle, Roman law, Thomas Aquinas, Hobbes, Locke and Kant.

While Sigmund mentions "reason" as only one possible understanding or aspect of "nature," I think that virtually all of the thinkers that he puts in the category of natural law theorists place considerable emphasis on some understanding of reason. At the same time, "reason" is a very protean concept. In particular, there is a fundamental difference between "instrumental rationality," which takes human ends as somehow given and then focuses on reason as the means to achieve them, and the broader, classical sense of reason as a capacity to grasp or perceive human ends as well as the capacity to devise means to achieve them.

Considering both classical (natural right and Thomistic natural law) and modern (natural rights) political philosophy as falling within the category of natural law, as Sigmund does, requires a broad definition of the essential features of natural law – only a shade narrower than the first definition above. The first concept of natural law focused on the idea of objective value, while the second concept adds that this objective value is rooted, somehow, in human nature, which also suggests that the value is permanent and universal. (It therefore excludes not only the positivistic and nihilistic approaches Hittinger considered excluded in the first concept, but also the notions of objective value that are rooted in essentially malleable notions of human nature, and especially modern or postmodern approaches that view human beings as characterized above all by the capacity for self-definition, and hence as not bound by any fixed nature.) Objective value rooted in nature need not entail a full or well-developed theory of the human good – it could simply be an identification of certain substantive evils to be avoided, as it is in natural rights theories that make self-preservation the fundamental law of nature.

8   Paul Sigmund, *Natural Law in Political Thought* (Lanham, MD: University Press of America, 1971), viii–ix.

But, as in the case of the first concept of natural law, the use of the term to encompass such a wide range of fundamentally differing philosophies limits its utility. Hittinger describes the theories that fall within the first two levels of natural law I have been describing as "minimalist natural law." He identifies their purposes (the roles they are meant to achieve), and argues that they are unsuccessful in achieving them.[9]

Natural Law and a Natural Order of Ends

A third notion of natural law, which has much more substantive content, is what thinkers in the natural law (Thomistic philosophy) and natural right (classical Greek philosophy) traditions have in common: an idea of a natural order, with various kinds of beings whose fulfillment or realization consists in developing and perfecting immanent capacities. This order is discovered, not created, by human beings. Human beings achieve a good life by living in accord with the natural order, and specifically by developing the capacities inherent in and distinctive of human nature. A flourishing human life is one of intellectual virtue (such as wisdom, developed in the philosophic life of dialectic and contemplation) and moral virtue (such as the cardinal virtues of prudence, justice, fortitude, and temperance).[10] Preeminent among the moral virtues is practical wisdom, whereby men, guided by a general perception of human goods and by right desire, choose the practical good, the right way of acting here and now. The common good (the good of the self-sufficient community – the polis, a broader political community, or even a universal Church) has a special eminence.

Natural right and classical natural law are both based on *epistemological realism*: human knowledge is not merely of appearances, much less a mere mental construction, but goes to the natures or essences of things. These approaches do, of course, recognize the plethora of obstacles to accurate human perception of reality, including the limits of the

---

9   Russell Hittinger, "Varieties of Minimalist Natural Law Theory," *American Journal of Jurisprudence* 34 (1989): 133–170.

10   While pleasure is recognized as good, it is always a derivative or secondary good attached to some more basic human good – good as a means, not an end – and it can be the source of disorder when it becomes an end in itself, as it often does for many human beings.

human intellect *per se* (for example, its dependence on sense and imagination, which makes knowledge of immaterial realities more difficult), cultural blinders, the weaknesses of given intellects, and the distortion of perception by disorder in the will (for example, the tendency of human beings to "see" what we *want* to see). But, despite all these obstacles, natural right and natural law philosophies maintain that the human mind is capable of approaching a grasp of reality itself.

Natural right and natural law share a similar philosophical *anthropology*. This understanding of human nature includes first, an internal ordering of the human faculties (reason–spirit–desire in the earlier, natural right tradition, or intellect–will–passions, in the Thomistic tradition), with reason or intellect exercising a directive function in well-developed human beings. Second, it views human beings as an integrated mind-body, so that it is neither reductionist (reducing mind to body as, for example, materialists do) nor dualist (separating them, and thereby viewing body and mind as "the ghost in the machine").

Natural law rooted in a natural order of ends is not (as it is sometimes misperceived) simply an identification of "typical patterns of behavior in nature" – what either animals or men "typically" do. Nor is it a theory based primarily on biological impulses or drives. "Nature" in natural right and classical natural law is understood as the full development of the inherent capacities of a being. The nature of a being is what it is when it is fully developed. In non-human beings, "their respective inclinations to their proper acts and ends" are simply "imprinted in their being," so to speak, and these ends are achieved without deliberation or choice (though some beings are defective and do not achieve their full natural development, due to internal defects or external obstacles – some acorns grow into oak trees, and others never make it that far). Man, a rational creature, on the other hand, having a "natural inclination to its proper act and end," must undertake deliberation and choice to achieve his ends – this sort of creature "partakes of a share of providence, by being provident both for itself and others."[11]

If the gap between the first two concepts of natural law is fairly small, the differences between those two concepts and this one are

11 Aquinas, *Summa Theologiae*, I–II, Q. 91, art. 2 (p. 997).

substantial. The common substantive content of natural law theories –
that is, the emphasis on natural ends (or teleology), virtue, and practical wisdom – on this understanding of natural law is much broader.
Still, there remain important differences within this category. For
instance, although classical thinkers like Aristotle and natural law
thinkers like Aquinas have so much in common that they could both be
said to inhabit this category – Aquinas's thought is often characterized
as "Christian Aristotelianism," and Aristotle is, for Aquinas, "the
Philosopher" – but they have some serious differences between them.
Some of these differences are the result of Aquinas's acceptance of
divine revelation (for example, Aquinas's typology of law, which
includes the divine positive law that comes from God intervening in
history) and others are perhaps differences that can be argued about
even within Aristotle's own framework of reason (e.g., the difference
between Aristotle's "Prime Mover" and Aquinas's "Creator" – the latter
being a concept accessible through reason, not just divine revelation).

Classical Thomistic Natural Law

The fourth and most determinate sense of natural law, strictly speaking,
is classical Thomistic natural law: human beings flourish and achieve
such happiness as is possible in this life by living good lives, following
a law inscribed in their being by their Creator: above all, lives of virtue
or excellence. They choose particular ways of living well, guided by the
self-evident basic principles of natural law, which they grasp through
practical reason and by right desire (largely the fruit of proper habitua-
tion).

This ethical order is rooted in an ontological order, an order of
being, though this natural law is not known or understood by "deduc-
ing" moral norms from a theoretical understanding of that order; rather,
it is grasped in the first instance by acts of the practical reason recognizing certain self-evident principles. In Aquinas's *Summa Theologiae*,
the most comprehensive order is the eternal law, which includes divine
positive law, which is derived from revelation, and natural law, which is
man's rational participation in the eternal law. According to Aquinas,
however, the broader context of the natural law is not only the truths of
divine revelation, but also the knowledge through natural reason of God

the Creator's existence, power, and providence – a "natural theology." Therefore, the term "natural law" is more properly used of Thomistic natural law than classical natural right (which rarely speaks of natural law), because it is understood to come from a "lawgiver," and it is in this sense that I primarily use the term.

Contemporary Liberalism

Given this background understanding of possible meanings of natural law, we can turn to the question at hand, examining two contemporary liberal thinkers – John Rawls and Ronald Dworkin – to see whether, or in what sense, they could be said to embody natural law thinking.

John Rawls

Rawls's *A Theory of Justice* (1971) resurrected social contract theory and gave it a more egalitarian form, drawing on Kant to provide a stronger foundation for liberal rights than the previously dominant form of liberal thought – utilitarianism – seemed able to do.[12] A particularly important element of Rawlsian political theory is the requirement that government be "neutral" on questions about the human good: government ought not to embrace any particular "comprehensive" theories (theological or philosophical) of the human good.[13]

Rawls's initial version of liberalism was subjected to powerful critiques from several different directions, and so Rawls revised his theory in articles that culminated in *Political Liberalism* (1993), in which he backed off what he conceded to be the "comprehensive liberalism" of *A Theory of Justice* and put forward a "political liberalism" that claimed not to rely on any comprehensive theories of the good. Central to this conception of political liberalism is the notion of "public reason." The idea of public reason is that, on issues of constitutional

12   John Rawls, *A Theory of Justice* (Harvard University Press, 1971). Rawls, and others, were bothered by the fact that the cost-benefit calculations of utilitarianism could result too easily in overriding the rights of individuals.

13   For an excellent and concise summary of Rawls, see Michael Pakaluk, "The Liberalism of John Rawls: A Brief Exposition," in *Liberalism at the Crossroads* eds. Christopher Wolfe and John Hittinger (Lanham, MD: Rowman and Littlefield, 1994).

essentials and questions of basic justice, citizens must "be ready to explain the basis of their actions to one another in terms each could reasonably expect that others might endorse as consistent with their freedom and equality."[14] This means that they cannot simply appeal to their own comprehensive religious and moral conceptions, which differ from those of many of their fellow citizens. Moreover, in making justifications, democratic citizens should "appeal only to presently accepted general beliefs and forms of reasoning found in common sense, and the methods and conclusions of science when these are not controversial."[15]

The apparent ground of the requirement of public reason is that, in its absence, society will inevitably collapse into internal warfare, as occurred in Europe during the time of the Reformation. The natural outcome of the use of reason in free societies, Rawls thought, is a deep pluralism of comprehensive views that threatens to make impossible a just and viable society. The alternative to political liberalism is an unstable "modus vivendi" in which different groups find it in their interest to accept a policy of tolerance toward each other in the short term, but are constantly jockeying for a position of dominance in which toleration can be dismissed.

Rawls is aware that a society that is "neutral" among competing comprehensive theories still promotes certain ways of life (e.g., tolerance). But, he argues, those ways of life are promoted, not because they correspond to some comprehensive theory of the good life, but because they advance a "political" conception of justice that is necessary for fair social cooperation among free and equal citizens.

From one perspective – that of a "minimalist" natural law – Rawls could be said to be a natural law thinker. For example, Rawls's theory includes the idea that there are certain "primary social goods," which are "things which it is supposed a rational man wants whatever else he wants." These primary goods include "rights and liberties, opportunities and powers, income and wealth" as well as "a sense of one's own worth."[16] Whatever else this entails, it entails at least "a more or less

14   John Rawls, *Political Liberalism* (New York: Columbia University Press, 1993), 218.
15   Ibid., 224.
16   *A Theory of Justice*, p. 92.

clearly articulated theory of human nature."[17] Moreover, Rawls's assumptions about the relative value of social peace, on one hand, and the pursuit of a social order based on some comprehensive conception of truth, on the other, likewise entail some theory of human nature.

On the other hand, from the broadest perspective, Rawls's political philosophy is strikingly "conventional" (based on common agreement, not nature). It simply assumes too much to be regarded as truly philosophical, as Pierre Manent has said.[18] Among other things, Manent writes, Rawls is of a breed of American thinkers who "take the democratic regime for granted."[19] Specifically:

> John Rawls does *not* qualify as a political philosopher. He certainly is a citizen in good standing of the American body politic, and a very commented-upon teacher and writer. He contributed to a revival of the debate about our social arrangements not only in the English-speaking world, but in the whole democratic world. But he *presupposes* the validity, truth, and excellence of our democratic principles and institutions, and so cannot do more than ingeniously tinker with parochial details.[20]

While Rawls and others are part of a recent "explosion of philosophical writing analyzing and justifying such matters as justice, democracy, rights, freedom, and equality,"[21] Manent says, "Who needs one more justifier for what he or she already believes? I need someone who is able to free me from the bondage of present conventions."[22] Of course, Rawls cannot get to the most fundamental issues of political philosophy because that would entail a comprehensive theory, which is

---

17 Hittinger, "Liberalism and the American Natural Law Tradition," 481. Hittinger is commenting on what is implicit in the work of David A. J. Richards, a constitutional scholar influenced by Rawls.

18 See Pierre Manent, "The Return of Political Philosophy," *First Things* 103 (May, 2000):15–22 and his response to several letters in *First Things* 106 (October 2000): 9.

19 From Manent's response to several letters in *First Things* 106 (October 2000): 9.

20 Ibid.

21 Ibid., quoting from a letter to which Manent is responding, from J. L. A. Garcia of Boston University, *First Things* (October, 2000): 7.

22 Ibid., 9.

too divisive, in his own view, to serve as the basis for a public philosophy.

From the perspective of a more substantive view of natural law, then, Rawls is certainly not a natural law thinker, as he would be the first to agree. The deeper question, of course, is whether Rawls's approach is superior to a natural law approach. I think one indication of the inadequacy of Rawls's theory is the weakness of his central concept of public reason, which I discuss at some length (with Robert George) elsewhere.[23] This weakness is on display when it is applied to issues such as abortion, slavery, and homosexuality.

While Rawls generally steers clear of controversial political issues, in *Political Liberalism* he suggested that any prohibition of abortion, at least in the first trimester of pregnancy, would fail the requirements of public reason. Later, however, he retracted this assertion in the introduction to the paperback edition of the book, conceding that an argument from public reason could be made to protect unborn life. (Others who follow him, such as Stephen Macedo, continue to believe that the question of the beginning of human life is so inherently controversial that no argument from public reason to prohibit abortion is possible. But proponents of the protection of unborn human life point out that what is "controversial" is not determined by a poll, but by the nature of the argument: even if overwhelming majorities find an argument unacceptable – as the humanity of black slaves was doubted in the pre-Civil War South – it may still meet the intrinsic requirements of public reasonableness.)

In "The Idea of Public Reason Revisited," Rawls contends, regarding the slavery debate, that it is a "misunderstanding" that "an argument in public reason could not side with Lincoln against Douglas in their debates of 1858." He simply asserts that "[s]ince the rejection of slavery is a clear case of securing the constitutional essential of the equal basic liberties, surely Lincoln's view was reasonable (even if not the most reasonable), while Douglas's was not."[24] But whether blacks

---

23   Robert P. George and Christopher Wolfe, "Natural Law and Liberal Public Reason," *American Journal of Jurisprudence* 42 (1997).

24   John Rawls, "The Idea of Public Reason Revisited, *"University of Chicago Law Review* 64.3 (Summer 1997): 802.

were fully human beings and appropriate subjects of "equal basic liberties" was precisely *the point of contention* in the slavery debate of that time (as it is the point of contention, in our time, regarding very young human beings still in the womb). Rawls is right about Lincoln and the rights of blacks, of course, in just the same way that those who today seek to protect the rights of the unborn are right. But it is not hard to imagine pre-Civil War southerners invoking a Rawlsian conception of public reason to maintain that Lincoln's arguments were illegitimate, because he could not reasonably expect them to accept those arguments, based on different comprehensive views about the humanity of black slaves.[25]

Ronald Dworkin

Is Ronald Dworkin a natural law thinker? Some people have thought so, since he is famous for arguing (in his first book, *Taking Rights Seriously*[26]) that there are "right answers" to "hard cases." And he says (not particularly unenthusiastically) that there might be some sense in which he could be called a natural law theorist, in his 1982 article "Natural Law Revisited."[27] In his later work, Dworkin rejects the anti-perfectionist liberal strategy that requires people to set aside their convictions about the good life when they act politically. The heart of his argument is that most people's ethical intuitions are best explained by a

---

25 In a very similar way, the U. S. Supreme Court's famous "mystery passage" in *Planned Parenthood v. Casey* makes no sense. It says: "These matters [such as abortion], involving the most intimate and personal choices a person may make in a lifetime, choices central to personal dignity and autonomy, are central to the liberty protected by the Fourteenth Amendment. At the heart of liberty is the right to define one's own concept of existence, of meaning, of the universe, and of the mystery of human life." (*Planned Parenthood v. Casey*, 505 U.S. 833, 851 [1992]). But a moment's thought shows us that this capacity of people to define personhood for themselves – defining an unborn human being as a non-person – would also allow them to "personally" define blacks as "sub-human."

26 Ronald Dworkin, *Taking Rights Seriously* (Cambridge, MA: Harvard University Press, 1977).

27 "If the crude description of natural law I just gave is correct, that any theory which makes the content of law sometimes depend on the correct answer to some moral question is a natural law theory, then I am guilty of natural law." Ronald Dworkin, "Natural Law Revisited," *University of Florida Law Review* 34 (1982): 165.

view of ethics that focuses not on the impact or consequences of a life but rather on meeting the challenge of living skillfully, and that this "challenge model" supports the ideal of liberal equality.

With some limited exceptions,[28] the challenge model leads to a rejection of "paternalism" – government forbidding or rewarding any private activity on the ground that one set of substantive ethical values is superior to others – because ethical value depends on free choice (this is the principle of "ethical integrity"). Nothing can improve the critical (true) value of a person's life unless it is seen as an improvement by the person whose life it is.

Liberal equality is grounded in a definite ethical position, so the challenge model does not begin with ethical neutrality. But it comes to neutrality in the course of its argument, denying the legitimacy of society outlawing a kind of life on the grounds that it is demeaning or corrupt, as long as it is not unjust. This neutrality can be generally accepted without people having to abandon what they believe is important to them, that is, their convictions of ethical identity and their substantive views about living a life well. People would only have to abandon views requiring them to force other people to act rightly – the "third-person beliefs" involved in "coercive critical paternalism" (laws forbidding or rewarding activity, based on an assumption of the superiority of certain moral views, and not on the injustice of the actions). Thus, liberal equality gives promise of consensus, since it is far less utopian to hope that people will give up their third-person than their first-person beliefs.

Dworkin acknowledges that liberal equality is not ethically neutral in its effects, since some lives will be more difficult or expensive in a liberal society (e.g., society need not tolerate the religious fanatic imposing his religion on others, or the racist imposing white supremacy) – but that is not in virtue of a condemnation of those lives but is due to liberalism's conception of justice. Liberal equality permits people to carry over their personal ethics into politics, but denies them one

---

28 It does leave room for short-range educational paternalism that looks forward to genuine endorsement – as when parents compel their children to practice the piano, in the expectation that the children will, in the future, "endorse" what their parents have done.

weapon: they may not forbid someone to live a life simply because they consider his ethical convictions wrong.

Hittinger again points out that this approach falls into a category of "minimalist" natural law:

> Dworkin hopes to avoid metaphysical swamps because the liberal principle, he insists, "does not rest on any special theory of the personality." But of course it does. Only with a certain view of the human personality can we suppose that governmental legislation on substantive views of the good are violative of individual liberty and personality. That is, *if* the value of humanity consists essentially in the individual's power to choose his or her own view of what is good in life (and I say essentially, because virtually no one argues or has argued that the good of choice is entirely accidental to personhood), *then* it follows that we cannot respect human persons by submitting their freedom to goals already chosen by others – whether God, nature, or community.[29]

Describing Dworkin as a natural law thinker in a less minimalist sense would be difficult, because Dworkin's description of the challenge model and ethical integrity is so formalistic: the challenge model of ethical life – life as a skillful performance, *irrespective of its specific content* – is superior to alternative models (Dworkin's straw man, the "impact" model, according to which a life is judged by its extrinsic results).

The real opposition, however, lies between two forms of the challenge model, which emphasizes "skillful performance": one that stresses objective, substantive criteria for skillfulness (there are acts that are good and those that are bad, by virtue of their objects) and another that denies that there are such objective, substantive criteria, focusing purely on "procedural" qualities of skillfulness (e.g., whether someone has really reflected on a problem seriously, grappled with its difficulties, etc.). In both cases, it is true that virtue does, in some sense, lie in skillful performance in the meeting of some challenge, but Dworkin has a very reductionistic and formalistic view of the criteria for skillfulness.

29 Hittinger, "Liberalism and the American Natural Law Tradition," 477.

Conclusion

It appears, then, that liberal theorists like Rawls and Dworkin are natural law thinkers only if one adopts a very minimalist view of natural law. This minimalist view is not unimportant, because, as Hadley Arkes frequently reminds us, it is a testimony to the inevitability of some sort of natural law. But the minimalist version of natural law is not ultimately very satisfying as political philosophy, especially because of the limited scope of its questioning, which assumes some fundamental starting points and refuses to engage other questions.

Isn't it enough that liberal theorists' conventional assumptions correspond to those of the community for which they write, i.e., Western constitutional democracies? I think not. First, from a short-term perspective, it might appear to be adequate, but short-term perspectives are inadequate to ground a public philosophy. We cannot simply assume that there will be no challenges to democratic assumptions, even in the relatively foreseeable future. For example, if American society were subject to dramatic stresses, such as severe economic depression or a successful terrorist assault of great magnitude (perhaps through biological or chemical weapons), challenges to democratic principles might well emerge. Resisting those challenges would require more than thinkers like Rawls and Dworkin have to offer their readers.

Second, the answers to more particular questions of public philosophy are not separable from the answers to the initial and broader questions. Some conception of free speech, for example, would be an essential part of any American public philosophy. But virtually no one believes that speech can never, under any circumstances, be prohibited or punished. What are the *reasonable* limits to free speech? The answer to that question will depend naturally on the *purpose* of free speech, and that, in turn, will require a much broader political philosophy that does not simply assume democratic institutions and practices (such as free speech).

Third, we should be more alert to the need for a political philosophy broader and deeper than contemporary liberalism, given the rise of international terrorism and aggressive anti-Western, anti-liberal democratic movements, governments, and cultures. For many years, the confrontation with Soviet communism was a considerable stimulus to Western political theory, requiring something more than assumptions of Western superiority – *arguments* were needed. With the fall of communism, liberal democracy temporarily appeared to be the only game in town, having vanquished its enemies. Now, liberal democracy confronts a more difficult opponent, rooted in a form of religious fanaticism that seems impervious to reason.

No amount of argumentation, of course, will "persuade" a religious fanatic. But it matters a great deal what people in such cultures – when they are invited to become religious fanatics – see as the alternative to it. If the alternative to religious fanaticism is a political community in which their deepest convictions about reality and human life are said to be false (as in comprehensive liberalism) or one in which those convictions are treated as politically irrelevant (except to the extent that they happen to harmonize with political liberalism) – if the political community is one in which the ideals of truth and goodness most important in their lives are relativized or privatized – then religious zealotry may seem to be the more tolerable option. Only if liberalism is able to put forward a face that makes public appeals to ultimate standards of truth and goodness possible will it be able to compete for the hearts and minds of many people in the world who are not simply raised with conventional Western ideas and attitudes. The challenge facing even this moderate or natural law liberalism – the challenge of convincing many people that freedom of conscience is good, even if moral relativism is not – will still be a great one. But I believe that there is a much greater possibility of successfully meeting that challenge with a natural law of substantive content (e.g., Classical Thomistic Natural Law) than there is of persuading them to accept comprehensive or political liberalism.

III. Religion, Liberal Democracy, and the American Project

Chapter 8:
Why the Natural Law Suggests a Divine Source
J. Budziszewski

Introduction

*They show that what the law requires
is written on their hearts . . .*[1]

Certain moral basics are not only right for everyone, but at some level known to everyone. Even false friends know that they should be faithful to their friends; even ingrates are at some level aware of the duty of gratitude; even skirt-chasers know that they ought to be faithful to their wives. These and other foundational principles have traditionally been called "natural law," because we know them through the way we are made, through the shared experience of lives that are structured by human nature. The fact that we know them naturally doesn't necessarily mean that we always follow them. Nor does it mean that our knowledge of them is clear: Though real as rain, it may be cloudy, latent, unreflective, and philosophically uninformed. But just as we all have an absent-minded feeling of weight even if we know nothing about the theory of gravitation, so we all have a dim awareness of the natural law even if we know nothing about the philosophy of natural law.

The argument of this chapter is that reality of the natural law gives

---

1   Romans 2:15a, RSV. I hope that nobody will suppose that just because each section is headed with a quotation from Scripture, the arguments rely on verbal revelation. It would have served as well to quote Shakespeare, if suitable quotations could be found. Those who do believe in verbal revelation may be interested to know that the Book of Scripture confirms the Book of Nature; those who don't may regard it as ordinary literature.

good reason to believe in the reality of God, even apart from verbal revelation. This is not to reject the possibility of verbal revelation; it is only to say that we are not presently considering it. Several of the revealed religions have vigorously explored the philosophy of natural law, but philosophers outside the revealed religions have pursued it too. This chapter considers the Book of Nature, not the Book of Scripture, and our suggestion is that, like its twin, it points back to its divine Author.

Four Modes of Natural Moral Knowledge

There is no speech, nor are there words;
their voice is not heard; yet their voice
goes out through all the earth.[2]

Before we investigate the suggestion that natural law points to God, a little more must be said about the natural law itself. How, exactly, is the natural law "natural" – how does "the way we are made" indicate right and wrong? In at least four ways, including the sheer recognition of human designedness, the deep structure of the human moral intellect, the other deep structures of our design, and what happens to us when we set ourselves at odds with our design. Some non-classical natural law theories emphasize one or two of these modes of natural knowledge at the expense of the others, and some even deny one or two of them. However, the mainstream of the natural law tradition affirms and integrates all four. Let us take a brief look at each one.

To return to the beginning, first is the simple fact that we recognize human nature to be not a blooming, buzzing confusion, but a deeply ordered, meaningful reality, a design. If the way we are were merely an arbitrary jumble of arbitrary processes with no meaning or purpose, then strictly speaking, we would have no nature. How could it possibly instruct us? How could we speak of following it if there were nothing to follow? We might just as well reprogram the mishmash, abolish our so-called nature – why not? But there is no good reason to believe that we are a mishmash. We do not experience ourselves that way; not only do we recognize order and structure in human life, but also it has value

2   Psalm 19:3–4a, RSV.

and significance to us. Some claim that this is nonsense, that the perception of moral meaning is an illusion, a way in which natural selection makes suckers of us, tricking us into carrying out its blind program.[3] Their idea is that animals who think they perceive meaning in their lives will be more strongly motivated to live and cooperate long enough to pass on their genes. But this explanation is circular. After all, the perception of meaning would strengthen the motive to live only if we *needed* to perceive meaning – only if we lost interest in living if we didn't perceive it. What adaptive value could such a tendency have? Wouldn't it have been more straightforward for natural selection to produce animals who didn't need to perceive meaning? If the evolutionary program is to make them live and cooperate so that they can pass on their genes, wouldn't it have been more economical simply to evolve a predisposition to live and cooperate? To put it another way, rather than first producing animals who lose their will to live unless they can see a meaning which isn't there, then making them think they *do* see a meaning which isn't there, why not just produce animals who want to live? A reasonable person concludes that we seek meaning not because it helps smuggle our genes into our descendants, but because there really is meaning – and because we are ordained to seek it and perchance to find it. One of the things that have meaning is our own nature, and part of this meaning is moral.

Second is the deep structure of the human moral intellect, of the power of moral reasoning. We might call this power deep conscience.

---

3   "It's amazing that a process as amoral and crassly pragmatic as natural selection could design [!] a mental organ that makes us feel as if we're in touch with higher truths. Truly a shameless ploy." Robert Wright, *The Moral Animal: The New Science of Evolutionary Psychology* (New York, NY: Random House, 1994), 212. "[O]ur belief in morality is merely an adaptation put in place to further our reproductive ends. . . . [E]thics as we understand it is an illusion fobbed off on us by our genes to get us to co-operate (so that human genes survive). . . . Furthermore the way our biology enforces its ends is by making us think that there is an objective higher code to which we are all subject." Michael Ruse and E.O. Wilson, "The Evolution of Ethics," *New Scientist* 108:1478 (17 October 1985): 51–52. For critique, see J. Budziszewski, "Accept No Imitations: Naturalism vs. Natural Law," *The Line Through the Heart: Natural Law as Fact, Theory, and Sign of Contradiction* (Wilmington, DE: ISI Books, 2009), 79–95.

Deep conscience is what tells us the basics of right and wrong, like "Never do gratuitous harm to your neighbor," "Punish only the guilty," or even more fundamentally, "Good is to be done and pursued, and evil avoided." It would be ridiculous to suggest that we work these out as conclusions from still deeper premises; *they are* the premises from which conclusions are worked out. It would be equally silly to suggest that we know these things only because our parents taught them to us. Certainly they did teach us, and that is important. But just as in the realm of arithmetic, no amount of perverse parental teaching could convince an intelligent child that the sum of ten plus ten is two, so in the realm of morality, no amount of perverse parental teaching could convince him that we owe loyalty to enemies and betrayal to friends.[4] And there is more. Not only does deep conscience teach us the foundational principles of right and wrong; it is how we discern that there is a distinction between right and wrong in the first place. Without it we would presumably be able to recognize a difference between what we want and what we do not want, but the possibility of a duty to do something *even though we do not want to* would escape us; we would be color-blind to the moral color "ought." In this sense, every mode of natural moral knowledge is built on deep conscience as a foundation – although, in another sense, every mode also depends on the recognition of designedness, which we have already discussed. For if deep conscience itself had no meaning, then why should we bother with it? Why not ignore it? If we find that we cannot ignore it, but that it gets in the way, then why not find a way to delete or disconnect it? We cannot help perceiving that this would be simply wrong. Conscience presents itself to us not merely as an inconvenient thought, but as an interior witness to a real law.

Third is how we are made more generally – the other features of the

4   Although we recognize the moral basics as true in themselves, it would incorrect to call them "innate." We are not born knowing them; the newborn infant does not reflect, "I ought to be faithful to my spouse, if I have a spouse, whatever a spouse is, and whatever faithfulness is." On the other hand, as soon as a child attains the age of reason – as soon as he is able to grasp the concepts to which such rules refer – he is able to see that the rules are true. Surely the mind must have a certain innate *structure* to be capable of such a feat. However, it is not pre-loaded with innate *ideas*.

human design, the other qualities of the human constitution. To mention but a few such features, we are persons rather than things; we come in two polar sexes; and we are imbued with a desire to know, which is moved not just by practical considerations, but by wonder. Each of these features makes a difference to how we should live. A striking fact about them is that each is ordered to a purpose, each of them stands in a "for the sake of" relationship to some human good. The difference of the sexes, for example, is ordained to the union of complementary opposites, and wonder is ordained to the seeking of wisdom. In fact, not only is our nature structured by "for the sake of" relations, it is in itself a kind of "for the sake of" relation. To be a person is to be ordained to meaningful freedom, to have value in myself rather than being merely an instrument or tool of someone or something else.

Fourth is the natural consequences of our actions, what happens when we set ourselves at odds with our design. In old-fashioned language, we reap what we sow. Amazingly, rather than being in conflict with deep conscience or the other features of our design, the system of natural consequences complements them – a fact to which we return later. Conscience bids me be faithful to my friends, but if I betray them all then I will have no friends. Wonder bids me seek wisdom, but if I am indifferent to wisdom I will become even stupider than I had intended. Awe and gratitude bid me acknowledge my divine Author, but if I lose Him I will ultimately lose myself. We may call the principle of natural consequences the "law of the harvest." It is the teacher of last resort, the testimony to natural law that kicks in after we have refused to pay attention to the other three.

Having already broached the subject of God, let us turn to some of the various ways in which the reality of the natural law points to a divine origin. I say "some" because these are only a sample; other arguments are possible as well. I call them "arguments" rather than "proofs" because the discussion is never finally closed; the best that philosophy can ever do is provide good reasons for believing that something is true, reasons which can then be investigated more fully. My aim, then, is not to anticipate and answer all possible objections to these good reasons – that would be impossible – but to bring them within grasp, to render them accessible to intuition.

The Argument from Natural Law as Order

He fixed their bounds which cannot be passed.[5]

Several different forms of the Argument from Natural Law as Order might be developed. The form in which I am presenting it makes it a special case of several other more general arguments for the existence of God.[6] In this form, it runs like this:

1. Natural law is a form of natural order, specifically, of natural *moral* order.
2. But every form of natural order requires a "cause," an explanation, and this form is no exception.
3. The most reasonable explanation for natural order is that nature itself has a cause which imparts such order to it.
4. This is what we call God.

Natural law, then, points to its divine origin in the same way that all natural order points to its divine origin. Let us consider each step of the argument in turn.

The most common objection to Step 1 is that the very expression "natural law" is misleading – that moral law is not a kind of *natural* order because, if it were, then everything that happens in nature would be moral, and obviously this is not the case. The objection misunderstands what is meant by calling moral law a kind of natural order. Two different kinds of statement describing natural order are commonly called "laws of nature," and at present we are referring to only one of them. What science calls the laws of nature – generalizations such as the law of gravity – describe how things *actually do* happen in the world. What ethics calls the laws of nature – generalizations such as the Golden Rule – describe how things *ought* to happen in the world, and serve as standards for the conduct of beings capable of grasping them. But how things ought to happen is just as truly a structure of reality as how they do happen, and just as truly knowable by the use of our natural intellect.

An example may help make this clear: What are eyes for? Obviously, for seeing. This is not just a wild guess, or an inference from

5   Psalm 148:5b-6, RSV.
6   The Argument from Order and the Cosmological Argument.

facts outside of nature. It is a reasonable inference from the facts of nature itself. What facts? Not *just* the fact that eyes do see (for in itself that would not be enough), but also the fact that without referring to their power to see, we would have no good way to explain why we have eyes in the first place. Now if the purpose of eyes is that they see, then eyes that see well are good eyes, and eyes that see poorly are poor ones; given their purpose, this is what it *means* for eyes to be "good." Moreover, good is to be pursued; the appropriateness of pursuing it is what it means for *anything* to be good. Therefore, the appropriate thing to do with poor eyes is try to turn them into good ones, and we ought to do so. Do you see what we have just done? We have reasoned from certain facts about what is (the function of the eyes) to certain conclusions about what ought to be done (helping them to fulfill their function). The conclusion, which is evaluative, turns out to be just as much a natural truth as the premise, which is descriptive. You may be thinking, "That can't be true, because I've always been told that an 'is' cannot imply an 'ought.'" This so-called rule of reasoning is overstated. Certainly not every kind of "is" implies an "ought." It really would be a fallacy, for example, to reason "rocks do fall on people, therefore rocks ought to fall on people." But attention to what we have just done shows that *some kinds* of "is" really do imply *some kinds* of "oughts." The fallacy lies not in reasoning from "is" to "ought" *as such,* but in drawing the wrong kinds of connection between these two kinds of proposition.

Concerning Step 2: It may seem that order does *not* require an explanation – that it can arise spontaneously, without anything bringing it about. Generally speaking, however, the achievement of the sorts of order we casually call "spontaneous" requires more design and contrivance, not less. If I toss nine three-inch-square blocks into a nine-inch-square box, then jostle the box, the blocks will spontaneously arrange themselves into a symmetrical three-by-three block grid. But they will do so only because they are just the right number, shape and size to fit – a set of features unlikely to arise by chance. In general, the more elaborate the spontaneous order, the greater the need to explain the circumstances which make it possible, so we have merely pushed the need for explanation one step back.

Concerning Step 3: It may seem that even if order does require an explanation, it does not require an *ultimate* explanation. Perhaps order is explained by cause A, cause A is explained by cause B, cause B is explained by cause C, and so on in an infinite regress. The problem is that requiring an infinite regress of explanations is equivalent to having no explanation at all. If order really does require explanation, then at some point the chain of explanations must terminate in a first cause or first explanation.

Concerning Step 4: It may seem that even if natural order requires a first cause or first explanation, this first cause may be something *else* in nature. If so, then why must the explanation resort to a Creator who is *different* from nature, who brought nature into order? Perhaps, instead of God, we should be thinking of, say, very powerful Martians, who are just as much a part of nature as we are. This objection overlooks a crucial distinction. Suppose it were true that for everything in nature, and for every kind of order among these things, we could find a cause or explanation which was also within nature. Even if this were true, it wouldn't explain enough. The *entire ensemble* of things and of kinds of order among them would remain to be explained, and the explanation would have to be distinct from the ensemble itself. To explain things in nature, it might, conceivably, be sufficient to resort to other things in nature; to explain nature *as such,* though, one must resort to something other than nature. This something is what we call God.

An interesting variation on the Argument from Natural Law as Order relies on the fact that the universe exhibits more than one kind of natural order – for example moral order, causal order, and teleological order. The various forms of natural order do correspond surprisingly closely; for example, I ought to be faithful to my friends (moral order), unfaithfulness tends to destroy friendship (causal order), and faithfulness is both part of friendship and practiced for its sake (teleological order). But the correspondence is not perfect. Our hearts are riddled with desires that interfere with our ultimate happiness, and we are sometimes strongly tempted to do what is wrong. The correspondence among the different kinds of order is itself a kind of order in need of explanation, and as such, points to a divine origin. On the other hand, the fact that the correspondence is less than perfect – the dislocation we suffer, which puts us at odds with ourselves – also requires explanation, an explanation which seems to go beyond the resources of natural law theory *as such.* This fact does not imply that natural law theory is untrue; it suggests only that it is not the *whole* truth about human nature, a point which natural law thinkers may gladly concede.[7]

The Argument from Natural Law as Law

. . . while their conscience also bears witness and their conflicting thoughts accuse or perhaps excuse them.[8]

The Argument from Natural Law as Law depends not on the fact that the natural law is one among many forms of natural order, but on the fact that it is a *specific* form of natural order, that is, law. The simplest but most suggestive argument version of the argument runs like this:

1. Natural law is really law.
2. Law requires enactment, therefore an enactor or legislator.
3. But law also requires promulgation, and natural law is promulgated through nature.
4. Nature could not serve as a means of promulgation unless the legislator fashioned it to do so.
5. Therefore, the legislator of the natural law must be the creator or fashioner of nature. This is what we call God.

The pillar of this argument is Step 1. Why should we accept it? Why should we believe that natural law is real law, rather than, say, a collection of urges or of interesting ideas? The most powerful reason to consider it a real law is the faculty of conscience. Conscience isn't merely something we pick up along the way; the experience is natural to us. Moreover, the experience is highly distinctive, utterly unlike any other – it presents itself not just as a medley of attractions and aversions, but as an interior witness to a standard which we do not make

---

7   To many thinkers, myself included, the interior dislocation suggests the need of *historical* explanation, an *event* – in Christian terms, a fall from grace.

8   Romans 2:15b, RSV.

up, which directs us and by which we are judged, and which we cannot change to suit ourselves.

It may seem that this confidence that conscience is what it seems to be is inflated: That it could not be what it seems to be, in the first place because it is not truly natural, in the second place because it is not truly distinctive. Rather than being natural, perhaps it is pumped in from the outside, an internal residue of lessons taught to us by others. Parents tell us things, teachers tell us things, and over time we accumulate a set of inclinations and inhibitions. And even if it is natural, rather than being a distinctive kind of experience, an interior witness, perhaps conscience is just a fancy name for some subset of mammalian instincts. Just as we have an instinct to eat when we are hungry, so we have an instinct, say, to do justice, the only difference being that we dress up the latter instinct by calling it a duty or a law.

Although these dismissive arguments are superficially plausible, they raise more questions than they answer. Certainly one can see why conscience might seem like a mere residue of socialization. After all, our sense of what is right and wrong is certainly influenced by how we are brought up and taught. But as we saw earlier, the only way to teach anyone anything is to build on something already there; unless conscience were partly natural, there would be nothing for the teachings to catch hold of, to take root in. "Don't hit your little brother," mother says to Johnnie, "you know better than that. How would you like it if he hit you?" The reason she says "You know better than that" is that Johnnie does know better than that. The reason she asks "How would you like it if he hit you?" is that even if he has never heard the Golden Rule, she can count on the underlying idea making sense to him. Teaching certainly helps, just as teaching helps us get the arithmetic sum "two plus two is four." Yet the reason the teaching works is that Johnnie can see for himself that he shouldn't do to his brother what he wouldn't want done to him – just as he can see for himself that two plus two is really four.

The classical term for the natural substrate of conscience is *synderesis,* and for what teaching plants in this rich soil, *conscientia.* As I suggested earlier, we may call the former "deep conscience"; to complete the pair, we may call the latter "surface conscience." Deep conscience makes it possible to reject false moral teachings because we see for ourselves that they are wrong. It is also the explanation for a fact that would otherwise be inexplicable: that the basics of conscience are the same everywhere. After all, if conscience were *only* a residue of what we are taught, why shouldn't it be completely variable? Why shouldn't the young in one country be taught "Treat everyone the same as you would wish to be treated," but in another "Treat everyone the opposite of how you would wish to be treated?" Why shouldn't they be trained in one land to be courageous, but in another to be cowards? Why shouldn't they hear in one culture that they should honor their parents, but in another that they should crush, despise, humiliate, crow over, and eat their parents? The moral codes of different times and places differ only in the details, and in the strictness with which people live up to what they believe – just as we would expect, if the possibilities of the acquired powers of moral judgment are shaped and limited by a natural substrate.

To return to the other dismissive argument, one can also see why deep conscience might seem like a fancy name for a subset of mammalian instincts. After all, haven't we just seen that deep conscience is natural after all? Yes. And isn't instinct the all-encompassing term for all natural impulses? Some people do use the term that way, but it is a misleading way to use it, because there is more than one kind of natural impulse, and we need distinctions. But why should we make *this* distinction – why should we distinguish deep conscience from instinct? There are at least two reasons.

In the first place, just as conscience may bid me to go against what I have been taught, so too it may bid me to go against my instincts. I may have an instinct to kill a man whom I resent, yet conscience warns that it is wrong to deliberately take innocent human life. I may have an instinct to run away from danger, yet conscience bids me stand and defend my friends. Someone might say that in cases like this, conscience is merely the strongest instinct. The problem with this explanation is that in some cases I have *conflicting* instincts, and conscience tells me which one to follow. Suppose that in certain circumstances, fighting would be more adaptive. Then why shouldn't I have evolved in such a way that in such circumstances, the instinct to fight automatically prevails? Something like this does seem to happen among the animals; behavioral biologists speak of an "order of prepotency" among the instincts, which varies according to the situation. In some situations one impulse has a higher rank, in other situations another one does. But conscience often tells a human like me to follow the *weaker* impulse! What is going on here? Why should evolution have followed such a tortuous and circuitous path, allowing me conflicting impulses, but also giving me a third thing that says "ignore that one and follow this one"? If this third thing is just *another* instinct, then what authority could it have to pass judgment? That which passes judgment upon instincts must be something different from an instinct.

In the second place, if conscience really were just an instinct, then why should we dress it up by giving it a fancy name? What adaptive value would there be in doing so? None. A better explanation for why we describe the impulses of conscience in terms of law is that they do reflect law. Not only is "I want to" different than "I ought to," but we also experience the violation of the former differently than we experience the violation of the latter. Ordinary slips of prudence lead merely to disappointment; violation of conscience leads to a sense of trespass, of breach, of transgression. The good that I betrayed was not merely commended by inclination, but commanded by authority. I am not only dismayed, I am accused. I have violated a real law.

Once we climb Step 1, the other steps in the argument are easy.

Concerning Step 2: Laws are caused by enactment, and enactment requires personal agency. Of course not all causes are personal. Rain, for example, is produced by an impersonal cause, the condensation of water from the atmosphere. By contrast, law is something addressed *to* a free and rational being *by* a free and rational being. If there is a law, then there must exist a personal agency competent to enact it, a legislator.

Concerning Step 3: The fact that the law is made known through nature – through how we are made, rather than by some other means such as verbal revelation – is the point of describing it as natural. To be sure, the same law might be made known to us by other means as well. The point is simply that whether or not it has been made known by other means, it has been made known by nature.

Concerning Step 4: In order to send a message by means of a written note, the sender must be able to write words and decide where they go on the page; otherwise, the recipients would receive not a message, but only a blank or a scribble. The same is true when the sender communicates by means of human nature, except that in this case the message is written on the recipient himself. He does not write the message, but he is the medium of expression.

Concerning Step 5: If the legislator is the one responsible for the promulgation of the law, and the law is promulgated through the design of nature, then the legislator must be the one responsible for the design of nature.

I cannot emphasize too strongly that this is not a "divine command theory," if by that term we mean the view that law is law just because God commanded it, and that He could have commanded anything, however evil, that he willed. Law, in the full sense of the term, is more than just an enactment by superior power; it must be an ordinance of reason, for the common good, made by legitimate public authority, and made known. To be confident that natural law is really law is to believe that it fulfills all four of these conditions, not just one. Interestingly, then, the Argument from Natural Law as Law not only points to the reality of God, but also tells us something about His character. If natural law is really law, then God must be reasonable, good, and worthy of obedience. If natural law is *First* Law, the law on which all other law depends, then He must be First Reason, First Good, and First Authority.

The Argument from Guilt and Forgiveness

Wilt thou hide thyself for ever?
How long will thy wrath burn like fire?[9]

The Argument from Guilt and Forgiveness depends not on the properties of natural law *as such* – for example that it is order, or that it is law – but on the properties of conscience, which announces it to us.

1. Violation of natural law generates awareness of guilt.
2. Awareness of guilt generates a natural desire for forgiveness.

9   Psalm 89:46b, RSV.

3. Since "nature makes nothing in vain,"[10] forgiveness must actually be possible.
4. However, only a personal agency can forgive.
5. The only personal agency which could forgive a violation of the natural law would be the creator and custodian of nature. This is what we call God.

To begin at the beginning, conscience works in more than one mode. In the cautionary mode it alerts us to the peril of moral wrong: "Don't do that!" In the accusatory mode, it indicts us for wrong we have already done: "Look what you did!" In the avenging mode, it punishes the soul who refuses to read the indictment: "Now you must pay." Conscience is so potent that clear vision of the natural law can be crushing; the first thing an honest man sees with this vision is how far he falls short of it.

Concerning Step 2: A strange thing about the accusation of conscience is that even though it is *my* conscience that accuses, it seems to speak to me with an authority greater than my own: I am not merely angry with myself, I find myself under wrath. I am aware of having breached a boundary which I did not make, but which my deepest self agrees with utterly. I spontaneously desire that the breach be sealed back up, that good relations between me and the law be restored, that I somehow return to the other side of transgression. Surprisingly, though, repentance along isn't enough; it turns out to be only a necessary and not a sufficient condition of the healing of the breach. I experience not only a need to be sorry, but a need for my sorriness to be accepted. What I want is reconciliation with the rule that I have crossed; what I desire is forgiveness. This desire is woven into the cloth of human nature. We don't just learn it from our culture, for it spontaneously arises in all cultures, even if not always with equal clarity.

Concerning Step 3: It would be absurd to suggest that just because I want something, there must be someone or something who can give it

---

10   Aristotle, *On the Generation of Animals*, Book 2, Chapter 5. I hope it will be needless to say that I am not endorsing the details of Aristotle's biology, only the observation that organisms are teleologically ordered.

to me. Suppose I conceive an irrational, delusional desire for pickled square roots; tough luck. In the case of *natural* desires, however, the case is different, because for every natural desire, there really does exist a possible satisfaction. To hunger corresponds food; to thirst, water; to wonder, knowledge. I may not *receive* food, water, knowledge, but at least such things exist; I *could* receive them. In fact, just as we saw earlier in the case of the desire for meaning, a natural desire for which there was no possible satisfaction would be pointless and maladaptive. There would be no reason for our nature to include it; it should not exist. So it is with the natural desire for forgiveness. If there were no such thing as forgiveness, the desire for it could not be woven into human nature in the first place.

Concerning Step 4: Not all of our attitudes, emotions, perceptions, and desires have to do with other persons, but many do. Consider the difference between pleasure and gratitude. I might find a cool breeze pleasurable even if I were the only person in the world, but I cannot be grateful for the cool breeze unless there is someone to whom gratitude is owed. The desire for forgiveness falls not into the former category but into the latter. I cannot *just experience* forgiveness, as I may *just experience* joy; I must actually be forgiven. I cannot be forgiven by a *thing,* as I may be given pain by a *thing;* I can only be forgiven by a person. Someone must actually forgive me.

Concerning Step 5: From what personal agency am I then to seek forgiveness when I have violated the natural law – with whom am I to seek reconciliation? There are three possibilities: Myself, other human beings, or God. The first possibility fails for the reason stated when we were discussing Step 2: Conscience speaks not with my own authority, but as with an authority that transcends me. The second possibility seems more promising, because I do, in fact, seek reconciliation with neighbors whom I have wronged, I can, in fact, receive it, and my neighbors are more than just me. If I hurt my wife's feelings, if I forget a promise to a friend, if I selfishly take credit that belongs to someone else, I know that I must not only change course, confess that I am in the wrong, and try to heal the injury, but ask forgiveness: "I am sorry;

please forgive me." But is this *enough?* No. Suppose I have been unfaithful to my wife, but she forgives me and takes me back, no longer holds my treason against me. Is everything fine? Somehow, it isn't. I haven't just transgressed against her; I have transgressed against something greater than either of us, against the right and good itself. It isn't just her wrath and sorrow that I feel; it is as though the law itself were wroth and sorrowful with me, as though I must be reconciled not only with the beloved wife whom I offended, but with the authority that made it wrong to offend her. The problem is that morality, by itself, has a heart of rock. I can no more be reconciled with law *as such* than I can offer atonement to the weather, or kiss and make up with the force of gravity. Only a personal agency can forgive; and the only personal agency with the authority to forgive the breach of natural law would be the Creator of Nature. This is what we call God.

Someone might say that the only reason I would want this kind of forgiveness is that I think there is a God. If I didn't believe in God, then I wouldn't long for such forgiveness. Yet how often have atheists protested to me that they *don't need* to believe in God to have a conscience that works just like mine? I not only concede their claim, I insist on it: Their consciences *do* work just like mine. This being the case, it is futile to suggest that we desire more-than-human forgiveness only because we believe in God. Rather it seems that we believe in God in part because we desire more-than-human forgiveness. We naturally experience the knowledge of guilt; we naturally desire forgiveness; but law by itself cannot forgive. The atheist, who supposes that there can be a law without a personal authority who is its source and custodian, must therefore suppose that forgiveness is both necessary *and impossible* – which is impossible.

But wait – don't some more radical atheists bite the bullet? Don't they *deny* conscience, reasoning that "if God is dead, then everything is permitted"? Certainly some do reason in such a way, but none can actually live in such a way; the experience of stricken conscience does not wait upon our theological assumptions. It presents itself to us in much the same way whether we believe in God or don't; the only difference is that the atheist lacks resources for explaining why it *should* present itself to him in that way, or why it should exist in the first place.

The Argument from Desire for Final Justice

Yet a little while, and the wicked will be no more;
though you look well at his place, he will not be there.[11]

The previous argument relied on the proposition that "nature makes nothing in vain," and so does this one. This time, though, we are considering a different feature of our nature: not the desire for forgiveness, but the desire for final justice.

1. When the natural law is violated, we naturally desire that justice be done to the wrongdoer.
2. For the reasons already given previously, such a desire could not exist unless justice could in fact be done.
3. But although human justice can partially requite wrongs, some wrongs are so heinous that human justice can never fully requite them.
4. There must then be another power which can fully requite them.
5. This power may be either personal or impersonal. If personal, then it is what we call God; if impersonal, then for reasons already given previously, it points to God as its cause or explanation.

The only likely confusion concerning Step 1 is the meaning of doing justice to wrongdoers. Society is justly ordered when each person receives what is due to him. Crime disturbs this just order, for the wrongdoer takes from people their lives, peace, liberties, dignity, and worldly goods in order to give himself undeserved benefits. Deserved punishment protects society morally by restoring this just order, compensating the victims and making the wrongdoer pay a price equivalent to the harm he has done. This is retribution. It must not be confused with revenge, which is prodded by a different motive. In retribution the spur is the virtue of indignation, which answers injury with injury for public good. In revenge the spur is the passion of resentment, which answers malice with malice for private satisfaction. The desire for retribution is natural, but the desire for revenge is merely its perversion.

---

11   Psalm 37:10, RSV.

Concerning Step 2: It is always best and safest to assume is that nothing in an organism's design is purposeless, even if its purpose is not yet known. Those who assume otherwise always get their comeuppance. Numerous functions have recently been discovered for those portions of the human genome once dismissed as "junk DNA."[12] Organs which were once called "vestigial," like the tonsils and appendix, have also turned out to have their own proper jobs in the body. Just as with the physical features of our nature, so with its non-physical features – in particular, our natural desires. They have purposes no less than the heart or the kidneys do, and for every desire there corresponds some possible satisfaction, or else they would be pointless. If we naturally long for forgiveness when we have done wrong, there must be a possibility of forgiveness; if we naturally pine for justice to the impenitent, there must be a possibility of justice.

Concerning Step 3: Yet human powers are insufficient to right all wrongs and bring all wrongdoers to justice. It isn't just that we don't catch all of them; the problem would remain even if none of them slipped from our grasp. As to the victims, some tears cannot be wiped away by anything within our puny strength; how can the memory of rape be purged, or the murdered dead be brought back to life? As to the perpetrators, what payment could be made to compensate inconsolable griefs? How then could true balance be restored? Not even the ancient formula "Whoever sheds the blood of man, by man shall his blood be shed" – which was not, by the way, an expression of contempt for life, but of respect for it[13] – fills the bill. Can the taking of his life, his only life, yet only one life, make up for his lethal gassing of twenty thousand? What we call public order is relative; what we mean by it is merely that the public is *less* disordered than in various other conditions with which we are familiar. One of the deepest counsels of wisdom (but one of the most difficult to learn) is that human powers are insufficient to achieve final justice.

12   Jonathan Wells, *The Myth of Junk DNA* (Seattle, Washington: Discovery Institute Press, 2011).
13   The passage ends, "for God made man in his own image" (Genesis 9:6, RSV).

Concerning Step 4: One might respond, "Even though human power cannot achieve final justice, the natural human longing for final justice is not in vain, because it moves us to do *what little we can* toward final justice." But if the purpose of the desire is merely to move us to do *what little we can* toward final justice, then why are we naturally endowed with a desire for *final* justice? Why should we not be endowed merely with a desire for what little we can do? Such a longing *could* be satisfied by human powers, because we would desire no more than we could reach; what we could not reach, we would not desire. Yet that is not in fact what we want. Our desire is for *final* justice, *perfect* justice. If we mistakenly suppose that for every natural desire there corresponds not just some possible satisfaction but some *purely natural* satisfaction, some satisfaction *within the scope of human powers,* then the desire for final justice is not only in vain but worse than in vain. Not only does it fail to help us, but it wounds us. Convinced that we can somehow achieve final justice by our own powers, yet persistently failing to achieve it by moral means, we come to think that we must resort to immoral means. Setting our hearts on utopia, we resolve to do evil so that good will result. So it is that among those convinced of the sufficiency of human powers, the natural desire for final justice finally generates an overmastering temptation to injustice. What shall we conclude? If it is really true that for every natural desire there corresponds some possible satisfaction – yet if it is also true that no satisfaction of the natural desire for final justice lies within human powers – what follows is that we must look to another power for its satisfaction.

Concerning Step 5: "Another power" is an ambiguous expression, because it may refer either to direct supernatural agency, or to a form of natural order. In the former case, we are speaking, again, of God. In the latter, it may seem at first that we are *not* speaking of God, but of something immanent and impersonal like Fate or Karma. But then these would be forms of natural order, and as we saw in the Argument from Natural Law as Order, such order itself points to God as its cause or explanation. Rather than of impersonal agencies like Fate or Karma, then, we are really speaking of His Providence.

In short, if it is really true that "nature makes nothing in vain," then it is impossible that the natural desire for final justice is in vain. If the desire cannot be satisfied by any human power, then it must be satisfiable by a power more than human. It turns out that the only plausible such power is the personal agency by which nature was made and endowed with its properties, the same agency that implanted the desire for final justice in us in the first place. This is what we call God.

Conclusion

Come now, let us reason together.[14]

I have already mentioned that the four paths we have traced from the reality of natural law to the reality of God are not the only paths possible. Perhaps I should also mention that they aren't a package deal. Although here and there, one of the arguments shares a piece with another, they are substantially independent, so it would be possible for some of them to be valid even if, on closer examination, some of them were not. It would even be logically possible to believe in God and yet think *none* of these four arguments was valid, although I do not think that is the case. I have advanced them because I believe them.

Questions like the reality of God arouse strong emotions, including, sometimes, resentment. However, the etymology of the word "philosophy" is not "love of crushing your opponent," but "love of wisdom." If God is real, it is profoundly important to know. If He were not real, it would be profoundly important to know that too – that is, on the assumption that anything could then be real or not-real at all (which I think might then become dubious, although that is another story). I hope, then, that if any reader thinks he has found insight in these arguments, he will take this insight seriously – but that if any reader thinks he has found errors in them, he will view his discovery not in the spirit of an athlete spiking the football in the end zone and shouting *Score!*, but in the spirit of a seeker for truth. The most important thing would be to discern what kind of errors they were: Were they truly fatal errors from which the argument could not recover, or were they technical errors which might be repaired so that the renovated argument was

14   Isaiah 1:18, RSV.

successful after all? Even in the case of fatal error, the job is not done. One must then ask what gave rise to it. A good deal about truth can be learned from fatal error, just as a good deal about health can be learned from the causes of bodily death. Errors have no resources in themselves to seem true; not even an error can be plausible unless some distorted bit of truth is mixed up with it. The important thing is to find out that bit is, and how it can be disentangled from the obscuring vines.

But what if there happen to be no fatal errors? I cannot help remembering a conversation in which someone asked me, "What if I just *know* the conclusion of an argument is false, but no matter how hard I try, I can't find anything wrong with the terms, the premises, or the reasoning?" The answer is, "Then you change your mind."

Chapter 9:
The Place of Religion among the American Founders[1]
Vincent Phillip Muñoz

First Amendment religion jurisprudence may have reached the height of its incomprehensibility on the last day of the Supreme Court's 2004 term. Faced with two separate cases involving Ten Commandments displays, the Court found postings of the Commandments in Kentucky courthouses unconstitutional but upheld a Ten Commandments monument on the grounds of the Texas state capitol.[2] To explain their different positions, the Court's nine justices issued ten separate opinions totalling nearly 150 pages. With one exception, every opinion included significant claims about the intentions of the Founding Fathers. Yet despite this common reliance on history, the justices invoked four different tests to determine the outcomes of the cases – the "Lemon" test, prevention of civic divisiveness along religious lines, no endorsement of religion, and no legal coercion – a disagreement that reflected the justices' divergent interpretations of the Founders. Most significantly, Justice David Souter, who wrote the majority opinion in the Kentucky case, claimed that the Founders' intentions made state-sponsored postings of the Ten Commandments unconstitutional. Justices Antonin Scalia and Clarence Thomas, who most thoughtfully opposed Souter, found history to counsel the opposite conclusion.

One might have expected that by now the Founders' views would be well understood and the meaning of the Constitution's religion

---

1   This article is adapted from portions of *God and the Founders: Madison, Washington, and Jefferson* (New York: Cambridge University Press, 2009).
2   McCreary County v. ACLU of Kentucky 545 U.S. 844 (2005); and Van Orden v. Perry 545 U.S. 677 (2005).

clauses would be decided. The Supreme Court first turned to Jefferson to interpret the Free Exercise Clause in 1879, and since the landmark Establishment Clause case *Everson v. Board of Education* in 1947,[3] both liberal and conservative jurists have repeatedly appealed to the Founding Fathers to guide church-state jurisprudence. The last three generations of scholarship and constitutional argument, however, have failed to reach a consensus on the historical record. If anything, the opposite has happened. Scholars and judges are more divided now than ever on how the Founders intended to protect religious liberty and what they meant by the separation of church and state.

One reason for our current confusion is that we have failed to understand that the leading Founding Fathers disagreed about how to best protect religious liberty. In the rush to claim the Framers for their own side, scholars and litigators have overlooked or downplayed the fact that there is not one uniform Founding position regarding how church and state should be related.

Our failure to account for the Founders' differences has led to two deleterious effects. First, advocates have been able to misrepresent the views of particular Founders as the "Founding view" more generally. This has allowed them to draw on the authority of history without fully or adequately presenting it. Second, by assuming that there is one Founding view and that it ought to determine contemporary controversies, we have failed to think through the Founders' arguments for ourselves. In doing so, we have failed to distinguish when their thought is profound from when it might be profoundly misguided.

Rather than deferentially appealing to our founding history, we need to learn how to critically engage it. The first step is to understand that the Founders championed different understandings of the proper separation of church and state. And there is no better place to begin than with the political thought of James Madison, George Washington, and Thomas Jefferson. Although they do not represent all the positions taken by members of the Founding generation, these three Founders have been cited frequently by the Supreme Court, and each articulated a distinct approach to protecting the right of religious liberty.

---

3   Everson v. Board of Education 330 U.S. 1 (1947).

James Madison: Libertarian

No Founder has been misinterpreted and misused more than James Madison, a fact that is particularly ironic given that Madison's church-state principle is simple and straightforward. For the Establishment Clause, Madison has been cited as the constitutional foreman who built Jefferson's "wall of separation." Justice Wiley Rutledge initiated this interpretation in *Everson*, when he declared that Madison was "unrelentingly absolute . . . in opposing state support or aid [to religion] by taxation."[4] For most of the last two decades, Rutledge's interpretation has been championed by Justice Souter, who has repeatedly invoked Madison to exclude religious entities from programs financed by the government (e.g., Christian groups receiving university student activity funds) and to eliminate religion's presence in the public square (e.g., public school graduation prayers, Ten Commandments displays).

For the Free Exercise Clause, Madison is said to support judicially granted exemptions from religiously burdensome laws. Michael McConnell, a former judge on the Tenth Circuit Court of Appeals and one of the nation's leading church-state scholars, has most forcefully presented this interpretation. McConnell contends that a Madisonian approach would exempt religious believers from burdensome but generally applicable laws, as long as a "compelling state interest" in the law's enforcement does not exist. For example, in the peyote case *Employment Service v. Smith* (1990),[5] McConnell contends that Madison would have opposed Justice Scalia's majority opinion and, instead, would have granted members of the Native American Church an exemption from the state's drug law, allowing them to use the otherwise illegal drug in their religious ceremonies.[6] Justice Sandra Day O'Connor adopted McConnell's interpretation of Madison in her 1997 opinion in *City of Boerne v. Flores*,[7] and in recent years, Justices Souter and Breyer have favored this interpretation as well.

4   *Everson*, 330 U.S. 1, 40 (Rutledge, J., dissenting).
5   *Employment Services v. Smith*, 494 U.S. 872 (1990).
6   Michael W. McConnell, "Free Exercise Revisionism and the *Smith* Decision," *University of Chicago Law Review* 57.4 (Autumn, 1990): 1109–1153.
7   *City of Boerne v. Flores*, 521 U.S. 507 (1997).

In truth, Madison was neither a strict separationist nor pro-exemptions. Madison's principle, which he articulated in his *Memorial and Remonstrance*,[8] was that the state had an obligation to remain noncognizant of religion. Just as advocates of a "color blind" constitution believe that the law should not take race into account, Madison said the state could neither legitimately privilege nor punish individuals or groups on account of their religious professions and actions (or the lack thereof).

Madison thought a "religion blind" constitution followed from a proper understanding of social compact theory and the place of the right to religious liberty within it. His emphasis on individual rights, however, was not opposed to religious duties. In fact, Madison's church-state philosophy begins by recognizing man's obligations to the divine. "It is the duty of every man to render to the Creator such homage and such only as he believes to be acceptable to him,"[9] Madison declares. This duty, he continues, "is precedent, both in order of time and in degree of obligation, to the claims of Civil Society."[10] Because men have a duty to the Creator to worship according to conviction and conscience, Madison says that they have an inalienable natural right to do so. The state, accordingly, cannot legitimately take cognizance of religion.

This understanding of religious freedom led Madison to oppose religious tests for political office and the abridgement of civil rights on account of religion. It also led him to remonstrate against special taxes to fund religious ministers and to declare his opposition to taxpayer-funded legislative and military chaplains. Madison opposed legislation that imposed special disabilities or extended particular benefits on account of religion.

Madison's resistance to taxpayer funding of religious ministers has been cited by separationists such as Justice Souter to indicate that Madison opposed all government aid to religion. But what Madison

---

8   James Madison, *Memorial and Remonstrance Against Religious Assessments* (1785), available at http://religiousfreedom.lib.virginia.edu/sacred/madison_m&r_1785.html.
9   Ibid.
10   Ibid.

actually opposed was the singling out of religious groups and individuals for special privileges. His principle of noncognizance requires that religious citizens be treated no better than non-religious citizens. But it also means that they be treated no worse. It demands no special privileges for religion and no particular penalties.

For this reason, a Madisonian approach would forbid special exemptions for religious citizens from generally applicable laws. To grant exemptions on account of religion requires that the state take cognizance of religion. A better approach from a Madisonian point of view would be to use non-religious criteria for exemption eligibility. Property tax exemptions for non-profit organizations, for example, would allow religious and non-religious groups to receive the same benefit on equal terms. It would also avoid state officials' need to determine what groups are and are not authentically religious.

Madison derived noncognizance from his understanding of man's religious duties and his corresponding natural rights, but he also thought it was politically prudent. The early history of Christianity, Madison said, demonstrated that it, at least, did not need the support of governmental to flourish. In 1823, over three decades after the adoption of the First Amendment, Madison claimed:

> We are teaching the world a great truth that Governments do better without kings and nobles than with them. The merit will be doubled by the other lesson: that Religion flourishes in greater purity without, than with the aid of government.[11]

In contemporary political terms, Madison was a libertarian in church-state matters. He thought that religion did not need state support. If anything, he believed government aid tended to corrupt religion by making it dependent on and beholden to state authorities. These practical observations were supported by his natural rights political philosophy. For Madison, theory and practice agreed that that the state should remain noncognizant of religion.

---

11   James Madison to Edward Livingston, July 10, 1822, in *Writings of James Madison*, ed. Gaillard Hunt , 9 volumes (New York: G. P. Putnam's Sons, 1910), 9: 102–103.

George Washington: Conservative

When one examines George Washington's politics regarding religion, one cannot help but be struck by how different they were from Madison's. While Madison attempted to make government noncognizant of religion, Washington consistently sought to use governmental authority to encourage religion and to foster the religious character of the American people. Washington, for example, initially was not opposed to Patrick Henry's general assessment bill, the proposed tax to fund religious clergymen in Virginia that sparked Madison to write the *Memorial and Remonstrance*. Writing to George Mason, a leading assessment foe, Washington explained,

> Altho [sic], no man's sentiments are more opposed to any kind of restraint upon religious principles than mine are; yet I must confess, that I am not amongst the number of those who are so much alarmed at the thoughts of making people pay towards the support of that which they profess, if of the denominations of Christians; or declare themselves Jews, Mahomitans or otherwise, and thereby obtain proper relief.[12]

Washington's strong endorsement of military chaplains reflects a second difference from Madison. Madison thought taxpayer-funded chaplains violated constitutional principles. Such a thought probably never crossed Washington's mind. As commander-in-chief of the Continental Army, Washington sought not only to procure chaplains for his soldiers but also to ensure that the Continental Congress offered a salary generous enough to attract "men of abilities." Chaplains, he believed, helped to improve discipline, raise morale, check vice, and to fortify courage and bravery, and at the same time, they helped to secure respectful obedience and subordination to those in command.

As president, Washington inaugurated the tradition of declaring special days of prayer and thanksgiving, which brings forth another sharp divergence from Madison. Madison followed the first president's

---

12   George Washington, *George Washington: A Collection*, compiled and ed. W.B. Allen (Indianapolis: Liberty Fund, 1988), chapter 109: To George Mason (3 October 1785), accessed from http://oll.libertyfund.org/title/848/101926.

example, but after he left the presidency Madison wrote that official religious proclamations violated the spirit of the Constitution. Washington took no such view. His first proclamation began by recognizing "the duty of all nations to acknowledge the providence of Almighty God, to obey His will, to be grateful for His benefits, and humbly to implore His protection and favor."[13]

Washington's official religious presidential proclamations not only reflect his understanding of the nation's duties, they also display his deliberate intention to sanctify solemn public statements and occasions. All of Washington's most important public addresses include religious language. A significant portion of his First Inaugural address, to take just one notable example, is a prayer.

The use of taxes to support religion, the appointment of military chaplains, the propriety of issuing religious presidential proclamations, and the deliberate inclusion of sacred language in public ceremonies reflect the distance between Washington and Madison on the proper disposition of government toward religion. Washington did not think that state actors must or should be noncognizant of religion. He agreed that religious worship was a natural right and that the purpose of government was to secure the rights of man, but he did not translate those general principles into Madison's specific limitations on the powers of government. Whereas Madison's libertarianism aimed to privatize religion, Washington sought to adorn the public square with vestments of sacred obligation and religiously inspired moral character.

It should not be surprising, then, that Washington's most definitive statement on church and state pertains not to the limits of state power but rather to the propriety of governmental support of religion. In his Farewell Address, Washington declared:

> Of all the dispositions and habits which lead to political prosperity, Religion and morality are indispensable supports. In vain would that man claim the tribute of Patriotism, who should labor to subvert these great pillars of human happiness, these firmest props of the duties of Man and citizens. The mere Politician,

13   Ibid., Chapter 183: Thanksgiving Proclamation (3 October 1789), accessed from http://oll.libertyfund.org/title/848/102090/2200511.

equally with the pious man ought to respect and to cherish them. A volume could not trace all their connections with private and public felicity.[14]

Religion and morality are indispensable because, Washington explains a few lines later, "'Tis substantially true, that virtue or morality is a necessary spring of popular government." Virtue and morality are needed for public felicity because without them, Washington asks, "where is the security for property, for reputation, for life, if the sense of religious obligation desert the oaths, which are the instruments of investigation in Courts of Justice?"[15]

Washington venerated virtue and morality because they prompt citizens to act in a decent, truthful, and law-abiding manner. Virtuous citizens govern themselves and they respect the rights of others, thereby reducing the need for security through the coercive force of law. Virtue and morality are indispensable because they make limited government possible.

And religion, Washington thought, was indispensable for cultivation of virtue and morality:

> And let us with caution indulge the supposition, that morality can be maintained without religion. Whatever may be conceded to the influence of refined education on minds of peculiar structure, reason and experience both forbid us to expect that National morality can prevail in exclusion of religious principle.[16]

Washington concedes that a few may be good on account of their "refined education," but he suggests that most men require religion to fortify their character. Washington therefore endorsed the use of religion to nurture patriotic and moral citizens, something that Madison thought was unnecessary and illegitimate. From Washington's perspective, Madison's position ignored the reality that republican government needs religion. To separate religious morality from state support would

---

14 Ibid., Chapter 178: Farewell Address (19 September 1796), accessed from http://oll.libertyfund.org/title/848/102077.
15 Ibid.
16 Ibid.

imprudently destabilize the foundation of the moral character upon which republican government is built.

For Washington, the right of religious liberty meant only that individuals should not be coerced to practice a religion to which they did not subscribe. As he declared in one of his letters to the Quakers, individuals "remain responsible only to their Maker for the Religion, or modes of faith, which they may prefer or profess."[17] Government endorsement of religion and even the funding of it, especially if it was directed to the taxpayer's own religion, did not violate Washington's understanding of the right to religious freedom.

Washington's embrace of positive state action does not mean he approved of sectarianism. In his public speeches and writings, he deliberately avoided specifically Christian language even though most Americans at the time were Christian. His First Inaugural includes fervent supplications to "that Almighty Being who rules over the universe," homage to "the Great Author of every public and private good," and humble supplications to "the benign Parent of the human race."[18] Washington sought to teach the young country that the American system of government, as he wrote to the Hebrew Congregation at Newport, "gives to bigotry no sanction, to persecution no assistance."[19] When he called on Congress to pass legislation authorizing military chaplains, he wanted chaplains of every denomination so that each soldier could attend his own religious services. If military commanders expected church attendance, soldiers should be provided clergymen of their own denominations. When President Washington addressed the American people using religious language, he spoke in a tongue that all Americans could appreciate and understand.

If we were to translate Washington's politics into a legal doctrine, it would be similar to those who suggest a "secular purpose" rule for ·

17 Ibid., Chapter182: To the Annual Meeting of Quakers (September 1789), accessed from http://oll.libertyfund.org/title/848/102088.
18 Ibid., Chapter 168: The First Inaugural Speech (30 April 1789), accessed from http://oll.libertyfund.org/title/848/102057.
19 George Washington's Reply to the Hebrew Congregation, Newport, Rhode Island (17 August 1790), available at http://gwpapers.virginia.edu/documents/hebrew/reply.html.

Establishment Clause jurisprudence. A Washingtonian approach would allow government to support (or hinder) religion as long as the state possesses a legitimate secular reason for its actions. Washington probably would have disliked the term "secular purpose," as the term itself can seem unnecessarily hostile toward religion; instead he might have favored "civic policy" or "the civic good" – government may support (or hinder) religion insofar as it does so in a manner that supports a legitimate civic good.

Washington would have fervently disagreed with today's strict separationists, who claim that government may not favor religion over irreligion. He also would have disagreed, though less emphatically, with nonpreferentialists, who claim government may support religion if it supports all religions equally. Washington's position is a bit more discriminating. Government should support religion because religion supports republican government. By implication, a Washingtonian approach would allow government not to support those religions that maintain principles hostile toward republicanism or advocate behavior contrary to good citizenship. That said, Washington also believed that when the state endorsed religion, it ought to be as ecumenical as possible.

On the question of exemptions from burdensome laws, Washington clearly would have favored measured legislative and executive accommodations of religion. As a military commander, he treated Quaker pacifists with the utmost care and respect. Yet in all his dealings with the Quakers, Washington never suggested that they had a natural or constitutional right to be exempt from legitimate generally applicable laws. If anything, he suggested the opposite. In his aforementioned 1789 letter to the Quakers, Washington declared that "while men perform their social duties faithfully, they do all that society or the state can with propriety demand or expect."[20] In the letter's next paragraph, he chided the Quakers for failing to share with others the burden of common defense. When the state remained within its legitimate sphere, Washington

---

20 Washington, *George Washington: A Collection*, Chapter 182: To the Annual Meeting of Quakers (September 1789), accessed from http://oll.libertyfund.org/title/848/102088.

suggested that it should, if possible, accommodate the demands of religious conscience, but that it did not have an obligation to do so.

Washington's prudential conservatism aimed to create a cooperative relationship between religion and government while keeping distinct the different ends of church and state. Insofar as religion could help nourish the moral citizenship that made limited democratic government possible, he believed the state could and should endorse religion. At the same time, Washington always maintained that individuals possessed a natural right to practice their religion according to the convictions of conscience and that within its own exclusive sphere, religion ought to remain free of government interference.

Thomas Jefferson: Progressive Liberal

If Washington was on the right in matters of religious liberty, Thomas Jefferson was on the progressive left. Placing Jefferson on the church-state political spectrum is difficult, however, because he is a bundle of contradictions. As in other areas in his life, so too with religious freedom: Jefferson said one thing but did something else.

What Jefferson publicly declared is encapsulated in his statute for religious freedom, the Virginia bill that was adopted by his home state in 1786.[21] In it, Jefferson recognizes five overlapping rights: that no individual shall be compelled to (1) frequent or (2) support any religious worship, place, or ministry; that individuals (3) shall not suffer or be punished by the state on account of religious opinions or beliefs, and that they (4) shall remain free to profess and by argument maintain their opinions in matters of religion; and that an individual's civil capacities (5) shall not be diminished, enlarged or affected by his religious opinions. While not the same as Madisonian noncognizance, protection of these rights would lead to the same results in many cases.

The complication with Jefferson is that the political actions he undertook to separate church and state were inconsistent with the rights he articulated. To take just one example, Jefferson repeatedly attempted to deprive clergymen of the right to hold public office, which contradicts

---

21 Thomas Jefferson, A Bill for Establishing Religious Freedom (1786), available at http://press-pubs.uchicago.edu/founders/documents/amendI_religions37.html.

the spirit, if not the letter, of the rule that an individual's civil capacities not be diminished on account of religious profession. Jefferson first designed to limit clergymen's civil rights in his 1783 draft constitution for Virginia. When the proposal crossed Madison's desk, Madison told Jefferson that it "violate[d] a fundamental principle of liberty by punishing a religious profession with the privation of a civil right."[22] Jefferson, however, was undeterred. Two years later in a private letter, he said the exclusion was needed because if clergymen were eligible to sit in the legislature, they would probably form its majority. That outcome had to be prevented, Jefferson continued, because the *esprit de corps* animating the clergy "has been severely felt by mankind, and has filled the history of ten or twelve centuries with too many atrocities not to merit a proscription from meddling with government."[23]

Jefferson failed to write his exclusion into the Virginia state constitution, but his efforts to restrict clergymen's civil rights and reduce their societal influence would resurface. In an 1817 bill establishing elementary education in the state, Jefferson sought a legal prohibition against clergymen serving on the board of visitors. He did not want the clergy directing or influencing Virginia's public schools. "History," Jefferson had written in 1813, ". . . furnishes no example of a priest-ridden people maintaining a free civil government."[24]

The legal exclusion of clergymen from political office was just one aspect of Jefferson's larger church-state reformation project. He also sought the transformation of Americans' religious opinions through public education. Jefferson insisted that young school children not read the Bible in Virginia's public schools. Young minds, he said, "are not sufficiently mature for religious inquiries." He recommended instead that children be taught morality with "the most useful facts from

22   James Madison, Observations on Jefferson's Draft of a Constitution for Virginia (15 October 1788), available at http://press-pubs.uchicago.edu/founders/documents/v1ch17s25.html.

23   Thomas Jefferson to Jean de Chastellux (September 2, 1785) in *The Papers of Thomas Jefferson*, ed. Julian P. Boyd (Princeton, NJ: Princeton University Press, 1953), 8: 470.

24   Thomas Jefferson to Alexander von Humboldt (December 6, 1813) in *Thomas Jefferson: Writings*, ed. Merrill D. Peterson (New York: The Library of America, 1984), 1311.

Grecian, Roman, European and American history."[25] Jefferson wanted Scripture banned from the curriculum so children's minds and imaginations would be kept free of miraculous truths and revealed dogmas, superstitions that he believed would inhibit the critical analysis of religion that he wanted more advanced students to undertake.

When planning his beloved University of Virginia, Jefferson designed the curriculum to minimize clerical influence. Instead of a professor of divinity, which was standard at the time, Jefferson proposed a professor of ethics. This would allow the university to teach morality without sectarianism and without hiring a member of the clergy. When Jefferson made his first round of faculty appointments, he caused a public stir by selecting a number of professors known for their heterodox religious opinions. Evangelical Christians' distrust of Jefferson ran so deep that Joseph Cabell, Jefferson's legislative ally in establishing the university, warned his friend that the clergy suspected "that the Socinians [Unitarians] are to be installed at the University for the purpose of overthrowing the prevailing religious opinions of the country."[26]

Jefferson was particularly keen to subjugate clerical influence in education because he thought that it stood as a barrier to progress in human thinking. He embraced the basic Enlightenment critique of religion and religious authority – that church authorities invented theological doctrines to disarm human reason and then used those dogmas and the power of the state to suppress the ideas and individuals that might threaten clerical power and influence. If men were freed from the artificial constraints that the clergy had imposed, Jefferson believed, they would be guided by science and reason alone. He was a true progressive insofar as he believed that to secure progress one only had to remove the "monkish ignorance" that arrested its development.[27]

---

25 Notes on the State of Virginia, Query XIV, in *The Portable Thomas Jefferson*, ed. Merrill D. Peterson (New York: Viking Penguin, 1975), 197.

26 Joseph Cabell to Thomas Jefferson (August 5, 1821) in John West, *The Politics of Revelation and Reason* (Lawrence, KS: University Press of Kansas, 1996), 63 n.265.

27 Thomas Jefferson to Roger C. Weightman (June 24, 1826) in *Portable Thomas Jefferson*, 585.

Jefferson's trust in the natural progress of reason is what led him, at the end of his life, repeatedly to predict that most Americans would become Unitarians. In 1822, he wrote, "I rejoice that in this blessed country of free inquiry and belief, which has surrendered it's [sic] creed and conscience to neither kings nor priests, the genuine doctrine of only one God is reviving, and I trust that there is not a *young man* now living in the US. who will not die a Unitarian"[28] (Jefferson's emphasis). Later that same year, he claimed, "that the present generation will see Unitarianism become the general religion of the United states [sic]."[29] Unitarianism, for Jefferson, represented the rejection of what he called the "hocus-pocus phantasm" of the Trinity and the episcopal structures of authority necessary to perpetuate it.[30] His prediction of a general acceptance of Unitarianism signalled his faith in the triumphs of reason over dogma and equality over hierarchy.

When the Supreme Court constructed Jefferson's "wall of separation" out of the First Amendment's text and then used that metaphor to remove prayer and Bible reading from the public schools, eliminate religious symbols from the public square, and prohibit religious organizations from receiving public funds, it resumed the liberal project that Jefferson himself began and expected to be completed within a generation or two of his death. Like the modern Court, Jefferson did not aim to be neutral toward religion. He intended his "wall" to restrict clerical authority, thereby diminishing the influence of irrational dogmas and institutions in American society. He sought to create a system of public education that would foster rationalism in religion and politics. Although Jefferson articulated natural rights principles in his famous Virginia Statute, his approach to religious liberty is better characterized as a politics that seeks, like modern liberalism itself, to aid the natural march of progress by transforming and overcoming traditional religion, thereby emancipating individuals to develop their minds and spirits according to the dictates of reason alone.

---

28 Thomas Jefferson to Benjamin Waterhouse (June 26, 1822) in *Jefferson's Extracts from the Gospels*, ed. Dickenson W. Adams (Princeton, NJ: Princeton University Press, 1983), 405–06. (Jefferson's emphasis).

29 Thomas Jefferson to James Smith (December 8, 1822) in Ibid., 409.

30 Ibid.

The Founders' Disagreement and First Amendment Jurisprudence

Whatever the merits of history-based jurisprudence, the leading Founders' disagreement means that no single church-state position can claim the exclusive authority of America's founding history and that no one Founder's position can be assumed to reflect the original meanings of the religion clauses. We should view jurisprudential appeals to any one Founder with a large dose of circumspection, especially if that appeal claims to represent "the views of the Founders." It is easy to pick and choose from the leading Founders to support different church-state jurisprudential results. Want to keep Bible reading out of public schools? Refer to Jefferson. Need a quotation to support religion in the public square? Washington's Farewell Address works perfectly. Too often a single quotation or an example from one Founder is used to imply that the entire founding generation stood for a particular under-standing of religious liberty.

The quintessential example of Founder abuse is *Everson v. Board of Education*, the 1947 Establishment Clause case.[31] In *Everson*, Justice Hugo Black asserted without *any* compelling evidence that the framers of the Constitution intended the First Amendment to achieve the same purpose as Jefferson's Virginia Statute for Religious Freedom. Then, in a second bald assertion, Black distilled the meaning of Jefferson's prin-ciple from his 1802 "wall of separation" letter to the Danbury Baptist Association. Black's selective history has been the cornerstone of the separationist jurisprudence that has guided much of the past sixty-plus years of Establishment Clause litigation. *Everson* remains a standing precedent to this day.

In a fundamental way, Justice Black got Jefferson right, but his claim that Jefferson's position represented the true meaning of the Establishment Clause was pure fiction. Jefferson had nothing to do with the actual drafting of the First Amendment. His closest ally on church-state matters, James Madison, sharply criticized a central tenet

---

31　For an evisceration of Justice Black's historical efforts in *Everson*, see Donald L. Drakman, *Church, State, and Original Intent* (New York: Cambridge University Press, 2010), 74–148.

of his approach. Few members of the founding generation shared his anticlericalism. To use Jefferson's "wall of separation" metaphor for the Establishment Clause was to rewrite the First Amendment, not to interpret it.

Black's use of Jefferson is not atypical of how the Founders are employed in church-state jurisprudence. A few fragments from the Founding era replace actual historical investigation and sustained constitutional reasoning. After long deliberation, one might find Jefferson's approach to religious liberty to be wise, prudent, and consistent with the Constitution's text and underlying purposes. But to show that it is any of these things requires a serious effort to present convincing reasons and arguments, not careless sloganeering. Throwing down a few Jefferson quotations as judicial trump cards simply does not suffice.

Because they disagreed, the leading Founders advanced arguments to defend their positions, and they made those arguments using philosophical reasoning and political considerations that can be as applicable today as they were over two hundred years ago. Understanding those arguments and considerations can help us think through the proper relationship between church and state for our times. The best type of originalism would take the Founders' competing positions seriously, evaluate their strengths and weaknesses, and integrate their most persuasive arguments with the Constitution's text and underlying principles. This approach to jurisprudence would be more honest insofar as judges would not cloak their substantive positions within an appeal to history. It would also be more true to the spirit of the Founders themselves, who sought to draft a constitution worthy of our sustained reflection and deliberate choice.

Chapter 10:
Freedom Under God: An American Understanding of Religious Liberty
Michael Novak

During the last decade, Muslims around the world, and especially in the Arab world, have been asking for help in formulating philosophical and religious arguments for religious liberty and other rights of the human person. I encountered this longing during a 2005 lecture in Casablanca, Morocco, to a group of Muslim intellectuals from around the region, and again during a set of lectures I delivered to the leaders of the resistance in Somalia.

They knew of two roadblocks in their path: 1) modern concepts (political, cultural, and religious) of religious liberty were not known in the seventh century, neither in Islam nor in the other world religions, and 2) in the modern period, almost everyone outside the United States identifies modern concepts of religious liberty with the French Revolution, not with the American tradition. French *laicisme* (the French style of secularism) is known almost everywhere as radically hostile to religion. Outside the United States (and perhaps even in significant precincts of some American law schools), the American way of keeping both the agencies of government free from control by any one religious body, while keeping religious bodies free from control by the state, is seldom distinguished from the French model, let alone emphasized.

Even now, in reflecting on these conversations with my eager Muslim interlocutors, I find myself plodding the intellectual paths of Hadley Arkes and my other mentors on natural law and natural right. It is precisely because natural law and natural right originate in human nature that they belong as much to Muslims as to Christians and Jews, not to mention Buddhists, Hindus, atheists, and agnostics.

In 2005, I found it most useful simply to present some of the major American documents, which were totally unknown to my new colleagues from the Arab world, while adding a running commentary. While many of these texts will be overly familiar to the readers of this volume, I think the experience of rereading them through the eyes of contemporary Muslims in the Arab world may shed fresh light on these texts, as they did for me. I have even been bold enough to include some of these basic texts in a kind of appendix for purposes of a similar exercise in re-recognition.

I should mention that of the twenty or so members of the Somalia Resistance in the week-long course I taught (in a safe neighboring country), slightly more than half were Muslims, in rebellion against a Taliban-like government in Somalia. Two of these leaders had been professors at the Sorbonne in France and McGill University in Canada. The others were all distinguished professionals. My colleagues at the seminar in Casablanca included scholars, journalists, and political and religious leaders, all very serious about the Muslim faith.

I would like to learn about how to think of religious freedom in Muslim terms. My task here is to explain religious liberty in American terms, but I do so in the spirit of trying to elicit from our Muslim colleagues around the world an account of how Islamic thinking about religious liberty is different from, analogous to, or perhaps even antithetical to the American views I am about to present.

Some Muslim friends have told me, for instance, that these are days in which there is a great deal of turmoil in the breast of Muslim peoples, a longing for public recognition of the dignity of individual conscience. They have insisted that this is a profound search, in four different dimensions: personal, religious, philosophical, and political.

They have said there is a growing thirst for liberty among these peoples, who at one and the same time wish to be both free and serious Muslims. I have heard Muslims say that they wish to be devout Muslims, live under the protection of the Universal Declaration of Human Rights, and enjoy the same liberties, dignity, and economic opportunity as other peoples on this earth. Since I believe that the God who gave us life gave us liberty at the same time, their words seem to me as though they must be true.

I have been told that there is a great inward pressure driving this longing for liberty. It comes from the last hundred years of bitter suffering, repression, the failure of many dreams, and much bloodshed among Muslim peoples. For decades, the human rights and sense of personal dignity among Muslim peoples may have been more seriously neglected by the world community than those of any other people. This *via negativa* is a harsh road, but a powerful incentive.

Two American Paths to Religious Liberty

Atheists in Europe, of course, have their own approach to religious liberty. They do not take religion seriously, naturally, but they do recognize it as a social reality that needs to be dealt with. Politically, their aims ever since the French Revolution of 1789 have been to expel religion from public life, to confine religion to the private sphere, and to non-recognition. They have attempted to place the state firmly over the church, synagogue, and mosque, in such a way that the state dominates all spheres of public life. They keep religious bodies toothless, on the margins. This process goes by the name (in Europe) of "laicization" and, more generally, "secularization." The secularists' unexpressed hope is that religion over time will wither away, along with other "old-fashioned" things that are inexorably being abandoned. They think that the future will be less religious, more secular than today – and that that will be a good thing.

In America, the pattern has been somewhat different. Some Anglo-American atheists share the sentiments of the French atheists. But most have recognized that religion has a serious place both in the public and in the private life of Great Britain and America. The Anglo-Americans have developed two different defenses of liberty of conscience, one of which is based on nonreligious premises, open to atheists as well as believers in God who value philosophical argument for its own sake. The other is based upon religious conceptions, and expressly on the Abrahamic vision of the Creator and Sovereign over all things.

The nonreligious view is that, by nature, each human person is responsible for accepting or rejecting evidence presented to his own consciousness; and each is responsible for deciding upon his own fundamental choice of a way of life. This responsibility gives rise to a human right to make such decisions and choices. And this right is inalienable. No one person can make those decisions or choices for any other. In this sense, the consciences of all must be respected as inviolable.

While this intellectual defense does not specifically mention "religious" liberty, it is a defense of liberty of conscience, and in this sense respects religious liberty as one serious option of conscience. Even if atheists reject this option for themselves, they see the social merit, and the intellectual consistency, in respecting it in others. They may not approve of the choices of religious people, but they respect their freedom to make those choices.

The religious defense of religious liberty or, more generally, liberty of conscience, is somewhat different. Here I follow the reasoning of Thomas Jefferson, George Mason, James Madison, and other Virginians who had a hand in drafting, arguing for, and getting accepted the Virginia Declaration of Religious Liberty of 1786. I have described this logic in more detail in my book, *On Two Wings: Humble Faith and Common Sense in the American Founding,* in "Epilogue: How Did the Virginians Ground Religious Rights?"[1] Allow me here to state the argument briefly.

In thinking about this question, these Virginians expressed the belief of most persons in America at that time (and also today), that the world was made by a benevolent Creator and Governor of all things. He wished to extend His friendship to men who are not slaves but free men, and wished to be thanked and worshiped in spirit and truth and purity of conscience. In other words, this God could not be deceived by mere outward acts, but saw directly into the human heart.

In brief, this outlook included four affirmations: the *greatness* of the Creator of all things; the *duty* of the creature to recognize, be grateful to, and adore that Creator; third, the *freedom* of soul that the Creator endowed in humans for such acts; and, fourth, the *friendship* with humans that God desired, and invited humans to share, and the freedom implied by such friendship.

With these background affirmations in mind, The Virginia

---

1   Michael Novak, *On Two Wings: Humble Faith and Common Sense in the American Founding* (San Francisco: Encounter Books, 2002), 127–142.

Declaration – and also the famous *Memorial and Remonstrance*[2] against Patrick Henry, the Governor of Virginia, circulated for signatures by James Madison – made the following argument. Every rational creature, contemplating the great gifts bestowed on him by the Creator, is conscious of a duty to give due worship to that Creator, in spirit and in truth, in the pure light of conscience, under no coercion whatever. Since this duty is sacred, and prior to all other duties either to civil society (even to one's own parents or friends) or to the state, and since it is a duty owed by the creature directly to the Creator, without intermediary, this duty also implies a right. For if a man has a duty to the Creator, it must be of a peremptory and prevailing sort, trumping all other duties; since this duty goes beyond any earthly power whatever, it must entail a right to exercise that duty, which may be abridged by no earthly power. It is an inalienable and an inviolable right. It is directly between the human soul and its own Creator. It must be exercised in conscience and without duplicity or coercion, in the direct sight of the Creator.

In all this, I have paraphrased, but not, I think, improperly. In any case, there are stunning parallels between the declarations of religious liberty by Jefferson and Madison, and those of the Second Vatican Council nearly 200 years later in *Dignitatis humanae*.[3] Let us examine the texts from Madison's *Memorial and Remonstrance* and Jefferson's *Bill for Establishing Religious Freedom*,[4] and place them side-by-side with the Vatican Council's affirmations. (All emphasis added in quotations below.)

Introductory Statements

The stunning similarities jump out right away in the introductory statements of each document. First, Jefferson's *Bill*:

2   James Madison, *Memorial and Remonstrance Against Religious Assessments* (1785), available at http://religiousfreedom.lib.virginia.edu/sacred/madison_m&r_1785.html.

3   *Dignitatis humanae* (December 7, 1965), available at http://www.vatican.va/archive/hist_councils/ii_vatican_council/documents/vat-ii_decl_19651207_dignitatis-humanae_en.html. All remaining references will appear in the text as DH.

4   Thomas Jefferson, *A Bill for Establishing Religious Freedom* (1786), available at http://press-pubs.uchicago.edu/founders/documents/amendI_religions37.html.

Well aware that Almighty God hath created the mind free; that all attempts to influence it by temporal punishments or burdens, or by civil incapacitations, tend only to beget habits of hypocrisy and meanness, and are a departure from the plan of the Holy Author of our religion, who being Lord both of body and mind, yet chose not to propagate it by coercions on either, as was in his Almighty power to do.

And here is the opening statement to Madison's *Remonstrance:*

Because we hold it for a fundamental and undeniable truth, "that religion or the duty which we owe to our Creator and the manner of discharging it, can be directed only by reason and conviction, not by force or violence." The Religion then of every man must be left to the conviction and conscience of every man; and it is the right of every man to exercise it as these may dictate.

Now compare those to the opening statement from *Dignitatis humanae:*

A sense of the dignity of the human person has been impressing itself more and more deeply on the consciousness of contemporary man, and the demand is increasingly made that men should act on their own judgment, enjoying and making use of a responsible freedom, not driven by coercion but motivated by a sense of duty. The demand is likewise made that constitutional limits should be set to the powers of government, in order that there may be no encroachment on the rightful freedom of the person and of associations. This demand for freedom in human society chiefly regards the quest for the values proper to the human spirit. It regards, in the first place, the free exercise of religion in society. (DH 1)

Duty Precedes Right

Both Madison's *Remonstrance* and *Dignitatis humanae* emphasize the idea that the fundamental rights of men are derived from preceding duties to the Creator. From *Remonstrance:*

It is the duty of every man to render to the Creator such homage and such only as he believes to be acceptable to him. **This duty is precedent, both in order of time and in degree of obligation, to the claims of Civil Society. Before any man can be considered as a member of Civil Society, he must be considered as a subject of the Governour of the Universe**: And if a member of Civil Society, do it with a saving of his allegiance to the Universal Sovereign. Compare with this portion of *Dignitatis humanae:*

> Further light is shed on the subject if one considers that the highest norm of human life is the divine law – eternal, objective and universal – whereby God orders, directs and governs the entire universe and all the ways of the human community by a plan conceived in wisdom and love. Man has been made by God to participate in this law, with the result that, under the gentle disposition of divine Providence, he can come to perceive ever more fully the truth that is unchanging. **Wherefore every man has the duty, and therefore the right, to seek the truth in matters religious in order that he may with prudence form for himself right and true judgments of conscience, under use of all suitable means.** (DH 3)

The Public Square

Both Jefferson and the Council recognized the importance of the right to freedom of religious expression – not just in the privacy of the home, but in the *public* square. *Dignitatis humanae* asserts that "the fact is that men **of the present day want to be able freely to profess their religion in private and in public,**" and "the religious acts whereby men, **in private and in public** and out of a sense of personal conviction, direct their lives to God transcend by their very nature the order of terrestrial and temporal affairs." (DH 15, 3) Therefore:

> Government therefore ought indeed to take account of the religious life of the citizenry and show it favor, since the function of government is to make provision for the common welfare. However, **it would clearly transgress the limits set to its power, were it to presume to command or inhibit acts that are religious.** (DH 3)

Nearly 200 years earlier, Jefferson's *Bill for Establishing Religious Freedom* did indeed take into account and show favor to the religious life of the citizenry:

> Be it therefore enacted by the General Assembly, That **no man shall be compelled to frequent or support any religious worship, place, or ministry whatsoever, nor shall be enforced, restrained, molested, or burdened in his body or goods,** nor shall otherwise suffer on account of his religious opinions or belief; but that **all men shall be free to profess, and by argument to maintain, their opinions in matters of religion,** and that the same shall in nowise diminish, enlarge, or affect their civil capacities.

Right of Conscience

All three documents recognize the right for every man to act in accordance with his conscience as formed by reason. First Madison's *Remonstrance:*

> Whilst we assert for ourselves a freedom to embrace, to profess and to observe the Religion which we believe to be of divine origin, **we cannot deny an equal freedom to those whose minds have not yet yielded to the evidence which has convinced us.** If this freedom be abused, it is an offence against God, not against man: To God, therefore, not to man, must an account of it be rendered.

And:

> **"The equal right of every citizen to the free exercise of his Religion according to the dictates of conscience" is held by the same tenure with all our other rights.**

Now from Jefferson's *Bill:*

> . . . that to compel a man to furnish contributions of money for the propagation of opinions which he disbelieves, is sinful and tyrannical; that even **the forcing him to support this or that teacher**

of his own religious persuasion, is depriving him of the comfortable liberty of giving his contributions to the particular pastor whose morals he would make his pattern, and whose powers he feels most persuasive to righteousness, and is withdrawing from the ministry those temporal rewards, which proceeding from an approbation of their personal conduct, are an additional incitement to earnest and unremitting labors for the instruction of mankind.

And from *Dignitatis humane:*

> In all his activity a **man is bound to follow his conscience in order that he may come to God, the end and purpose of life. It follows that he is not to be forced to act in manner contrary to his conscience.** Nor, on the other hand, is he to be restrained from acting in accordance with his conscience, especially in matters religious. (DH 3)

Truth

But, as Both Jefferson and the Council Fathers were eager to emphasize, with the freedom of conscience comes the responsibility of each man to seek the truth through debate and right reasoning. First read Jefferson:

> **Truth is great and will prevail if left to herself,** that she is the proper and sufficient antagonist to error, and has nothing to fear from the conflict, unless by human interposition disarmed of her natural weapons, **free argument and debate, errors ceasing to be dangerous when it is permitted freely to contradict them.**

Now compare that to one of the most famous and important lines to come out of the entire Second Vatican Council:

> **The truth cannot impose itself except by virtue of its own truth, as it makes its entrance into the mind at once quietly and with power.** (DH 1)

It is quite clear, then, that the religious foundation for religious liberty in America begins with the nature of God (the sovereign Creator, who wishes to be worshiped in spirit and truth, without deception or coercion; and who offers to humans His friendship, to accept or to reject in inner liberty, but with full responsibility for the eternal consequences of their choice). It also sketches out a set of convictions about the nature of human beings: that man was born free, and equal to all other men in his freedom before God, and, independently of the state or any Caesar whatever, owes duties to his Creator. Based upon these convictions, the religious justification of religious liberty, as expressed by the Virginians aforementioned, is founded upon the natural rights endowed in human beings by their Creator.

So thorough and profound are these rights, moreover, they are not limited to Jews or Christians, but to all human creatures of the Creator – to Muslims, Hindus, Buddhists, and also atheists and agnostics. For all were given their liberty directly by the Creator, in the act of creating human beings. From before time was, the Creator knew each individual by name, and called each to Himself – but allowed to each the duty, and the right, to accept or to reject that invitation, according to their own conscience.

I believe that this justification is particularly beautiful because those who first came to it proposed it for formal ratification and established it for all other human beings equally, far beyond their own immediate circle. They claimed nothing for themselves that they did not recognize also belonged to all other human beings. That is why they referred to *natural* rights. These are founded not in culture nor ethnicity nor tribe nor religious denomination, but in all human beings equally. Their historical root may have been discovered by one particular religious group in human history, but their philosophical and practical application (if they are true) is universal.

Some Reflections on "Church and State" ("Mosque and State"?)

The early Americans were composed of not only the Virginians, but also the Pennsylvanians, who in some ways solved some problems of religious liberty even more successfully, and the men of Massachusetts, who put in place yet another alternative, and so with virtually each of the other thirteen original states. When they put together the Constitution of the United States, in 1787, and even more explicitly with the Bill of Rights appended in 1792, they did manage to declare the federal Congress incompetent to make any law respecting the establishment of religion, or inhibiting the free exercise thereof. This is the way in which they provided for the so-called "separation of church and state." They did not want the *federal Congress* to impose any one religion upon them. They took the government out of the business of religion. In this way, too, they also prevented any one religion from becoming the official, "established," and in some way mandatory religion of the people as a whole. (The individual states had the option to establish a religion if they wished. Some did, for a generation or so, but that practice soon proved to be impracticable and irksome, both to the church and to the state.) Experience showed them that both the church and the state prospered more when the officials of the church did not make political decisions with the authority of the state, and when the state did not make authoritative religious statements. The leaders of each, church and state, were better off humbly sticking to their own lasts, and not attempting to do the job of the other. Certainly, the churches have prospered better under such a system in America than the more or less established churches of Europe.

The American solution, however, is not properly described as the "separation" of church and state. Its actual practice is more like an "accommodation," each treating the other to public acts of mutual exposure and mutual respect. At many religious ceremonies, officials of the state are often present in formal ways. At many state functions, ceremonies begin with a prayer led by a clergyman. Quite often a sermon by a clergyman is written into the program, or at least appropriate religious remarks, and often conclude with a religious blessing. The British writer and humorist, G.K. Chesterton, once described America as "a nation with the soul of a church."[5] He noted that the Declaration of Independence and the Constitution were treated like sacred texts. And that Americans spoke easily and often of an "American creed," and solemnly pronounced such things as "We hold these truths to be

5   G.K. Chesterton, *What I Saw in America* (New York: Dodd, Mead and Company, 1923), 12.

self-evident . . ." Above all, politicians in America speak often of God, and sometimes with observable seriousness and devotion – and at times in a more or less perfunctory, or even a seemingly insincere way. But speak of God they almost all do, even – or rather, especially – on formal political occasions.

The American way of relating church and state is not like the French way. It is more accurately described as mutually respectful, even accommodating, but quite jealous of the liberty and independence of each, in its own place. Citizens of America find it relatively easy to discern what belongs to God and what belongs to Caesar – although, of course, each generation has its own arguments about where exactly the lines should be drawn.

It has often been remarked, for instance, that President George W. Bush seemed unusually serious about religion, and spoke of God fairly openly and with great respect. But close observers have also noted that President Bill Clinton used to speak about God even *more* often than Bush, and was perhaps even rather more ostentatious in being certain to be seen in church each Sunday. The fact is every American president has felt the duty to speak of God, since that is what the American people, who are a quite religious people (outside of Hollywood movies and television entertainment), want and expect of them.

In a word, the separation of church and state is in part a misnomer, although it does point to an important differentiation of function and public role. To be sure, it is not the same thing as the interpenetration of religion and society, even in public places such as great sporting events, at which it is common for prayers to be offered. *Church* and *state* do not cover the same territory as *religion* and *society*. They are narrower, institutional concepts, as compared with much larger realities of daily life. Citizens in U.S. society have a right to the free exercise of their religion in private and in the full range of the public activities of civil society. They also have a right to follow their religious conscience in their public life, consistent with fidelity to their public duties and to the Constitution of the United States. And they have a right to argue in the public square, in accord with the rules of democratic give-and-take and the civic virtues of civility of manner, for their own convictions, religious or secular, about the full range of issues of our common life, including laws concerning marriage, birth, and death, among other matters. Civic life can be quite alive with religion, the more so for being uncoerced by the state.

Some Public Prayers of American Presidents

To present a few samples of how the American accommodation of religion and society, church and state, has actually worked out in practice, let me mention that in the earliest days of Washington, D.C., beginning with the Jefferson Administration (1800–1808), the largest church service in the whole United States was held in the U.S. Capitol Building every Sunday, with music provided at government expense by the U.S. Marine Band. President Jefferson was often in attendance. Both before and after Jefferson, both the U.S. Congress and the presidents have often by decree urged Americans in an hour of need to pause for a Day of Thanksgiving, or fasting and humiliation. To give a few examples of such moments, allow me to quote at some length from the Thanksgiving Proclamation of President Washington in 1789, following upon a Decree from the Congress urging him to issue it:

> Whereas it is the duty of all Nations to acknowledge the providence of Almighty God, to obey his will, to be grateful for his benefits, and humbly to implore his protection and favor . . . . therefore I do recommend and assign Thursday the 26th day of November next to be devoted by the People of these States to the service of that great and glorious Being, who is the beneficent Author of all the good that was, that is, or that will be. That we may then all unite in rendering unto him our sincere and humble thanks, for his kind care and protection of the People of this country previous to their becoming a Nation, for the signal and manifold mercies, and the favorable interpositions of his providence, which we *experienced* in the course and conclusion of the late war, for the great degree of tranquility, union, and plenty, which we have since enjoyed, for the peaceable and rational manner in which we have been enabled to establish constitutions of government for our safety and happiness, and particularly the national One now lately instituted, for the civil and religious liberty with which we

are blessed, and the means we have of acquiring and diffusing useful knowledge and in general for all the great and various favors which he hath been pleased to confer upon us.[6]

In his proclamation establishing Thanksgiving Day in 1863 – during the middle of the American Civil War – Abraham Lincoln beseeched Americans on both sides to pause, reflect, and give thanks to the Almighty for the blessings of life despite the devastation of the war:

> No human counsel hath devised nor hath any mortal hand worked out these great things. They are the gracious gifts of the Most High God, who, while dealing with us in anger for our sins, hath nevertheless remembered mercy.
>
> It has seemed to me fit and proper that they should be solemnly, reverently and gratefully acknowledged as with one heart and voice by the whole American people. I do therefore invite my fellow citizens in every part of the United States . . . to set apart . . . a day of Thanksgiving and Praise to our beneficent Father who dwelleth in the Heavens. And I recommend to them that . . . they do also, with humble penitence for our national perverseness and disobedience, commend to his tender care all those who have become widows, orphans, mourners or sufferers in the lamentable civil strife in which we are unavoidably engaged, and fervently implore the interposition of the Almighty Hand to heal the wounds of the nation and to restore it as soon as may be consistent with the Divine purposes to the full enjoyment of peace, harmony, and tranquility and Union.[7]

President Lincoln continued to emphasize the common grounds of religion until the end of the war between the northern and southern states, in an effort to reconcile their differences. This is perhaps most evident

---

6   George Washington, *George Washington: A Collection*, compiled and ed. W.B. Allen (Indianapolis: Liberty Fund, 1988), Cchapter 183: Thanksgiving Proclamation (3 October 1789), accessed from http://oll.libertyfund.org/title/848/102090/2200511.

7   Abraham Lincoln, Proclamation for Thanksgiving (3 October 1863), available at http://teachingamericanhistory.org/library/index.asp?documentprint=32.

in his Second Inaugural Address (March 4, 1865), which, sadly, was also one of his final speeches to the American people:

> Neither party expected for the war, the magnitude, or the duration, which it has already attained. . . . Both read the same Bible and pray to the same God; and each invokes His aid against the other.
>
> It may seem strange that any men should dare to ask a just God's assistance in wringing their bread from the sweat of other men's faces; but let us judge not that we be not judged.
>
> The prayers of both could not be answered; that of neither has been answered fully. The Almighty has His own purposes . . .
>
> With malice toward none, with charity for all, with firmness in the right as God gives us to see the right, let us strive on to finish the work we are in, to bind up the nation's wounds, to care for him who shall have borne the battle and for his widow and his orphan, to do all which may achieve and cherish a just and lasting peace among ourselves and with all nations.[8]

References to religion have by no means been abated in the more recent presidencies of Bill Clinton, George W. Bush, and Barack Obama. Addressing the nation for the first time as president, Bill Clinton laid out his plan for his presidency, seeing the work of Americans as a response to God's call to serve (January 20, 1993):

> And so, my fellow Americans, at the edge of the 21st Century, let us begin with energy and hope, with faith and discipline, and let us work until the work is done. The scripture says, "And let us not be weary in well-doing, for in due season, we shall reap, if we faint not."
>
> From this joyful mountaintop of celebration, we hear a call to service in the valley. We have heard the trumpets. We have changed the guard. And now, each in our own way, and with God's help, we must answer the call.[9]

8 Abraham Lincoln, Second Inaugural Address (4 March 1865), available at http://www.gutenberg.org/dirs/etext90/linc211h.htm.

9 William Jefferson Clinton, First Inaugural Address (20 January 1993), available at http://www.presidentialrhetoric.com/historicspeeches/clinton/first_inaugural.html.

President George W. Bush consistently drew upon religious faith in his public speeches and addresses. In his 2003 State of the Union address, President Bush proclaimed (January 28, 2003):

> Americans are a free people, who know that freedom is the right of every person and the future of every nation. The liberty we prize is not America's gift to the world, it is God's gift to humanity.
>
> We Americans have faith in ourselves, but not in ourselves alone. We do not know – we do not claim to know all the ways of Providence, yet we can trust in them, placing our confidence in the loving God behind all of life, and all of history.
>
> May He guide us now. And may God continue to bless the United States of America.[10]

While President Obama does not typically speak in Christian accents in ways that Bush and Clinton did, he took special pains during his campaign to quote from Biblical texts – the story of the Sermon on the Mount is a particular favorite of his – and make an unusual number of references to religion. This was thought to be a special virtue of his presidential campaign.

At the same time as the presidents continue the tradition of accommodation between religion and society, and even church and state, in American life, it must be acknowledged that a small but important tide of unbelief, secularism, and even antagonism toward religion has been growing among important sectors among American elites, especially in circles of entertainment (cinema and television), journalism, and the academy. If the people of America remain remarkably religious in observance, the class of *glitterati* becomes more boldly antireligious. Of course, this is all part of a permissible and healthy pluralism and diversity. But it is not without its mortal dangers. For it was precisely in the café culture of European intellectuals in the 1920s that the nihilism was most tenderly cultivated, into which Fascism and Marxism plunged their deepest roots (more so than in the fabled proletarian

---

10 George W. Bush, State of the Union Address (28 January 2003), available at http://www.washingtonpost.com/wp-srv/onpolitics/transcripts/bushtext_012803.html.

class). Ideologies of terror, violence, and murder required for their unchecked growth a preliminary diminution of all concepts of natural law, any morality of reason, and religion. For raw power to emerge as the fulcrum of action – and this was the moral essence of both those ideologies – reason and religion had to be ridiculed into social insignificance.

The Problem of Secularism

In 2005, the new Pope of the Roman Catholic Church, Pope Benedict XVI, and and then president of the Italian Senate, Marcello Pera, teamed up to publish two books, *Without Roots*[11] and *Christianity and the Crisis of Cultures*,[12] concerning the moral crisis prompted in the West by the rise of secularism and, along with it, a fresh revival of relativism and even nihilism. To borrow an American drollery, this is *déjà vu*. We have been there. We lived through its awful fruits. Why go there again?

To begin with, secularism seems like a healthy advance, providing a path to peaceful pluralism, at the end of a long historical series of religious wars – or at least wars in which religion played some part. Similarly, atheism and agnosticism at first seem benign, for many who embrace them go on living almost as if they still were religious. They live according to civilized values of the religious past, with mercy, charity, compassion, and other high qualities. Sometimes they seem even more moral than religious people of their own generation.

Atheism, however, as Benedict points out, may be a position of passionate commitment, but it cannot be a position of reason. No man knows enough about the conditions of existence to know for certain that there is no God. For this reason, too, agnosticism seems like a far more tenable intellectual position, and a more plausible and attractive moral position as well. It seems modest and humble, open and thoughtful. There seems to be much in agnosticism to admire.

Still, the Pope goes on, theory is one thing and practice (or *praxis,*

11   Joseph Ratzinger (Pope Benedict XVI) and Marcello Pera, *Without Roots: The West, Relativism, Christianity, Islam* (New York: Basic Books, 2007).
12   Joseph Ratzinger (Pope Benedict XVI) and Marcello Pera, *Christianity and the Crisis of Cultures* (San Francisco: Ignatius Press, 2006).

as the Europeans seem to prefer) is another. Agnosticism may be attractive as a theory, because of its modesty, but in practice a man cannot be so neutral. In practice, a man must live either as though God exists or as if God does not exist (*etsi Deus aut daretur aut non daretur*). Which of these practical roads an agnostic chooses to follow makes a great difference in his actual conduct. A mind open to God tends to be open to many arguments; arguments that to one who lives as if there is no God are likely to seem dim and obscure.

Pope Benedict puts matters this way. A purely secular society living as if there is no God tends to value individual liberty before any other good. This preference is proposed as public policy on the grounds that it is the most democratic principle, and on the grounds that all other policies are more dangerous threats against democracy. But this preference cannot be long maintained, without falling into impossible contradictions.

For instance, the individual woman who chooses to have an abortion may seem to be exercising a fundamental human right of choice, and by reason of various complexities in her own life even be entitled to our sympathies. Still, her choice necessarily demands the destruction of another individual life, that of the infant in formation in her womb, whose DNA is significantly different from hers, and utterly unique to that unborn individual. In this way, secularism ends up not treating all individuals as equals, but rather as privileging some human individuals more than others.

In addition, secularism ends up destroying a fundamental principle of democracy, in the very process of boasting that it alone protects democracy. For in granting the more powerful party (the individual woman) the right to exercise violence to destroy the weaker party (the infant in formation in her womb), it privileges might over right. But it is the fundamental democratic principle, its very foundation, to privilege right over might. Secularism thus ends up, in its moral self-contradictions, destroying what it claims to love above all, democracy and pluralism. And abortion is not the only instance of this self-contradiction.

The greatest danger of secularism is that it steadily undercuts all concepts of natural law, moral reason, and religion, in the name of privileging personal preference, taste, and selection. It tends firsts toward moral relativism, and then begins sliding toward moral nihilism. There remains little or nothing in the moral arsenal of secularism to slow a cultural tendency toward decadence, or to empower a wave of moral awakening. Mesmerized by: 1) the glowing attraction of the individual as the central unit of moral analysis, 2) the focal point of personal preference rather than objective reason, and 3) the priority of will over intelligence, secularism tends to hold that moral truth cannot be grasped by the human mind. All there is to rely upon is personal preference. In matters of social conflict, then, it is inexorable that power must become the ultimate adjudicating force: power, stripped of appeal to objective reason.

Although this is the inner logic of secularism, we are saved from its most dire effects for a time by the slow drag of tradition and cultural inhibition. While the road of decline is slippery, in a strong culture total decadence takes time. But the logic does tend to rush onward, meeting ever less resistance.

Secularism is no firm basis for democracy. It does not have any moral foundation on which to base democracy. Nor has it sufficient resources to inspire the virtues necessary for the practice of democracy. What Abraham Lincoln called "the silent artillery of time"[13] wears down the strengths secularism has borrowed from the past.

Not to put too fine a point upon it, there are few resources in secularism for justifying the claim that all men are created (or born) equal – which certainly flies in the face of empirical observation. Nor the appeal to fraternity. Nor the appeal to liberty, at least in the sense of liberty which applies only to human beings and not to the other animals – moral liberty, as opposed to sensate, appetitive, instinctual animal liberty. Nor that crucial value of modern progressive liberalism, compassion for the poor and the weak. And on what precise basis does secularism determine what constitutes the measure of progress, particularly moral progress? Mere preference does not really advance that argument.

13 Abraham Lincoln, "Address Before the Young Men's Lyceum of Springfield, Illinois: The Perpetuation of Political Institutions" (27 January 1838), in *Collected Works of Abraham Lincoln*, ed. Roy P. Basler et al. (New Brunswick: Rutgers University Press, 1953), 1:115.

What the West calls secularism is in large measure a heavy draw upon the religious heritage of Abrahamic religion. That is the deepest source of current liberal ideas of liberty, fraternity, equality, compassion, and progress. In fact, it is more owing to the specifically Christian values of the past that Communism was decisively defeated, bloodlessly, by Solidarity, the Polish labor union, and other dissidents, who at last refused to be complicit in the Soviet regime of the Lie. ("Even in giving weather reports, the regime lied.") Both Fascism and Communism ran aground upon the natural law of human existence, being based upon false, inadequate, and stunted moral anthropologies. It proved impossible for humans to live under such false philosophies. And, thus, even contemporary secularism owes its current peaceful thriving to the recent victory over Fascism and Marxism by the very religions, and their morality of nature and reason, that it despises.

In order for democracy to thrive, it does not need to be based upon secularism. Secularism is a most unsure basis for democratic survival.

The European way of laicism is destructive of religions liberty. The classic American way, as Tocqueville pointed out, has been to keep the spirit of liberty together with the spirit of faith, each one reinvigorating one another to the very depths of their being.

Chapter 11:
Veritatis Splendor:
Exceptionless Moral Norms,
Human Rights, and the Common Good
Gerard V. Bradley

The focal point of this chapter is from the papal encyclical *Veritatis Splendor*[1] where Pope John Paul II made a startling – breathtaking, really – assertion about moral truth and human equality. It is the most important statement by the Catholic Magisterium bearing on social and political questions since Leo XIII. It is not about the economy or constitutions or "just wars" or Marxism. It is nonetheless indispensable to any sound understanding of law, government, and the common good.

I

In VS 96 the Pope writes: "*When it is a matter of the moral norms prohibiting intrinsic evil, there are no privileges or exceptions for anyone.* It makes no difference whether one is the master of the world or the 'poorest of the poor' on the face of the earth. Before the demands of morality we are all absolutely equal." VS 97 states that the "commandments of the second table of the Decalogue in particular – those which Jesus quoted to the young man of the Gospel (cf. Mt. 19:19) – constitute the *indispensable* rules of *all* social life." The exceptionless moral prohibitions of adultery, intentional killing, theft, lying (as John Paul II also said in VS 97) are the "unshakeable foundation and solid guarantee of

---

1   John Paul II, *Veritatis Splendor* (August 3, 1993), available at http://www.vatican.va/holy_father/john_paul_ii/encyclicals/documents/hf_jp-ii_enc_06081993_veritatis-splendor_en.html. All remaining references will appear in the text as VS. Any emphases are in original unless otherwise indicated.

just and peaceful human coexistence, and hence of genuine democracy.
. . . [C]ivil authorities . . . never have authority to violate the fundamental and inalienable rights of the human person." (VS 97)

Let us consider now some corollaries, implications, and entail-
ments of the "master of millions" passage. Here are ten.

First. In VS 96 Pope John Paul II explains that "genuine democracy"
"can come into being and develop only on the basis of the equality of
all its members." The "master of millions" statement establishes this
equality. By its force not only are all persons (master as well as servant)
bound to observe the same moral norms in their treatment of others
(masters as well as servants), but also by its force those protected by
these moral duties – call them beneficiaries or rights holders – are
equally protected: no one whomsoever may be intentionally killed, lied
to, tortured, dismembered, made the subject of sexual abuse, and so on.
We all have equal rights against being made victims of such monstrous
evils.

Second. The moral obligations confirmed by the "master of millions"
passage suggest most immediately a bar to rulers' exploitation of members of their own societies. But the passage just as certainly prohibits
the same wrongs against residents of another nation. VS does not speak
in geographical terms or of domestic politics. So there is to be no
enslaving of the indigenous peoples in a colony or dependent territory,
no attacks upon the civilian populations of an enemy, no torture of
enemy combatants.

VS 96 thus points both rulers and ruled toward the *universal common good.* As the Pope said in VS: "only a morality which acknowledges certain norms as valid always and for everyone, with no exception, can guarantee the ethical foundation of social coexistence, both on
the national and international levels." (97)

Third. The universal reach of VS serves to curb the common tendency
of citizens of one nation to prefer themselves to those of other nations,
to side with their own – especially when it comes to hard moral choices. The Truman Administration's decision to drop the atomic bomb on

Japanese cities, for example, was motivated by a desire to end the war. But Truman seems to have been most highly motivated to end the war in a manner that saved the lives of American combatants. He did not worry about targeting Japanese civilians in order to do so. He ordered the bombs to be dropped.

I do not mean to argue here that bombing Hiroshima was immoral (though I think it was). My point is that any decision to bomb Hiroshima (or a hamlet in Afghanistan or a house in Basra or a meeting hall in Gaza) must respect the moral truth that *everyone* has an equal right not to be intentionally killed. Any such decision must comport, too, with the truth that each human life is due equal respect when deciding whether it is fair to accept lethal side effects – "collateral damage" – of acts which are not excluded by the norm against intentional killing.

I do not mean to say that bombing an Afghan hamlet on suspicion that some Al Qaeda members are there is necessarily wrong. But when a wedding party is in progress in the hamlet, the key moral question is whether we would bomb the hamlet if the wedding party were American – if the hamlet were in, say, Pennsylvania or Indiana.

Fourth. The "master of millions" passage forecloses any possibility of a distinct "public morality": a separate set of moral norms or set of exceptions to them specific to the statesman. Call this implication the *unicity* of morality.

The Pope's intervention was in this regard timely and courageous. VS was promulgated when the idea of a distinctive "public reason" appropriate to deliberation and choice about public affairs was widely accepted in the academy. John Rawls was the most influential of many philosophers who were defending a fundamental discontinuity between "private" and "public" morality. Separation of morality was a commonplace of political life, too. Perhaps the most prominent of many recent examples was the Democratic Presidential candidate in 2004, John Kerry. Kerry (and before him Mario Cuomo and Ted Kennedy, among others) affirmed his belief in Church teaching on marriage and abortion. But Kerry also affirmed his party's contradictory positions on the same issues. Kerry said that his personal moral code had to be separated from his decisions on behalf of a democratic society. He did not cite John Rawls, although he could have.

Fifth. The *assimilation* of "public" to "private" morality – what I have called the *unicity* of morality – is complete as far as it goes. But it does not mean that there is no such thing as "public morality." There are two senses of the term "public morality" which remain valid and useful after VS.

The first is "public morality" understood as the complex web of cultural and legal expectations and prohibitions that make up a society's ambient moral ecology. Protecting this is among the most important responsibilities of public officials. *Dignitatis humanae*[2] describes "protection of public morality" as "basic" to the common good, part of what is called "public order." (DH 7)

The second surviving sense of "public morality" refers to the unique moral responsibilities of the public official. This sense has to do not with a distinct morality but rather with, first, choices having no "private" analogue and, second, with the distinctive complexity of other unique choices.

(1) The *Catechism of the Catholic Church*[3] lists the criteria of a "just war," for instance, and then states that the "evaluation of these conditions for moral legitimacy belongs to the prudential judgment of those who have responsibility for the common good." (2309) This peculiar responsibility implies no special moral license or dispensation from the obligations of morality. The "master of millions" passage denies any such license. It is clear, too, that only public authority may punish criminals.

While an individual Christian may choose to bear witness to the Kingdom by being a pacifist, pacifism is not an option for one who has

2   *Dignitatis humanae* (December 7, 1965), available at http://www.vatican.va/archive/hist_councils/ii_vatican_council/documents/vat-ii_decl_19651207_dignitatis-humanae_en.html. All remaining references will appear in the text as DH. Any emphases are in original unless otherwise indicated.

3   *Catechism of the Catholic Church: Revised in Accordance With the Official Latin Text Promulgated by Pope John Paul II*, 2nd ed. (Washington, DC: United States Conference of Catholic Bishops, 2000). All remaining references will appear in the text as *Catechism*. Any emphases are in original unless otherwise indicated.

undertaken to protect society from its enemies, internal and external. (*See Catechism* 2306.) An individual Christian may choose (and sometimes be morally obliged to choose) to turn the other cheek. The *Catechism* recognizes that public authorities must not be pacifistic. The sheriff and the soldier have the "right and duty to impose on citizens the obligations necessary for national defense." (2310) Public authority "should," however, provide for alternative service for those conscientiously scrupulous of bearing arms. (2311)

(2) The practical application of universally binding moral norms – such as avoiding formal and unfair material cooperation in another's wrongdoing, avoiding scandal, and bearing sound witness to the faith – are *refracted* in peculiar ways in making choices about public affairs. Let us take abortion as an illustration. Abortion is always wrong. But is it always wrong for a legislator to vote for a law that says: "abortion is permitted up to sixteen weeks of pregnancy; after that abortion is prohibited"? Yes, this law is objectively unjust. A fully just law would prohibit all abortion. But *voting* for this *imperfect* (less than fully just) law is not necessarily wrong. Voting for it is morally permissible where the *existing* law permits abortion up to twenty-four weeks, and where the legislator's intention is to *restrict* abortion by voting for the new bill, so long as the legislator avoids scandal by making clear that abortion is, indeed, always an injustice.

Sixth. VS 96 belies any attempt to relieve public officials of the *kind* of moral responsibility which ordinary people shoulder, and which public officials carry in their non-public acts. Call this (if you like) a second aspect of the *unicity* of morality.

There are two particulars.

One is that VS undermines reading Romans 13 as if it gives public officials a moral prerogative (of a dispensing nature) predicated of God.[4]

---

4   The passage in question states: "Let every person be subject to the governing authorities. For there is no authority except from God, and those that exist have been instituted by God. Therefore he who resists the authorities resists what God has appointed, and those who resist will incur judgment. For rulers are not a terror to good conduct, but to bad. Would you have no fear of him who is in authority? Then do what is good, and you will receive his approval, for he is God's ser-

According to this view, the Prince may and sometimes must do things – kill an innocent or torture the terrorist – which are ordinarily wrong but which (by hypothesis) God as sovereign of the universe may choose, would choose, and in this instance willed that it be so. God's earthly assistant is then said to be empowered by divine commission to carry out the choice. This reading of Romans would hold that, in carrying out a death sentence, the public executioner does not *intend* to kill. He instead intends to carry out God's judgment.

This hypothesis of course requires one to hold that God might intend to kill a human person and that, somehow, this judgment could be and sometimes is effectively communicated to one bearing the instrument of death.

In VS Pope John Paul II refutes this way of thinking. He says (in VS 9) that God "preferred the correction rather than the death of the sinner." The central burden of sections 95–97 is clearly to state that human actions including those of public authority are to be judged according to the Decalogue. The upshot of these passages is this: either God possesses a dispensing authority, in which case VS makes clear that it has *not* been delegated. Or God does not possess such authority; effectively, that God does not kill. In that case there is nothing of the relevant dispensing nature to be delegated.

A second mistaken reading of Romans 13 would relieve public officials of ordinary moral responsibility by making a disinterested motive the decisive feature of moral analysis. Contemporary philosophers would say that the substitution is that of an *agent*-centered focus of moral evaluation for an *act*-centered focus. The idea here seems to be that *because* an army interrogator, for example, would be acting for the public good and not for any base reason or personal motive when torturing a suspected terrorist, the interrogator would be acting blamelessly

vant for your good. But if you do wrong, be afraid, for he does not bear the sword in vain; he is the servant of God to execute his wrath on the wrongdoer. Therefore one must be subject, not only to avoid God's wrath but also for the sake of conscience. For the same reason you also pay taxes, for the authorities are ministers of God, attending to this very thing. Pay all of them their dues, taxes to whom taxes are due, revenue to whom revenue is due, respect to whom respect is due, honor to whom honor is due."

and, even, rightly. A simple way of expressing the thought would be to say that the interrogator "referred his work to the common good."

But everyone (including a brutal interrogator) who does what he or she believes to be right acts blamelessly. The questions have to do with objective reality: what *is* it that you are doing? Is *that* right and wrong?

VS 76 makes clear in its general analysis of acts and moral evaluation of them that the *object* of the act, and not the motive or interest of the actor, settles *what* it is that anyone is doing for moral evaluative purposes. Consider VS 97: "[e]ven though intentions may sometimes be good, and circumstances frequently difficult, civil authorities and particular individuals *never* have authority to violate the fundamental and inalienable rights of the human person." The "master of millions" passages settles which evaluative norms apply.

Seventh. What if it is true that targeting civilians (such as at Hiroshima) saves many more lives than are taken in the atomic blast? What if the only way to save the riders of a subway train is to threaten and if need be carry out the threat to mutilate a terror suspect in custody? (This is often called the "ticking bomb" scenario.)

Notwithstanding the potentially heartbreaking quality of these situations, the conclusive answer is supplied by St. Paul: do not do evil that good may come of it.[5] The Church firmly teaches it is *never* morally permissible to intentionally kill an innocent person. There is nonetheless a certain tradition in ethics that, paradoxically, holds that one could be *obliged* to do what is in truth morally evil. This complex of ideas is most often called the "dirty hands" thesis. It is more often displayed in works of art and literature than in discursive analyses of ethics. As Brian Mooney recently wrote: "Much of Greek tragedy is concerned with the issues provoked by 'dirty hands.' More recently the works of writers such as Brecht, Sartre, and Camus have fully engaged with the problematic as too Styron in *Sophie's Choice*."[6]

---

5   "And why not do evil that good may come? – as some people slanderously charge us with saying. Their condemnation is just." (Rom. 3:8 – RSV).

6   T. Brian Mooney, "Torture, Tragedy, and Natural Law," in *Responding to Terrorism*, eds. Robert Imre, T. Brian Mooney, and Benjamin Clarke (Burlington, VT: Ashgate, 2008), 66.

One problem with the thesis is expressive: it is not so much para-doxical as it is incoherent. To say that it would be wrong to do something is to exclude the possibility that one *may* do it, much more certainly to exclude the conclusion that one is obliged to do it.

"Dirty hands" is something of a moralist's theodicy. It seems to rec-oncile a firm commitment to cognitivism in ethics with the satisfaction (if that is what it should be called) of being morally at liberty to com-mit an "injustice" to stave off still worse – even though in some sense one knows that doing so is "wrong." But "dirty hands" is more than that. It is a rhetorical bait and switch. The thesis goes beyond express-ing justifiable regret at the loss of something valuable in the course of doing what truly has to be done (say, killing in self defense). It coun-sels one to, finally, do what one feels one must do, or can't help doing. But the "something" is either a suppressed "proportionalism" or some form of emotivism. But if one could reasonably affirm either propor-tionalism or emotivism then we would not need a "dirty hands" thesis at all; either of those two moral theories would permit us to do evil that good may come of it.

Eighth. The "master of millions" passage belies some traditional Catholic metaphors for understanding the relationship of the individual to the political society in which he or she lives. I have in mind chiefly organic descriptions of the polity. In these depictions individuals are said to be parts of the whole, or that each of us is related to society as is one's "limbs" to one's "body." The appeal of such metaphors is obvious enough. They serve to restrain selfishness and to encourage sacrifice for the common good. They rightly indicate the dependence of each upon the greater society, both for survival and for flourishing. No man is an island. They point helpfully to the moral truth that political society is more than an aggregation of individuals and institutions that service their needs – as if the state were a giant K-Mart. The polity and its administrative arm – the state – have a richer moral status than does the mall.

The great appeal of the organic metaphors owes partly (for Christians, at least) to their resonance with St. Paul's sublime descrip-tion of the Body of Christ in I Corinthians 12:12–31. St. Paul uses the metaphor of the One Body composed of many members to establish the equality of all the disciples. From "apostles" all the way down to "those who speak in tongues," each makes a distinctive but nonetheless "indispensable" contribution to the flourishing of the whole: "God has set each member of the body in the place he wanted it to be."

Despite the laudatory tendencies of the organic metaphor and the truths to which it points, the metaphor is fundamentally mistaken. Political society is not a "body" of any sort. There is no membrane firmly separating inside from outside, and its "parts" are not in any useful sense hard-wired for smooth organic functioning. Political society is not a natural community or basic good, in the way that some other communities – marriage, friendship, the Church - are. The political common good is commodious. But it is limited, and even instrumental to the flourishing of human persons and their communities. (See *Catechism* 1906 and *Gaudium et spes.*[7]) Individual persons are surely *not* usefully described for *any* moral analytical purpose as limbs or organs of the human body. Each and every one of us is an end unto himself or herself.

Is the metaphor harmless? I think not. It often confirms or supports mistaken moral conclusions, such as those of Thomas and others in the Catholic tradition, about capital punishment. (*See* the last of these ten points, below.) I say "supports" or "confirms" advisedly, because the metaphor is obviously not an argument, and no responsible author would use the metaphor as more than illustrative of conclusions reached on other grounds. The problem is that the concepts used by the Apostle suggest that a "member" could reasonably be viewed as an instrumental part of the greater whole. No less an authority than Thomas Aquinas suggested that capital punishment be seen morally as the elimination of a diseased member for the sake of the body.

Some contemporary Catholic writers maintain that organic images are a healthy corrective to modern "rights talk."[8] Maybe so. These writers have in mind an excessive individualism or rights-consciousness in

7   *Gaudium et spes* (December 7, 1965), 24, available at http://www.vatican.va/archive/hist_councils/ii_vatican_council/documents/vat-ii_cons_19651207_gaudium-et-spes_en.html. All remaining references will appear in the text as GS. Any emphases are in original unless otherwise indicated.
8   See, e.g., Mary Anne Glendon, *Rights Talk: The Impoverishment of Political Discourse* (New York: The Free Press, 1991).

society. A corrective of some kind is indeed in order. But the baneful tendencies associated with "rights talk" can be sufficiently corrected without introducing the distortions of organic metaphors. The bad tendencies of modern jargon and thought are corrected, for example, by saying that persons should do their fair share for common projects in society, and not arbitrarily prefer their interests to those of others.

Ninth. Organic metaphors obscure an essential truth about law and the whole political common good: they are *for* persons – not the other way around. The Roman philosopher Justinian said that "[k]nowledge of law amounts to little if it overlooks the persons for whose sake law is made."[9] He was right: law is for persons and for their flourishing or perfection. Law is also for those communities that are indispensable *to* persons' flourishing, chiefly the family rooted in marriage and religious congregations – and above all the Catholic Church.

Tenth. The Catholic moral tradition stretching at least back to Aquinas excluded all acts of "private" persons which acts were intended to kill. Anyone might rightly use lethal force where necessary to legitimate defense. Thomas and the tradition after him clearly held, however, that in those situations the death of the aggressor had to be outside the intention of the defender who used lethal means. The tradition held that intentional killing was morally permissible in three cases: just war, capital punishment, and armed rebellion against unjust government authority. The common thread in these cases is the common good: intentional killing on behalf of the *community* was sometimes permissible. But not otherwise.

II

What effect does (should? might?) the "master of millions" proclamation have on the tradition of morally justified intentional killing?

A great effect. It seems to me that we are in the middle of an important transition within the tradition, the end point of which will someday

---

9   Justinian, *Institutes* 1.2.12, as quoted in John Finnis, *Intention and Identity: Collected Essays Volume II* (New York: Oxford University Press, 2011), 19.

be this interpretation of the Fifth Commandment: *intentionally killing any human person is always wrong.* No exceptions, not even for the "master of millions."

I recognize that recent authoritative Church teachings on killing – notably *Evangelium Vitae*[10] and the *Catechism* – often express the relevant norm against "intentional" (or "direct") killing to those victims who are deemed "innocent." (*See, e.g.,* EV 53, 57; *Catechism* 2263) These sources also confirm the perennial teaching on the possibility of "just war" (even if a bit reluctantly in light of the massive destructive capabilities of modern weapons systems). These sources do not entirely exclude the possibility of capital punishment either, however "rare, if not practically nonexistent" it might become. And capital punishment surely seems to involve the intentional killing of another human being. I recognize, in other words, that the interpretation of the Fifth Commandment which I anticipate will someday be binding – and which I defend here – is not *now* the Church's clear teaching. Authoritative clarification is in order.

Now, one permissive account of capital punishment within the Catholic tradition held that the condemned party forfeited by his heinous acts his right to life. Some commentators more colorfully said that the malefactor had descended to the status of "beast." This way of speaking was never meant to be understood literally; our ontological status as a human person (and not as a hamster or a turnip) never depends upon our acts, choices, and opinions.

The traditional image is stripped of any validity by contemporary Church teaching: "*Not even a murderer loses his personal dignity,*" Pope John Paul II said in EV 96. "God himself pledges to guarantee this." (96) The traditional account no doubt was meant to convey the proposition that a murderer (for example) *deserved* to die. But even a punishment that is in some sense deserved can be morally excluded by a moral norm unrelated to theories of punishment and desert. We do not castrate rapists. We do not torture or mutilate people guilty of grievous assaults.

10   John Paul II, *Evangelium Vitae* (March 25, 1995), available at http://www.vatican.va/holy_father/john_paul_ii/encyclicals/documents/hf_jp-ii_enc_25031995_evangelium-vitae_en.html. All remaining references will appear in the text as EV. Any emphases are in original unless otherwise indicated.

The emerging teaching on capital punishment seems to be of this sort: apart from what anyone deserves, moral truth prohibits even the "master of millions" from intentionally killing another human being.

I think that the best way to understand the emerging teaching on capital punishment is to see it precisely as an implication of the "master of millions" declaration. In this view, capital punishment is morally excluded, save in the very few cases where it constitutes the last means of defending against aggression. "Aggression" would in this understanding mean an actual impending or threatened physical attack which cannot be forestalled by non-lethal means – say, where a society does not have the wherewithal to safely isolate a murderous criminal for the rest of his natural life, but must nonetheless protect society from him, somehow.

In this chapter I can offer only a brief summary of the evidence to support my claim that the keystone of this teaching is the assimilation of the ethics of capital punishment to what heretofore was the ethics of "private" killing.

The Pope begins the discussion of capital punishment in EV by recognizing the moral authority of ordinary persons to use deadly force. This is question of "legitimate defense" which the text makes clear refers to the use of force *without* intending to kill. The Pope's citation includes St. Thomas's statement that an "act of self-defense can have a double effect: the preservation of one's own life; and the killing of the aggressor. . . . The one is intended, the other is not." The portion of the *Catechism* to which the Pope refers continues:

> Someone who defends his life is not guilty of murder even if he is forced to deal his aggressor a lethal blow. "If a man in self-defense use more than necessary violence, it will be unlawful: whereas if he repels force with moderation, his defense will be lawful. . . . . Nor is it necessary for salvation that a man omit the act of moderate self-defense to avoid killing the other man, since one is bound to take more care of one's own life than of another's." (2264)[11]

The Pope in EV cites this passage for the textual proposition that "the

---

11   Quoting St. Thomas Aquinas, *Summa Theologiae,* II-II, Q64, art7.

fatal outcome is attributable to the aggressor whose action brought it about," even if the aggressor is morally irresponsible due to lack of the use of reason (EV 55) – suggesting that the category of "innocence" or guilt is not relevant.

Both EV and the *Catechism* treat private defense of "persons" and of the family as belonging to the same moral species as defense of "societies" and "state" (see EV 55; *Catechism* 2263). Public authority's use of force is a species (or an instance) of anyone's moral authority to do what is needed to forestall aggression, on the strict condition (as the tradition always held) that there be no *intent* to kill. Public authority is more surely subsumed within the authority to use lethal force by the Pope's statement: "This is the context in which to place the problem of the death penalty" (EV 56): "render[ing] the aggressor incapable of causing harm." (EV 55)

The *Catechism* also says: "The fifth commandment forbids *direct and intentional killing* as gravely sinful." (2268) "The fifth commandment forbids the intentional destruction of human life." (2307) The *Catechism* also confirms the tradition's developing limitation of the moral justification for war to defense against aggression: "'[A]s long as the danger of war persists and there is no international authority with the necessary competence and power, governments cannot be denied the right of lawful self-defense, once all peace efforts have failed.'" (2308, quoting GS 79)

This passage gives no quarter to a justification defended by St. Augustine and St. Thomas Aquinas: retributive or punitive war, undertaken by one country to discipline or chastise another. Morally justified warfare is now limited to cases of defense. The *Catechism* seems to anticipate, too, a time when all wars will be police actions of a superintending, international authority.

Pope John Paul II's statements on when capital punishment is permissible confirm the *unicity* of moral norms governing deadly force. It is permissible only "in cases of absolute necessity: in other words, when it would not be possible otherwise to *defend society*"; and (2) "If bloodless means are sufficient to *defend human lives against an aggressor and to protect public order and the safety of persons*, public authority must limit itself to such means . . ." (EV 56, emphasis added).

III

Someone might object to the "master of millions" passage by saying: surely public authority possesses the moral authority to *punish* criminals. Even if this moral authority does not include capital punishment, it must be the case that public officials are permitted to intentionally harm basic goods, in apparent violation of the negative, exceptionless moral norms. After all, public authorities have long resorted to painful and even disfiguring corporal punishments – whippings, branding, the rack. Imprisonment for long terms without regular contact with one's spouse and children must count as an attack upon the good of marriage and family. Imprisonment itself, this objector might conclude, is inescapably intended to deprive persons of freedom, autonomy, and time.

This objection is serious and plausible. It deserves a careful reply. The central part of any adequate reply is a sound understanding of the moral justifying aim of punishing criminals: retribution. We can imagine that in the absence of any established political order, people would do whatever they pleased. Yet their choices would not necessarily render society the uncontrollably selfish state of nature anticipated by Hobbes.[12] Absent political order, some people would likely act reasonably, maybe even altruistically, and seek cooperation to achieve common benefits. But there would be no means through which to structure that cooperation; each person would have to exercise personal judgment about the appropriate way to cooperate. Political society, by contrast, provides an authoritative scheme for structuring cooperation, a scheme that thereby excludes all reasonable alternatives. Under such a system, individuals naturally accept these restrictions on their freedom to act on their own personal judgments about successful cooperation.

The following simple example captures this concept. Neither driving on the left side of the road nor on the right is immoral. Either side could easily be chosen as the rule of the road. Both cannot be chosen without disastrous consequences, and refraining from all authoritative choice would be catastrophic. A choice has to be, and is, made. After determining that driving shall occur on the right side of the road,

---

12 *See* Thomas Hobbes, *On the Citizen* (1642), eds. Richard Tuck and Michael Silverthorne (New York: Cambridge University Press 1998): 26–31

political authority may then appropriately penalize those who continue to drive on the left. Legal norms such as this one guide people by specifying the exact form that fair cooperation with others should take; they make general moral obligations more concrete and explicit.

One entailment of these propositions is that justice requires individuals within the society to accept the common pattern of liberty and restraint specified by public authority. By accepting the established apparatus of political society and by observing its stipulations for the common good, legal liberty for all is equalized. Stepping outside the common pattern put in place by authority amounts to a usurpation of liberty, a self-preference, an *unfair* advantage. The central wrong in commission of a crime is, therefore, not that a criminal causes harm to a specific individual. It is that the criminal unfairly usurps liberty to pursue his own interests and plans in a manner contrary to the common boundaries delineated by the law. (Alternately, where the crime is one of negligence, the offender demonstrates that he is unwilling to make the requisite effort to stay within the legally or morally required pattern of action or restraint.) From this perspective, it is clear that the entire community – save the criminal – is victimized by crime. The criminal's act of usurpation is equally unfair to everyone else, in that he has gained an undue advantage over those who remain inside the legally required pattern of restraint.[13]

Depriving the criminal of this ill-gotten advantage is the central aim or focus of punishment. Since that advantage primarily consists of a wrongful exercise of freedom of choice and action, the most appropriate means to restore order is to deprive the criminal of that freedom. The essence of punishment is precisely to restrict a criminal's will by depriving him of the right to be the sole author of his own actions. The goal of punishment is to undo the criminal's bold and unjust assertion of his own will. Punishment assures society both that crime does not pay and that observing the law is important; by doing so, it restores fundamental fairness and equality.

Punishment may include sensory deprivation, inconvenience,

---

13 Punishment may appropriately include an order of restitution to a person specifically harmed by a given criminal act, but any such specific harm is *in addition* to that caused to society at large.

unpleasantness, even transient pain, all of which is likely to be experienced by the criminal as "suffering." It should be; that is the basic idea. But pain as such is not an evil; its presence is sometimes beneficial to persons (as a sign of illness or infection) and even sought out by fitness buffs as an indication that they are really getting a workout. Imposing pain as punishment for a crime is thus not absolutely excluded by any basic moral norm. In no case, however, is intentional mutilation, dismemberment, or permanent impairment of organic functioning morally permitted, even as punishment for the most serious crimes. Care must be taken as well to avoid visiting these harms upon prisoners as an *effect* of some licit form of punishment.

It is easy to see from the short introduction to the moral aim of punishment (above) that invasions of bodily integrity and physical health would qualify as *punishments;* they would indeed impose upon the criminal's will and choice in a way likely to set things right with society. But it is also easy to see that such impositions are not morally *necessary* to impose a fit punishment; some other gross imposition is almost always going to be available to the punishing authority. But mutilation and the like are morally wrong for the same reason that capital punishment is wrong: all these acts would intentionally attack a basic aspect of human well-being.

As to the balance of the objection: though lengthy incarceration no doubt impedes and damages family life, especially of those prisoners who are married and more for those who also have children, that deprivation can be a morally acceptable effect of punishment *intended* as isolation – as "doing time." Neither time nor the freedom to do what one wishes is a basic human good. Nor is the money or property confiscated by public authority or collected as a fine. Intentionally depriving a criminal of these *instrumental* goods is not excluded by the basic exceptionless norms. They are highly valued by most people; that is one reason why depriving criminals of them serves as punishment. They are *not* basic goods in any event.

IV

GS defined the common good as "the sum total of social conditions which allow people, either as groups or as individuals, to reach their fulfillment more fully and more easily." (26) This account excludes the view that the political common good is or includes the fulfillment of all persons in all possible ways – as if the polity were a complete or potentially perfect community. It is true that those responsible for the common good would be best equipped to discharge their responsibility if they understood what human fulfillment truly is. But that does not imply that they are charged with perfecting people. They are not. They are responsible for maintaining "conditions" conducive to people perfecting themselves.

The limited and subsidiary quality of the political common good arises from the primary responsibility other non-political actors have for the inculcation of virtue. Parents have the first duty and natural right to direct the education of their children. The state's role in this undertaking is not only secondary to that of the parents. It is conditional as well. Only where the parents ask for help or are incapable of discharging their primary responsibility may the state intervene. The state cannot justly be said to have charge of educating kids in virtue because parents have a natural right to educate their own children in virtue. The state's job is to *help* parents perfect themselves in raising their children to be perfect as the heavenly Father is perfect.

It is true to say that the purpose or function of law and government is "peace and justice." But there are many reasons why the state's jurisdiction even over justice and peace may rightly be limited to a portion of what justice permits and/or to maintaining a measure of peace. Justice would permit the state to prohibit "victimless" immoralities such as gambling, fornication, the sale of erotic literature, and so on. But for sound reasons involving the difficulties of enforcement and popular opposition – and for better or for worse – most modern societies tolerate them instead.

Sometimes it is best for the law to prohibit some acts which justice might, in discrete circumstances, require. Assume for the moment that "Affirmative action" programs that take account of racial identity in public hiring, are occasionally morally justifiable. Prudent constitution writers could still judge that, given the tendencies of human nature and the prevalence of racial prejudice in their society and the necessary uncertainty of who will exercise political power under the Constitution in the future, it is better to stipulate that law be "color-blind" than to chance things by authorizing racial discrimination in "exceptional" circumstances or for "compelling reasons." Better, these constitution writers might conclude, to tolerate the occasional injustice (where race *could* and perhaps *should* be taken into account) then to open the sluice gates to abuse.

The state's competence in religious matters is limited by everyone's natural right to immunity from coercion in religious affairs (the first part of DH). Public authority is obliged to show favor to the religious life of the people. But it is forbidden to take charge of that life and to direct persons' spiritual acts. The Church also claims for herself (in the second part of DH) an unconditional right by virtue of its divine mission to evangelize people and to care for her own members' spiritual welfare without state interference.

Does this mean that state recognition of the true faith is *within* the limited and instrumental common good described by GS and DH? This is not the place to argue the point. But even if a state could justly recognize Catholicism to be *true*, a law that forbade state recognition of Catholicism or any other particular faith as true (our First Amendment, for instance) could still be just. Many prudential reasons could support a limiting condition such as that found in our First Amendment.

In both these instances – the First Amendment and in the hypothetical about affirmative action – morality would require that people adhere to the law, though the law could have *justly* been more ambitious in promoting virtue. These two cases also indicate that there are two basic modes or stages of the "common good" of a particular political society. The common good of a political society *as such* is likely to be different from the common good of any real society because of contingent constitutional limitations. This is the distinction between what it is *naturally* (or philosophically; as a matter of unrestricted reason) and what it is by *stipulation.*

A good example is the United States of America. Two hundred-odd years after the founding, our government in Washington, D.C. is still *not* a government of general or plenary jurisdiction. In our constitutional law that would be a sound description of *state* governing authorities. The national government is a genuine and complete government, and there is a national common good. But that common good is attenuated, limited, partial. The national common good is ascertainable not from philosophical reflection, but mainly from looking at the United States Constitution. That foundational document sets out the limited, enumerated powers of the national government.

The basic point of these observations is that it can be and often is *reasonable* for the members of a political society to charge their government with care for *less* than the whole common good of society. Where this assignment is made in an authoritative manner (usually in a constitution), it is not only reasonable for those exercising public authority to care for the common good only within those limits. It is ordinarily *unjust* to act beyond the assigned competence – *ultra varies*.

Conclusion

The "master of millions" passage is a startling truth that, in my judgment, should be seen as the keystone in the arch of Catholic – and indeed, all sound – thinking on the political common good. But it is at times a very hard truth to follow. It is difficult enough for anyone to decline every invitation to do evil that good might come of it. But it can seem to be morally irresponsible for one charged with care of the common good to accept devastating consequences *to others* as the cost of maintaining one's own (it might be said) moral purity. (Think of Harry Truman, or of the "ticking bomb" scenario.) The "dirty hands" thesis responds to this apparent waste of what are, in truth, goods of great worth – the lives of innocents, for example. Sacrifice the many for the sake of, what, one's own moral vanity? Is there anything more to be said in response to the dire moral predicaments which fidelity presents? What solace is there for those who are willing to sacrifice all – humanly speaking – for the sake of moral integrity? GS tells us in its eschatological proclamation in section 39:

> For after we have obeyed the Lord, and in His Spirit nurtured on earth the values of human dignity, brotherhood and freedom, and indeed all the good fruits of our nature and enterprise, we will find them again, but freed of stain, burnished and transfigured, when Christ hands over to the Father: "a kingdom eternal and universal,

a kingdom of truth and life, of holiness and grace, of justice, love and peace." [Preface of the Feast of Christ the King]. On this earth that Kingdom is already present in mystery. When the Lord returns it will be brought into full flower.

GS here teaches that the goods protected by the exceptionless moral norms – truthfulness and thus genuine community; marital friendship; human life and thus the precondition of all other human rights – last forever. We shall find them in the heavenly Kingdom. We shall find them there burnished and purified and preserved from corruption forever. We shall find the goods that fulfill us as human persons on earth somehow constitutive of the Kingdom. And, as Gandalf said one time to Frodo, "that is an encouraging thought."

Now, the truth about heaven does not supply or affect the *content* of any exceptionless moral norm, such as those in the Second Table. If that were so, one could only know these moral truths by revelation or by prior acceptance of religious authority (because unaided reason could never discover what heaven is like). But the natural law is known to reason; in fact, it is *revealed* that people do not need revelation to know the moral truths of the Decalogue. (Romans 2: 14–15). The truth found in GS 39 is not what *makes* those norms exceptionless. If that were so, the norms would (again) depend for their cogency upon revelation or upon prior acceptance of religious authority. But they do not.

What difference does the truth about heaven make?

The truth about the Kingdom found in GS 39 *enhances* the rational appeal of the "master of millions" passage. It allows us to make sense of adhering to the exceptionless moral norms, in season and out, no matter what the consequences of fidelity might be. GS 39 also supplies an additional reason to stand fast when facing difficult moral choices. By doing so we cooperate with Jesus in His work of preparing the world to be given to His Father at the end of the age.

IV. Communities, Persons, and Institutions

Chapter 12:
On the Moral Purposes
of Law and Government*
Robert P. George

The obligations and purposes of law and government are to protect public health, safety, and morals, and to advance the general welfare – including, preeminently, protecting people's fundamental rights and basic liberties.

At first blush, this classic formulation (or combination of classic formulations) seems to grant vast and sweeping powers to public authority. Yet, in truth, the general welfare – the common good – requires that government be limited. Government's responsibility is primary when the questions involve defending the nation from attack and subversion, protecting people from physical assaults and various other forms of depredation, and maintaining public order. In other ways, however, its role is *subsidiary*: to support the work of the families, religious communities, and other institutions of civil society that shoulder the primary burden of forming upright and decent citizens, caring for those in need, encouraging people to meet their responsibilities to one another while also discouraging them from harming themselves or others.

Governmental respect for individual freedom and the autonomy of nongovernmental spheres of authority is, then, a requirement of political morality. Government must not try to run people's lives or usurp the

---

* This chapter is the prepared text of the 2007 Erasmus Lecture the author delivered for the Institute on Religion and Public Life. A highly edited and abridged version of this text was published as the article, "Law and Moral Purpose," in *First Things* (January 2008).

roles and responsibilities of families, religious bodies, and other character- and culture-forming authoritative communities. The usurpation of the just authority of families, religious communities, and other institutions is unjust in principle, often seriously so, and the record of big government in the twentieth century – even when it has not degenerated into vicious totalitarianism – shows that it does little good in the long run an frequently harms those it seeks to help.

Limited government is a key tenet of classic liberalism – the liberalism of people like Madison and Tocqueville – although today it is regarded as a conservative ideal. In any event, someone who believes in limited government need not embrace libertarianism. The strict libertarian position, it seems to me, goes much too far in depriving government of even its subsidiary role. It underestimates the importance of maintaining a reasonably healthy moral ecology, especially for the rearing of children, and it misses the legitimate role of government in supporting the nongovernmental institutions that shoulder the main burden of assisting those in need.

Still, libertarianism responds to certain truths about big government, especially in government's bureaucratic and managerial dimensions. Economic freedom cannot guarantee political liberty and the just autonomy of the institutions of civil society, but, in the absence of economic liberty, other honorable personal and institutional freedoms are rarely secure. Moreover, the concentration of economic power in the hands of government is something every true friend of civil liberties should, by now, have learned to fear.

There is an even deeper truth – one going beyond economics – to which libertarianism responds: Law and government exist to protect human persons and secure their well-being. It is not the other way round, as communist and other forms of collectivist ideology suppose. Individuals are not cogs in a social wheel. Stringent norms of political justice forbid persons being treated as mere servants or instrumentalities of the state. These norms equally exclude the sacrificing of the dignity and rights of persons for the sake of some supposed "greater overall good."

But since we are going back to first principles, we might ask: *Why not* subordinate the individual to the ends of the collectivity or the state?

Here we see how profound is the mistake of supposing that the principle of limited government is rooted in the denial of moral truth or a putative requirement of governments to refrain from acting on the basis of judgments about moral truth. For our commitment to limited government is itself the fruit of moral conviction – conviction ultimately founded on truths that our nation's founders proclaimed as self-evident: namely "that all men are created equal, that they are endowed by their Creator with certain unalienable rights, and among these are life, liberty, and the pursuit of happiness."

At the foundation is the proposition that each human being possesses a profound, inherent, and equal dignity simply by virtue of his nature as a rational creature – a creature possessing, albeit in limited measure (and in the case of some human beings merely in root or rudimentary form) reason and freedom – powers that make possible such human and humanizing phenomena as intellectual inquiry, aesthetic appreciation, respect for self and others, friendship, and love. This great truth of natural law, which is at the heart of our civilizational and civic order, has its theological expression in the biblical teaching that man, unlike the brute animals, is made in the very image and likeness of the divine creator and ruler of the universe.

It is critical to bear this great truth in mind. We must not adopt a merely pragmatic understanding or speak only of practical considerations in addressing the pressing issues of our day. Sound positions cannot be effectively advanced and defended by citizens and statesmen who are unwilling or unable to engage moral arguments. That is why we should, in my opinion, rededicate ourselves to understanding and making the moral argument for the sanctity of human life in all stages and conditions, and the dignity of marriage as the conjugal union of one man and one woman.

Please do not misunderstand me. I am not saying that practical considerations should or even can be left out of the argument. In a proper understanding of morality, practical considerations are not "merely" practical. The moral case for the reform of unilateral-divorce laws, for example, includes reference to the devastating, poverty-inducing, crime-promoting social consequences of the collapse of a healthy marriage culture and the role of unilateral divorce in contributing to the collapse. The moral argument for restoring legal protection to the unborn includes reference to the adverse psychological and, in some cases, physical consequences of abortion on many women who undergo the procedure. Our task should be to understand the moral truth and speak it in season and out of season. We will be told by the pure pragmatists that the public is too far gone in moral relativism or even moral delinquency to be reached by moral argument. But we must have faith that truth is luminously powerful, so that if we bear witness to the truth about, say, marriage and the sanctity of human life – lovingly, civilly, but also passionately and with determination – and if we honor the truth in advancing our positions, then even many of our fellow citizens who now find themselves on the other side of these issues will come around.

To speak of truth frightens some people today. They evidently believe that people who claim to know the truth about anything – and especially about moral matters – are fundamentalists and potential totalitarians. But, as Hadley Arkes has patiently explained, those on the other side of the great debates over social issues such as abortion and marriage make truth claims – moral truth claims – all the time. They assert their positions with no less confidence and no more doubt than one finds in the advocacy of pro- lifers and defenders of conjugal marriage. They proclaim that women have a fundamental right to abortion. They maintain that "love makes a family" and make other strong and controversial moral claims. The question, then, is not whether there are truths about such things as the morality of abortion and the nature of marriage; the question in each case is, What is true?

What is centrally and decisively true about human embryos and fetuses is that they are living individuals of the species *Homo sapiens* – members of the human family – at early stages of their natural development. Each of us was once an embryo, just as each of us was once an adolescent, a child, an infant, and a fetus. Each of us developed from the embryonic into and through the fetal, infant, child, and adolescent stages of our lives, and into adulthood, with his or her distinctness, unity, and identity fully intact. As modern embryology confirms beyond any possibility of doubt, we were never mere parts of our mothers; we were, from the beginning, complete, self-integrating organisms that developed to maturity by a gradual, gapless, and self-directed process. Our foundational principle of the profound, inherent, and equal dignity of every human being demands that all members of the human family be respected and protected irrespective not only of race, sex, and ethnicity but also of age, size, location, stage of development, and condition of dependency. To exclude anyone from the law's protection is to treat him unjustly.

And so it seems to me that justice demands our resolute opposition to the killing of human embryos for biomedical research and to elective abortion. If we would do unto others as we would have them do unto us, then we will insist that law and public policy respect the lives of every member of the human family, including those at what the late Paul Ramsey called, the edges of life – the unborn, the severely handicapped, the frail elderly.

Of course, politics is the art of the possible. And, as Frederick Douglass reminded us in his tribute to Lincoln, public opinion and other constraints sometimes limit what can be done at the moment to advance any just cause. The pro-life movement has in recent years settled on an incrementalist strategy for protecting nascent human life. So long as incrementalism is not a euphemism for surrender or neglect, it can be entirely honorable. Many lives have been saved, and many more can be saved, by laws forbidding the public funding of abortions; laws requiring parental consent or at least notification for abortions performed on minors, and mandating full disclosure to women contemplating abortions of factual information regarding fetal development and the possible physical and mental health consequences of submitting to abortion; laws forbidding late-term abortions and particularly gruesome methods of abortion, such as live-birth and partial-birth abortion, and laws banning the production of human beings by cloning or other methods for purposes of research in which they are destroyed in the embryonic or fetal stages. Moreover, as Hadley Arkes has taught us by both precept and example, planting premises in the law whose logic demands, in the end, full respect for all members of the human family can be a valuable thing to do, even where those premises seem modest.

Let me turn to the other great moral question we confront today: marriage. The institution of marriage is battered in our culture, but it is not lost. Private pro marriage forces, such as Marriage Savers, are doing important work through churches and other institutions. Much damage was done by bad legislation and policy, almost always in the name of reform. That legislation and policy is now itself in need of reform.

If we are to restore and secure the institution of marriage, we must recover a sound understanding of what marriage is and why it is in the public interest for law and policy to take cognizance of it and support it. Marriage is a pre-political form of association – what might be called a natural institution. It is not created by law, though law recognizes and regulates it in every culture. Nowhere is it treated as a purely private matter.

Some on the libertarian fringe toy with the idea that marriage could be privatized, and even some who are not on the fringe wonder whether that might be the best solution to the controversy over same-sex marriage. I understand why someone would consider this idea, but it strikes me as a bad one. There is a reason that all cultures treat marriage as a matter of public concern and even recognize it in law and regulate it. The family is the fundamental unit of society. Governments rely on families to produce something that governments need – but, on their own, they could not possibly produce: upright, decent people who make honest, law-abiding, public-spirited citizens. And marriage is the indispensable foundation of the family. Although all marriages in all cultures have their imperfections, children flourish in an environment where they benefit from the love and care of both mother and father, and from the committed and exclusive love of their parents for each other.

Anyone who believes in limited government should strongly back government support for the family. Does this sound paradoxical? In the absence of a strong marriage culture, families fail to form, and when they do form they are often unstable. Absentee fathers become a serious problem, out-of-wedlock births are common, and a train of social pathologies follows. With families failing to perform their health, education, and welfare functions, the demand for government grows, whether in the form of greater policing or as a provider of other social services. Bureaucracies must be created, and they inexorably expand – indeed they become powerful lobbyists for their own preservation and expansion. Everyone suffers, with the poorest and most vulnerable suffering most. The effective defense of marriage against the current onslaught will require an understanding of marriage as a matter of moral truth. Practical or pragmatic arguments are legitimate and important. But too few pro-marriage politicians are willing to say much about what marriage actually is. This gives those who would abolish the conjugal conception of marriage an important advantage in public debate. They hammer away with their rhetoric of "love makes a family" and demand to know how anyone's marriage would be threatened if the same-sex partners next door were also allowed to marry.

Everyone agrees that marriage, whatever else it is or does, is a relationship in which *persons* are united. But what are persons? And how is it possible for two or more of them to unite? According to the view implicit in sexual-liberationist ideology, the person is understood as the conscious and desiring aspect of the self. The person, thus understood, inhabits a body, but the body is regarded (if often only implicitly) as a subpersonal part of the human being – rather than part of the personal reality of the human being whose body it is. The body is viewed as serving the interests of the conscious and desiring aspect of the self by functioning as an instrument by which the individual produces or otherwise participates in satisfactions and other desirable experiences and realizes various objectives and goals.

For those who formally or informally accept this dualistic understanding of what human beings are, personal unity cannot be achieved by bodily union as such. Persons unite by uniting *emotionally* (or, as those of a certain religious cast of mind say, *spiritually*). And, of course, if this is true, then persons of the same sex can unite and share sexual experiences together that they suppose will enhance their personal union by enabling them to express affection, share the uniquely intense pleasure of sex, and feel more intensely by virtue of their sex play.

The alternate view of what persons are is the one embodied in both our historic law of marriage and what Isaiah Berlin once referred to as the central tradition of Western thought. According to this view, human beings are not nonbodily persons (consciousnesses, minds, spirits, what have you) inhabiting and using non-personal bodies. Rather, a human person is a dynamic unity of body, mind, and spirit. The body, far from being a mere instrument of the person, is intrinsically part of the personal reality of the human being. Bodily union is thus personal union, and comprehensive personal union – marital union – is founded on bodily union. What is unique about marriage is that it truly is a comprehensive sharing of life, a sharing founded on the bodily union made uniquely possible by the sexual complementarity of man and woman – a complementarity that makes it possible for two human beings to become, in the language of the Bible, "one flesh," and for this one-flesh union to be the foundation of a relationship in which it is intelligible for two persons to bind themselves to each other in pledges of permanence, monogamy, and fidelity.

So, then, how should we understand what marriage *is*? Marriage, considered not as a mere legal convention or cultural artifact, is a one-flesh communion of persons that is consummated and actualized by acts that are procreative in type, whether or not they are procreative in effect. Its nature and normative structure are determined by its being the kind of relationship that is naturally fulfilled by conceiving and rearing children together (and it remains precisely this kind of relationship whether or not it is de facto possible for a particular married couple to conceive). It is an intrinsic human good, and, precisely as such, it provides a more than merely instrumental reason for choice and action.

The bodily union of spouses in marital acts is the biological matrix of their marriage as a comprehensive, multilevel sharing of life: a relationship that unites the spouses at all levels of their being. Marriage is naturally ordered to the good of procreation (and is, indeed, uniquely apt for the nurturing and education of children) as well as to the good of spousal unity. At the same time, it is not a mere instrumental good whose purpose is the generating and rearing of children. Marriage, considered as a one flesh union, is *intrinsically* valuable.

To understand how it can be the case that, on the one hand, the generating and rearing of children is a perfection of marriage and not something merely incidental to it, and, on the other, marriage is not a mere means to the good of generating and rearing children, it is important to see that the procreative and unitive goods of marriage are tightly bound together. The one flesh unity of spouses is possible *because* human (like other mammalian) males and females, by mating, unite organically – they forma single reproductive principle.

It is a plain matter of biological fact that reproduction is a single function, yet it is carried out not by an individual male or female human being, but by a male and female as a mated pair. So, in respect of reproduction, albeit not in respect of other activities (such as locomotion or digestion), the mated pair is a single organism; the partners form a single reproductive principle: They become one flesh. Some people desperately want to deny this. But consider this thought experiment: Imagine a type of bodily, rational being that reproduces, not by mating, but by some individual performance. Imagine that for these beings, however, locomotion or digestion is performed not by individuals, but only by biologically complementary pairs that unite for this purpose. Would anybody acquainted with such beings have difficulty understanding that in respect of reproduction the organism performing the function is the individual, while in respect of locomotion or digestion the organism performing the function is the united pair? Would anybody deny that the unity effectuated for purposes of locomotion or digestion is an organic unity? Precisely because of the organic unity achieved in marital acts, the bodies of persons who unite biologically are not reduced to the status of extrinsic instruments of sexual satisfaction or expression. Rather, the end, goal, and intelligible point of sexual intercourse is the intelligible good of marriage itself as a one-flesh union.

On this understanding, the body is not treated as a mere instrument of the conscious and desiring aspect of the self whose interests in satisfactions are the putative ends to which sexual acts are means. Nor is sex itself instrumentalized. The one-flesh unity of marriage is not a merely *instrumental good*, a reason for acting whose intelligibility as a reason depends on other ends to which it is a means. This unity is an *intrinsic good*, a reason for acting whose intelligibility as a reason depends on no ulterior end. The central and justifying point of sex is not pleasure, however much sexual pleasure is rightly sought as an aspect of the perfection of marital union; the point of sex, rather, is marriage itself, considered as an essentially and irreducibly bodily union of persons – a union effectuated and renewed by acts of sexual congress conjugal acts. Because sex is not instrumentalized in marital acts, such acts are free of the self-alienating qualities that have made wise and

thoughtful people from Plato to Augustine and from the biblical writers
to Kant, treat sexual immorality as a matter of the utmost seriousness.

In truly marital acts, the desire for pleasure and even for offspring,
are integrated with and, in an important sense, subordinated to the central and defining good of one-flesh unity. The integration of subordinate goals with the marital good ensures that such acts effect no practical dualism that separates the body from the conscious and desiring
aspect of the self and treats the body as a mere instrument for the production of pleasure, the generation of offspring, or any other extrinsic
goal.

But one may ask, what about procreation? On the traditional view
of marriage, is not the sexual union of spouses instrumentalized to the
goal of having children? It is true that St. Augustine in certain writings
seems to be a proponent of this view. The conception of marriage as an
instrumental good was rejected, however, by the mainstream of philosophical and theological reflection from the late Middle Ages forward,
and the understanding of sex and marriage that came to be embodied in
both canon law and civil law does not treat marriage as merely instrumental to having children. Western matrimonial law has traditionally
and universally understood marriage as consummated by acts fulfilling
the behavioral conditions of procreation, whether or not the nonbehav-
ioral conditions of procreation happen to obtain.

By contrast, the sterility of spouses – so long as they are capable of
consummating their marriage by fulfilling the behavioral conditions of
procreation (and, thus, of achieving true bodily, organic unity) – has
never been treated as an impediment to marriage, even where sterility
is certain and even certain to be permanent. Children who may be conceived in marital acts are understood not as ends extrinsic to marriage
but rather as gifts – fulfilling for the couple as a marital unit and not
merely as individuals – that supervene on acts whose central defining
and justifying point is precisely the marital unity of spouses. I and others have elsewhere developed more fully the moral case for the conjugal conception of marriage as the union of one man and one woman
pledged to permanence and fidelity and committed to caring for children who come as the fruit of their matrimonial union. I have argued
that acceptance of the idea that two persons of the same sex could

actually be married to each other would make nonsense of key features of marriage and would necessarily require abandoning any ground of principle for supposing that marriage is the union of only two persons, as opposed to three or more. Only a thin veneer of sentiment, if it happens to exist (and only for as long as it exists), can prevent acceptance of polyamory as a legitimate marital option once we have given up the principle of marriage as a male-female union.

To those arguments, I will here add an additional reason to reject the idea of same-sex marriage: The acceptance of the idea would result in a massive undermining of religious liberty and family autonomy as supporters of same-sex marriage would, in the name of equality, demand the use of governmental power to whip others into line. The experience of Massachusetts and other states, as well as foreign jurisdictions, is that once marriage is compromised or formally redefined, principles of nondiscrimination are quickly used as cudgels against religious communities and families who wish to uphold the conjugal conception of marriage as the union of husband and wife.

Part of the trouble pro-marriage politicians and others have in defending marriage follows from the fact that these pathologies that afflict the marriage culture are widespread, and supporters of marriage, being human, are not immune to them. This is not to excuse anyone from personal responsibility.

But the fact is that sustaining a marriage despite the collapse of many of its social supports is difficult. In trying to stand up for marriage, political leaders, intellectuals, and activists who have had marital problems of their own are subjected to charges of hypocrisy. Many therefore censor themselves. As a result, the pro-marriage movement loses the leadership of some of its most talented people. The question of same-sex marriage is critically important, but rebuilding and renewing the marriage culture goes far beyond it. By abolishing the basic understanding of marriage as an inherently conjugal union, legal recognition of same-sex marriage would be disastrous. But many would say that such recognition would simply ratify the collapse of marriage that followed from widespread divorce, non-marital sexual cohabitation, and other factors having nothing to do with homosexual conduct. It is certainly true that the origins of the pathologies afflicting marriage lie in such factors. Rebuilding the marriage culture will require careful, incremental legal reforms to roll back unilateral divorce, accompanied by herculean efforts on the part of nongovernmental institutions – especially churches and other religious bodies – to prepare couples more adequately for marriage, help them nurture strong marital relationships, and assist those who are dealing with marital problems. Public-private partnerships will be essential, in my view, to cutting the divorce rate. This won't be easy. If marriage weren't so important, it wouldn't be worth trying.

As with abortion, same-sex marriage is being advanced by socially liberal activist judges who impose their own beliefs and values under the pretext of enforcing constitutional guarantees. That gives us reason to pursue with new dedication the larger fight against the judicial usurpation of democratic legislative authority – another profound abuse of governmental power. Judicial usurpation, beginning with the Massachusetts Supreme Judicial Court, has put into operation a chain of events that will result in the radical redefinition of marriage unless action is taken at the national level, beginning with a vigorous defense of the Defense of Marriage Act (which is under attack in the federal courts), and perhaps including a pro-marriage federal constitutional amendment.

The defense of life against abortion and embryo destructive research calls America back to the founding principles of our regime and to reflection on the justifying point and purposes of law and government. The defense of marriage, meanwhile, shores up the cultural preconditions for a regime of democratic republican government dedicated to human equality, fundamental human rights, and principled limits on governmental powers. These causes should not be regarded as distractions from other pressing goals, such as economic growth, assistance to the needy, environmental protection, and the defense of the nation against terrorism. They are, rather, causes that spring from the foundational moral purposes of law and the state. They are today among the most urgent causes.

Chapter 13:
The Justice of the Market and the Common Good:
Justice Sutherland's Debate
James R. Stoner, Jr.

Introduction: History, Philosophy, and Constitutionalism

The contemporary economic crisis, and the fiscal crisis that is in part
its consequence and perhaps in part its cause, have turned public attention in the United States once again to fundamental questions about the
nature of economic life, the character of commercial society, and the
role of government. Reflection on these matters takes place against the
background of the twentieth century: a century that began with a growing consensus among the intelligentsia that nineteenth-century laissez-
faire capitalism had spawned enormous social dislocation and was in
need of serious reform or radical revamping; that witnessed the rise and
then the fall of revolutionary socialism – communist or national –
across much of Europe and Asia, accompanied by unprecedented violence and world war; and that ended, amidst the collapse of the Soviet
Union, with a resurgence of global capitalism, sometimes methodic and
regulated, sometimes inventive and untamed. At the turn of the new
century, academic commentary focused on a neo-liberal consensus, but
the crisis has made the political parties in America seem more polar-
ized than they have been in years: Democrats became less reluctant to
see their aspirations described as socialistic, while Republicans are
drawn to libertarian notions of a minimal state. Except among hardened
ideologues, even a mild version of Marxist historicism today is uncon-
vincing as a science of economy, society, and polity, but no social or

political theory of comparable scope has achieved widespread acceptance. Pragmatism – sometimes favoring market solutions, sometimes designing regulatory regimes – seems to be the order of the day.

However much being pragmatic might be the counsel of prudence in a particular situation, pragmatism as a philosophy tells us nothing about what is good or bad, or what is just or unjust, even in market society or the modern state. That demands an analysis of first principles, and among contemporary philosophers the analysts typically split into two camps. On the one side are deontologists, who consider rights to be absolute and construct justice as a system for their protection; they claim the lineage of Immanuel Kant and include modern thinkers such as John Rawls, but they might be found on the political right as well as the left, among libertarians as well as among advocates of social justice. On the other side are utilitarians, who follow John Stuart Mill in defining justice always in terms of its contribution to the general good, against whose claims no individual can succeed; they, too, can be found on both sides of the political spectrum, wherever people pride themselves in being pragmatists and scoff at any fixed principle besides the greatest good for the greatest number.[1] The utilitarian defense of free markets stresses markets' success in generating wealth, their tendency to promote technological development, and the real gains in human welfare that wealth and technology entail, not only in highly developed nations but in places such as China and India, which experienced widespread poverty before the recent resurgence of global capitalism. The deontological supporters of capitalism emphasize property rights, which underlie and enable free markets precisely when rights are widely spread around society. The utilitarian critics of markets concentrate on market failures, not only the chronic instability of the business cycle but also the tendency of wealth to concentrate and to seek special privilege, thereby distorting the very markets that created it. Deontological

---

1   For this way of characterizing the debate, see John Rawls, *A Theory of Justice* (Cambridge: Harvard University Press, 1971), and Michael Sandel, *Justice: What's the Right Thing to Do?* (New York: Farrar, Straus, and Giroux, 2009). Utilitarian defenses and critiques of the market are myriad. Rawls offers a deontological critique; for a deontological defense, see Robert Nozick, *Anarchy, State, and Utopia* (New York: Basic Books, 1974).

market critics cite the lack of social justice, noting the extremes of inequality that market societies seem to enable and the consequent pressure on personal rights besides the right to property, for example rights to self-expression or even to basic human dignity, not to mention rights to a decent minimum by which to live, and to goods such as education and health care.

Although differences between utilitarians and deontologists characterize contemporary philosophic discourse about states and markets, classical political philosophy typically did not dichotomize justice and the common good but instead stressed the harmony between them. For Plato and Aristotle, justice is the common good – justice understood both as the right order of the city and as a virtue in the soul. To be sure, human beings seek external goods and bodily goods as well as goods of the soul, and cities depend on those as well as upon virtue; but they are conditions for virtuous living, which is in turn the source of true happiness. The right order of justice would be one that recognizes the best things as intrinsically choiceworthy, and recognizes other goods merely as means to higher ends.[2] In somewhat different language and with a more universal aim, Thomas Aquinas shared the classical confidence in the harmony of the good and the just. He defined law as "an ordinance of reason for the common good"; explained that "since every part is ordained to the whole, as imperfect to perfect; and since one man is a part of the perfect community, the law must needs regard properly the relationship to universal happiness"; cited Aristotle's *Ethics* and *Politics*; and concluded "every law is ordained to the common good."[3] All three philosophers recognize the need for private property and marketplaces in the actual world – Plato makes the case for communism in his *Republic* to illustrate its impossibility – but for them these were mere presuppositions for human thriving, subordinate to politics, which was charged with securing the common good and justice. And there

---

2   Allan Bloom, tr., *The Republic of Plato* (New York: Basic Books, 1968); Aristotle, *The Politics*, tr. Carnes Lord (Chicago: University of Chicago Press, 1985); Robert C. Bartlett and Susan D. Collins, trs., *Aristotle's Nicomachean Ethics* (Chicago: University of Chicago Press, 2011).

3   St. Thomas Aquinas, *Summa Theologiae* (New York: Benziger Bros. 1948), tr. Fathers of the English Dominican Province, I-II, q. 90, art. 3, 5.

was even a good above common human happiness – for Aquinas, beatitude, for Plato and for Aristotle, philosophy – that transcended the city, even the best city, whose justice might in turn be only a precondition for the higher things.

The American Founders seem to accept the modern distinction between the common good and justice – they were certainly friendly both to market development and to rights protection – but like the classics they admired, they aimed to achieve a balance between them. In the Declaration of Independence, rights are introduced as fundamental and the end of government is their security; as many have noted, happiness itself is not initially promised, only the right to pursue it equally, perhaps with each individual defining happiness for himself. But within a sentence, forms of government are said to secure to the people as a whole their "safety and happiness," and both the traditional institutions to which the signers appeal – most especially the jury – and their "mutual pledge to each other [of] our lives, our fortunes, and our sacred honor" indicate a communal dimension to their enterprise, as does their expressed "firm reliance on the protection of divine providence." When Publius mentions the ends of government in *The Federalist*, justice and the common good are almost always paired, sometimes in variants – for example, in the definition of faction as a group of people opposed to "the rights of other citizens [justice], or to the permanent and aggregate interests of the community [common good]" – sometimes simply by formula.[4] The authors, especially James Madison and Alexander Hamilton, carry no brief for "utopian speculations," which they denounce, but neither are they hardened realists who excuse injustice for the sake of overall advantage. Instead, they seem to insist that both goals be pursued together and give neither priority over the other: After all, both "establish[ing] justice" and "promot[ing] the general·welfare"

---

4   Alexander Hamilton, James Madison, John Jay, *The Federalist*, ed. Jacob Cooke (Middleton, Conn.: Wesleyan University Press, 1961), No. 10, p. 57. For examples of the pairing, see No. 10, p. 60 ["justice and the public good"]; No. 14, p. 88 ["private rights and public happiness"]; No. 26, p. 164 ["combines the energy of government with the security of private rights"]; No. 44, p. 300 ["in proportion to his love of justice, and his knowledge of the true springs of public prosperity"]; No. 51, p. 353 ["justice and the general good"]; No. 58, p. 397 ["justice or the general good"]; etc.

are, according to the Constitution's Preamble, among its aims. Indeed, one way of understanding American politics is to see constitutional government itself as the country's overarching common good, the key not only to its understanding of justice but also of all the other ends enumerated in the Preamble, liberty and its blessings not least of all.

This would explain, at any rate, why fundamental political questions in the United States are so often treated as judicial questions, invoking the Constitution in a court of law. The distinction between wisdom and constitutionality runs deep in the American tradition, too, and fundamental policy choices are often left to Congress and the legislatures in the states. But it is no accident that in times of crisis, when serious innovation is possible because the old order seems to have failed, constitutional challenges are brought against new legislation. This was true in the 1930s, and in fact in the decades preceding as well. Today we see something similar occurring in the cases concerning the Affordable Care and Patient Protection Act of 2010 ("Obamacare"), now at the time of this writing slowly working their way through the courts in different circuits around the country.[5] The basic question before the country may be the benefits and costs of the free market versus those of central planning and regulation, compounded by questions of justice or injustice in the policies under consideration. But in America this will soon involve the Commerce Clause and the Spending Clause, doctrines of indirect effects and coercive conditions, the Due Process rights of individuals, and much more. While the current crisis remains unresolved, the crisis of the Great Depression generated critical Supreme Court precedents in these matters, precedents held to govern even to our day. And it was also no accident that Hadley Arkes turned to these cases long before the current crisis, in the context of the reemergence of the prestige of the free market as the Cold War ended, investigating the jurisprudence of one of the

---

5   Thomas More Law Center v. Obama, No. 10–2388 (U.S. Ct. of App., 6th Cir., decided June 29, 2011); State of Florida v. U.S. Dept. of Health and Human Services, No. 3:10–cv-91–RV/EMT (U.S. Dist. Ct., N. D. of Fla., decided Jan. 31, 2011) (on appeal to the 11th Cir.); Virginia ex rel. Cuccinelli v. Sebelius, No. 3:10CV188–HEH (U.S. Dist. Ct., E.D. Va., decided Aug. 2, 2010), and Liberty University v. Geithner, No. 6:10–cv-00015–nkm (U.S. Dist. Ct., W.D. Va., decided Nov. 30, 2010) (together on appeal to the 4th Cir.).

most articulate justices of the earlier period, George Sutherland.[6] This essay, too, will look at Justice Sutherland, with particular attention to his disagreements with other conservative or other Republican-appointed justices. The issues involve the constitutionality of legislation, but every major question about the justice and desirability of markets and commercial society appears as well.

The Moral Liberty of Contract

As Arkes describes in his book, *The Return of George Sutherland*, the justice who gave the clearest defense of market principles came to the Supreme Court by a unique path.[7] Born in England, he immigrated to the United States as a child, his father having converted to Mormonism and moving the family to Utah. Young Sutherland received his education at Brigham Young University and studied law at the University of Michigan, where the faculty included Thomas Cooley, the leading constitutional lawyer of his generation, known for his treatise, *Constitutional Limitations*. Sutherland returned to practice law in Utah and commenced a political career that included serving in the territorial legislature, the new state's senate, the United States House of Representatives, and two terms in the U.S. Senate. Failing to be re-elected after passage of the Seventeenth Amendment, he lectured at Columbia University, practiced law in Washington, D.C., served as President of the American Bar Association, and was appointed to the Supreme Court by Warren Harding in 1922. In the Senate, Sutherland had distinguished himself by his legal knowledge, but he was also known as an advocate of women's rights, staunchly supporting the extension to women of the right to vote, established in the nineteenth century in Utah and extended to the country as a whole with the ratification of the Nineteenth Amendment in 1920.[8]

On the Court, Sutherland's first major case – which became, in a

---

6　Hadley Arkes, *The Return of George Sutherland: Restoring a Jurisprudence of Natural Rights* (Princeton, N.J.: Princeton University Press, 1994).

7　See ibid., ch. 1; also John Fox, "Biographies of the Robes: Alexander George Sutherland" http://www.pbs.org/wnet/supremecourt/capitalism/robes_sutherland.html. The account that follows draws from these sources.

8　See Arkes, *The Return of George Sutherland*, 5 ff.

sense, his signature – was *Adkins v. Children's Hospital*, decided together with *Adkins v. Lyons*, in 1923.[9] At issue was the constitutionality of congressional legislation creating a Minimum Wage Board for the District of Columbia, empowered to declare minimum wage standards for women "adequate to supply the necessary cost of living . . . to maintain them in good health and to protect their morals." Writing for a majority of five, Sutherland struck the Act as a violation of the liberty of contract implicit in the Due Process Clause: "In making . . . contracts [of employment], generally speaking, the parties have an equal right to obtain from each other the best terms they can as the result of private bargaining."[10] It is not that the freedom of contract is absolute, for Sutherland. He notes that individual liberty "must frequently yield to the common good," acknowledges that minimum wage legislation is said to be "required in the interest of social justice," even "concedes" "the ethical right of every worker, man or woman, to a living wage." What he insists is that liberty of contract is "the general rule and restraint the exception."[11] "To sustain the individual freedom of action contemplated by the Constitution is not to strike down the common good but to exalt it; for surely the good of society as a whole cannot be better served than by the preservation against arbitrary restraint of the liberties of its constituent members."[12] The burden of his argument in the case, then, is to show that the restraint on wages in the statute does not fall within the appropriate exceptions, but instead is an arbitrary assault on the rule.

The exceptions had been established by previous cases, and Sutherland shows to his satisfaction that none applies to the D.C. law: it is not limited to businesses "impressed with a public interest," but instead applies to all employment except domestic work; it does not specifically concern government employment; it does not merely regulate "the character, methods, and time for payment of wages," which would have been acceptable; it does not fix hours of labor, something which the Court had allowed in employments determined to threaten injury to health; nor is the act temporary, intended to meet "a sudden

9   261 U.S. 525 (1923).
10 Ibid., 545.
11 Ibid., 546.
12 Ibid., 561.

and great emergency."[13] Instead, the general rule applies, so the controlling case is *Lochner v. New York*, the 1905 case in which the Court struck down a New York statute that would have limited the hours a baker could work, a case that Sutherland quotes at length.[14] Government cannot rightly interfere with labor contracts simply to favor one side; that would be an arbitrary denial of the basic equality that the Constitution commands, a special privilege as wrong when favoring labor as when favoring capital. The statute overlooks "the moral requirement implicit in every contract of employment, viz., that the amount to be paid and the service to be rendered shall bear to each other some relation of just equivalence."[15] Showing concern for women's needs and nothing else, the legislature not only ignores the claim of just equivalence, but overrides any woman's unforced choice to accept a lesser wage on her own terms. Chief Justice Taft in dissent interprets the law as a legislative attempt to prevent substandard employment conditions known as the "sweating system," but Justice Sutherland relies on testimony in the companion case to show that the woman challenging the law there is happy with part-time work and satisfied with the wage. Contracts are individual arrangements and thus allow for the exercise of individual rights, while legislative pronouncements have a general sweep, and even when administered, as here, by a board entitled to issue exceptions, they make the individual subservient to the legislature's purpose. The dissenters – Holmes as well as Taft – see no distinction between maximum hours legislation and minimum wage laws, since both regulate the terms of employment, but Sutherland disagrees: "the heart of the contract [is] the amount of wages to be paid and received," and statutory limitations on hours of work can be taken into account when compensation is negotiated.[16] In short, for Sutherland, the police power of the state can circumscribe the power to contract one's labor, but the essence of the labor contract must be free.

There is a more particular reason Sutherland needs to distinguish

13   Ibid., 551.
14   198 U.S. 45 (1905).
15   Adkins v. Children's Hospital, at 558.
16   Ibid., 554.

restrictions on hours and on wages. A 1908 case, *Muller v. Oregon*, had qualified the ruling in *Lochner* as applied to women, who it held fell peculiarly under the protective power of the state.[17] The argument for state authority in *Muller* had been made by Louis Brandeis, who produced a thorough accounting in the best science and social science of the day of the social harm that follows from women's working long hours outside the home. By the time of *Adkins*, Brandeis is on the Court (though he declines to sit on this case), but the argument is made by his protégé, Felix Frankfurter. Sutherland, however, will have none of it, not only because hours and wages are different issues, but because the Nineteenth Amendment has changed the way law can differentiate women and men. Without enacting an Equal Rights Amendment by judicial fiat, Sutherland nevertheless takes note of "the great – not to say revolutionary – changes which have taken place since [*Muller*] in the contractual, political and civil status of women." To subject "women of mature age . . . to restrictions upon their liberty of contract which could not lawfully be imposed in the case of men under similar circumstances . . . would be to ignore all the implications to be drawn from the present day trend of legislation, as well as that of common thought and usage, by which woman is accorded emancipation from the old doctrine that she must be given special protection or be subjected to special restraint in her contractual and civil relationships."[18] The liberty of contract, then, is an equal right, in some ways the most fundamental of rights, since many if not all human relationships – including government itself, according to the Declaration – are built upon consent or contract. The law may police contracts, to be sure they are not executed to do harm, but to suppress them is to substitute paternalism for freedom. Particularly for women in the early twentieth century, as for African Americans a couple generations earlier, and as for propertyless white men a couple generations before that, the liberty of contract was as essential to civil freedom as the right to vote was to political freedom. It is not a guarantee of happiness, but it is the condition of a free and therefore of a moral life.

17   208 U.S. 412 (1908).
18   Adkins v. Children's Hospital, 553.

The Public Interest in a Changing World

Three years later, Justice Sutherland again wrote for the Court in an important case involving property rights: *City of Euclid v. Ambler Realty Co.*[19] At issue was the constitutionality of a local zoning ordinance, or more precisely, of a zoning ordinance that involved "the creation and maintenance of residential districts, from which business and trade of every sort, including hotels and apartment houses, are excluded."[20] The common law had presumed in every owner of real estate a right to the full and free use of his property, under the restriction that he was not to be a nuisance to his neighbors; the maxim was *sic utere tuo ut alienum non laedas*, so use your own as not to harm others. The aim of zoning law was to ensure proactively that economic growth and development would be orderly, defining what parcels of land could be used for what purposes – in the ordinance in question the basic categories were residential, commercial, and industrial, with gradations within several of these – rather than allow haphazard development and the abatement of consequent nuisances only after lawsuits, or, depending on the rigor of the courts, rather than discourage vigorous development because of uncertainty as to whether nuisance would be discovered and improvements canceled. To the opponents of zoning, however, pre-emptive government control of land use impeded the natural course of economic growth and thus deprived astute developers of the rightful value of their land without compensation; in the words of the attorneys for the realty company, zoning "enacts arbitrary considerations of taste . . . into hard and fast legislation," and tends to create monopolies, too.[21]

Given his staunch defense of the liberty of contract, one might suppose Justice Sutherland would vote to strike zoning as a violation of Due Process property rights, particularly as the designation of residential districts created commerce-free zones, but instead he voted to uphold the legislation, at least against the attempt to seek an injunction against its implementation. Acknowledging that the zoning regulations now upheld "probably would have been rejected as arbitrary and

19   272 U.S. 365 (1926).
20   Ibid., 390.
21   Ibid., 371.

oppressive" "a century ago, or even half a century ago," Sutherland freely admits that times have changed:

> Such regulations are sustained, under the complex conditions of our day, for reasons analogous to those which justify traffic regulations, which, before the advent of automobiles and rapid transit street railways, would have been condemned as fatally arbitrary and unreasonable. And in this there is no inconsistency, for while the meaning of constitutional guaranties never varies, the scope of their application must expand or contract to meet the new and different conditions which are constantly coming within the field of their operation. In a changing world, it is impossible that it should be otherwise.[22]

From the utilitarian or pragmatic point of view, there is no little irony in this: Free markets fuel economic development, but development crowds the world and requires more extensive regulation. But Sutherland is thinking here like a Progressive without being a pragmatist. The question of right does not change; the principle is still the prevention of nuisance or harm, and so the police power is limited to what "bears a rational relation to the health and safety of the community," not allowed to range arbitrarily to serve any conceivable public purpose without regard to the basic rights of ownership. Still, in the condition of modern cities, it is easy enough to sustain residential zoning: children and others might be better protected from injury and sustained in health, disorder can be suppressed, the danger of fire might be reduced, also the danger of traffic, and so forth. Quoting a case about New Orleans, he finds a city might secure better police protection, economy in street paving, prevention of noise and the "malodorous" and "unsightly," and the elimination of vermin by excluding businesses from residential neighborhoods through a city ordinance, rather than relying only on adjudication of nuisances.[23] Let the voters change the

---

22   Ibid., 387.
23   Ibid., 392–393. Sutherland resists the respondent's invitation to consider whether zoning can be undertaken for aesthetic reasons alone without violating Due Process; in the Louisiana case, about residential neighborhoods in New Orleans, the Supreme Court of Louisiana affirms it can. State ex rel. Civello v. City of New Orleans, 154 La. 271 (1923).

law if they do not like the policy, said the Louisiana court; Sutherland agrees that property rights are not imperiled either way. Nor do such ordinances fail because "some industries of an innocent character might fall within the proscribed class"; "the inclusion of a reasonable margin to insure effective enforcement, will not put upon a law, otherwise valid, the stamp of invalidity."[24]

Is Justice Sutherland consistent in sustaining zoning laws that seriously restrict the use a person can make of his own property, and that consequently might impede its value, while rejecting minimum wage laws on the grounds that they interfere with the liberty of contract? Both, after all, were central planks of the Progressive platform, and both were rejected by the most conservative members of the Supreme Bench: Justices Van Devanter, McReynolds, and Butler all dissent in *Euclid*, albeit without opinion. Zoning does seem to reverse the presumption of the rule and the exceptions, if the common-law rule was "full and free use," and the exception was the abatement of nuisance, for now the rule becomes legally designated use in order to prevent nuisance from arising, with general liberty of use allowed only in a single zoning category. Still, the key to Sutherland's opinion is his recognition that no honest use is wholly banned, only displaced: Even "a nuisance may be merely the right thing in the wrong place – like a pig in the parlor instead of the barnyard."[25] Indeed, for Sutherland, liberty of contract is more fundamental than ownership of property, because it is the means by which property is acquired, as well as the means by which it is exchanged. A carefully-drawn zoning statute, like the one at issue in *Euclid*, especially when it operates prospectively, as in that case, actually expands the choice available to individuals. Rather than reinforce an entrenched distribution of ownership and the ancient customs of places, it encourages orderly development and growth.

Natural Right and Constitutional Change

Still, Justice Sutherland's opinions in *Adkins* and *Euclid*, though reconcilable, seem to issue from two different attitudes towards the

24   Euclid v. Ambler Realty, 388–389.
25   Ibid., 388.

Constitution: the first emphasizing the permanent or natural rights that the Constitution embodies, the second illustrating how changing circumstances can reverse, not the Constitution's meaning, but its application. Sutherland faced these two attitudes in confrontation with one another in the case of *Home Building and Loan Ass'n v. Blaisdell*, decided in the early years of the Great Depression.[26] At issue was the constitutionality of the Minnesota Mortgage Moratorium, a statute enacted by the state in 1933 instructing courts to delay foreclosure of mortgages in arrears, up to two years, provided some payment is continued, though less than the terms of the mortgage contract required: Did this not violate Article I, section 10, of the Constitution, which provided "No State shall . . . pass any . . . Law impairing the Obligation of Contracts"? Justice Sutherland thought that it did. True, the law was passed in the context of an economic crisis, but the Constitution with its Contract Clause was formed in the midst of a crisis, too: "A candid consideration of the history and circumstances which led up to and accompanied the framing and adoption of this clause will demonstrate conclusively that it was framed and adopted with the specific and studied purpose of preventing legislation designed to relieve debtors especially in times of financial distress."[27] While this sounds harsh to one in need, Sutherland shows that to the Founders, "a violation of the faith of the nation or the pledges of the private individual . . . was equally forbidden by the principles of moral justice and of sound policy. . . . Indiscretion or imprudence was not to be relieved by legislation, but restrained by a conviction that a full compliance with contracts would be exacted." Helping the irresponsible through legislative action contributes to a general collapse of the value of notes and property, and thus deepens the economic distress it is meant to relieve. Sutherland not only quotes many of the leading Founders in support of exact performance of contracts and exacting collection of debts – Madison, Sherman, Ellsworth, Hamilton, Pinckney – but also cites cases from the 1840s in which the Supreme Court struck down debt relief statutes passed by the states after the panic of 1837, quoting favorably the comments of Supreme Court historian Charles Warren:

26   290 U.S. 398 (1934).
27   Ibid., 453.

> Unquestionably, the country owes much of its prosperity to the
> unflinching courage with which, in the face of attack, the Court
> has maintained its firm stand in behalf of high standards of busi-
> ness morale, requiring honest payment of debts and strict perform-
> ance of contracts; and its rigid construction of the Constitution to
> this end has been one of the glories of the Judiciary.[28]

But in *Blaisdell*, Justice Sutherland was in dissent, joining the same
three justices who had rejected his opinion in *Euclid*. The Opinion of
the Court was written by Chief Justice Charles Evans Hughes, who had
resigned from the Court to run for President in 1916 but now had
returned as Chief Justice by President Hoover's appointment, after the
death of Taft. Gary Jacobsohn has noted that during the interval he was
in civilian life, Hughes gave a series of lectures about the Court in
which he quoted favorably Sutherland's discussion in *Euclid* of changing circumstances in the application of constitutional principles, and he
now puts his colleague's reasoning to use against his conclusions in the
case at hand.[29] Hughes takes judicial notice of the Depression, but
argues, not that times of economic distress are something new, but that
the character of the modern economy has changed the meaning of contractual relations, making Sutherland's moral concern with "indiscretion and imprudence" inapt in describing the situation of an honest
debtor in the face of a modern economic crisis. The heart of Hughes's
opinion is worth quoting at length:

> It is manifest from this review of our decisions that there has been
> a growing appreciation of public needs and of the necessity of
> finding ground for a rational compromise between individual
> rights and public welfare. The settlement and consequent contrac-
> tion of the public domain, the pressure of a constantly increasing
> density of population, the interrelation of the activities of our

28   Ibid., 467, quoting Charles Warren, *The Supreme Court in United States History*,
     vol. 2, rev. ed. (Boston: Little, Brown, 1926), 104.
29   Gary J. Jacobsohn, *Pragmatism, Statesmanship, and the Supreme Court* (Ithaca,
     New York: Cornell University Press, 1977), 182. In the pages that follow,
     Jacobsohn gives a thoughtful analysis of Hughes's and Sutherland's opinions in
     Blaisdell.

people and the complexity of our economic interests, have inevitably led to an increased use of the organization of society in order to protect the very bases of individual opportunity. Where, in earlier days, it was thought that only the concerns of individuals or of classes were involved, and that those of the State itself were touched only remotely, it has later been found that the fundamental interests of the State are directly affected; and that the question is no longer merely that of one party to a contract as against another, but of the use of reasonable means to safeguard the economic structure upon which the good of all depends.[30]

Treating the "economic structure" of society as a common good that the police power can support does not make Hughes a socialist, although he speaks of the "organization of society" as a public responsibility, not the spontaneous result of the economic decisions of individuals; as Jacobsohn points out, Hughes interprets the statute as a modification of the judicial remedy for collecting payment in arrears, not as an impairment of the contract's obligation. The police power "may be exercised – without violating the true intent of the provision of the Federal Constitution – in directly preventing the immediate and literal enforcement of contractual obligations by a temporary and conditional restraint, where vital public interests would otherwise suffer."[31] The basic structure of private property and freely made judicially enforced contracts remains in place, in *Blaisdell* as in *Euclid*, for Hughes, even though social and economic development is now thought to require more legislative and administrative monitoring than in the past.

Full Circle: Private Rights and Common Good in the Free Economy

The debate between Chief Justice Hughes and Justice Sutherland is revived three years later in the case of *West Coast Hotel v. Parrish*, which upholds a Washington State minimum wage law for women and overturns *Adkins*.[32] Decided March 29, 1937, while President Franklin

---

30   Home Building & Loan v. Blaisdell, 442.
31   Ibid., 398.
32   300 U.S. 379 (1937).

Roosevelt's "court-packing" plan was pending in Congress, this case was hailed as the "switch in time that saved nine" and the signal of a "Constitutional Revolution," although jurisprudentially its ground had been prepared three years before, not only in *Blaisdell* but in *Nebbia v. New York*, where the Court upheld a state's power to fix milk prices in an opinion by Justice Roberts, over a McReynolds dissent.[33] In *West Coast Hotel*, Hughes notes that the Due Process Clause mentions liberty simply, not liberty of contract, and explains that "the liberty safeguarded is liberty in a social organization which requires the protection of law against the evils which menace the health, safety, morals, and welfare of the people. Liberty under the Constitution is necessarily subject to the restraints of due process, and regulation which is reasonable in relation to its subject and is adopted in the interest of the community is due process."[34] Hughes accepts the continued authority of *Muller v. Oregon* and agrees with Taft in rejecting the distinction between minimum-wage and maximum-hours limitations on contractual freedom, then adds: "We may take judicial notice of the unparalleled demands for relief which arose during the recent period of depression and still continue to an alarming extent despite the degree of economic recovery which has been achieved. . . . The community is not bound to provide what is in effect a subsidy for unconscionable employers. The community may direct its law-making power to correct the abuse which springs from their selfish disregard of the public interest."[35] Sutherland in dissent reiterates the key points of his *Adkins* opinion, distinguishing the general rule of contractual liberty from the exceptions, insisting on the continued viability of the distinction between a minimum-wage and maximum-hours legislation, and reminding the Court that "women today stand upon a legal and political equality with men," but he knows he is speaking to deaf ears: "it is the right of the minority to disagree, and sometimes, in matters of grave importance, their imperative duty to voice their disagreement at such length as the occasion demands."[36] Within a year, he had retired from the Court.

33   291 U.S. 502 (1934).
34   West Coast Hotel v. Parrish, 391.
35   Ibid., 399–400.
36   Ibid., 411, 402.

Since *West Coast Hotel*, the Supreme Court has never invoked the Due Process Clause to strike legislation as interfering with the liberty of contract. A few weeks later, in *NLRB v. Jones & Laughlin Steel*, an opinion by Chief Justice Hughes that echoed *Blaisdell* and *West Coast Hotel*, insisting the Court not "shut our eyes to the plainest facts of our national life," the Court began erasing many of the distinctions it had used earlier in the twentieth century to limit the commerce power of Congress.[37] By 1942, with Hughes also retired, the Court in *Wickard v. Filburn* held that the aggregate effect of a farmer's feeding his own animals the grain he grows on his own farm is sufficient to trigger the interstate commerce power and allow Congress to limit the acreage he puts into production.[38] That case remains unchallenged precedent today, although since 1995 the Court has limited the commerce power to economic regulations, striking several federal criminal statutes targeting matters only indirectly related to economic activities.[39] Of course government price-fixing schemes have been generally discredited as a policy tool and, except for rules against gouging, have been largely abandoned, and farm policy, too, has largely reverted to market pricing, though regulations remain in place to ensure the healthiness of food and increasingly to label its ingredients and explain the conditions of its production. None of this has happened as a result of constitutional law, only as a matter of policy: Congress's constitutional power over the economy is held to be plenary on a national scale, even though they sometimes choose deregulation instead of regulation for political reasons and to utilitarian ends.

Is anything lost by the abandonment of judicial protection for constitutional limits on the legislative power concerning property and its uses? If the argument at the outset was sound that justice and the common good in relation to the economy need to remain in balance, and if the dialogue between Justice Sutherland and his interlocutors made that dynamic balance its focus, then the collapse – after Hughes – of principled limits on congressional power is a matter for concern, both from

---

37   301 U.S. 1 (1937), 41.

38   317 U.S. 111 (1942).

39   See United States v. Lopez, 514 U.S. 549 (1995); United States v. Morrison, 529 U.S. 598 (2000); Gonzales v. Raich, 545 U.S. 1 (2005).

the perspective of individual property rights and from the perspective of the public welfare. Of course property rights and economic liberties are defended every day in Court, but for the most part the rights are legislated, not constitutional; even the Takings Clause, revived in the 1990s to scuttle zoning legislation that takes away all economically viable use from a piece of property, serves rather as a focus for popular outcry against a Court decision permitting a city to take unblighted homes for its downtown development plan than as a barrier to government action.[40] Whether the Supreme Court will be faced with a case challenging the constitutionality of the new national mandate to buy health insurance, and if so, whether it upholds or overturns the mandate, remains to be seen.

From the point of view of political liberty, our greatest constitutional good, perhaps it is not a bad thing for constitutional property rights to rest on the settled opinion of the people rather than a 5–4 margin on the Supreme Court. While the government's immediate response to the financial crisis of September and October 2008 relied on the broad constitutional powers anchored in the precedents that came from the New Deal, it has been interesting to see that the American people, or at least what appears to be a clear majority of them, even across the party lines, remain persuaded that economic health requires a recovery of healthy markets, not their replacement by the sort of central planning that was championed in that earlier age. Perhaps this judgment is only pragmatic: markets produce a lot of wealth and distribute it widely, and the bureaucratic alternative has produced a lot of misery, and in some places, much worse. But following pragmatism without principle is like trying to walk straight while watching only one's feet. Even to allow markets to recover, and to address the fiscal crisis now at hand, will require attention to the justice of markets, and to the limits of the justice that markets supply on their own. We Americans pursue our interests and enjoy our liberties, but we can never thrive without attention to first things.

---

40   Lucas v. South Carolina Coastal Council, 505 U.S. 1003 (1992); cf. Kelo v. City of New London, 545 U.S. 469 (2005).

Chapter 14:
The Unborn and the Scope of the Human Community
Christopher Tollefsen

Through a long and distinguished career, Hadley Arkes has been widely known and praised for his work – philosophical, political, and legal – on what is arguably the single most important social issue of our day, that of the rights of the unborn and the morality of abortion. Nor has this work been without practical consequences; it has not been Professor Arkes's role to spin dry theories in a hermetically sealed university office. Rather, Professor Arkes was the primary motivating force behind one of the most important pro-life victories of recent decades, the Born-Alive Infants' Protection Act. He recounts both some of the theory and some of the practice that went into this vital piece of legislation in his book – essential to any pro-life thinker – *Natural Rights and the Right to Choose (NRRC)*.[1]

In this essay, I trace five key steps of an argument that supports the rights – legal as well as moral – of the unborn against those who wish them harm. Two steps concern matters of fact; two steps concern matters of morality; and a final step concerns matters of the law. The argument reveals what would be owed to the unborn and legally protected for them, were the law to be achieving its primary purpose. But the law, as Professor Arkes notes, is not at present achieving that purpose. And so, at the conclusion of this essay, I note three further points to which Professor Arkes has drawn our attention, concerning the relationship of the law to the rights of the unborn under our present circumstances –

---

1   Hadley Arkes, *Natural Rights and the Right to Choose* (Cambridge: Cambridge University Press, 2002).

that is, under circumstances in which full justice for the unborn is neither given nor immediately obtainable.

All five steps to the core argument may be found in Professor Arkes's work, although he has, of course, focused to varying degrees on each of them. The great differences, then, between my accounting of the argument and that of Professor Arkes are these: where my prose will be somewhat pedestrian, his is always vibrant. Where my essay will limit itself to a philosophical argument, his is always placed within a larger tapestry of American history and political thought. And where I have few, if any, good stories, anecdotes, or even witty one-liners in my account, Professor Arkes's book, like his public lectures and his private conversations, is chock-a-block full of them – to a greater degree than is perhaps fair for any one mortal. Saddled with such burdens of comparison, I nevertheless struggle ahead.

Each of my five theses can be framed most effectively by asking a question; the answer to each provides one of the five key steps. I will, as necessary and possible, attempt to justify in each case my answer to each question.

What are you and I essentially?

By "essentially" in this question, I mean the following. You, the readers of this book, and I, the author of this essay, are many things: students, teachers, husbands, wives, lawyers, runners. Yet all of these descriptions could cease to be true of us, without you or I ceasing to exist. When my running career comes to an end – because of arthritis or weariness with the sport – I will still continue to exist, and when you cease, as may be, to be a student, you will still continue to exist – perhaps as a professor, or as a member of some other occupation. I am not essentially, but only contingently or accidentally, a runner, just as you are not essentially a student.

What then are we such that we would cease to exist if we ceased to exist as *this* sort of thing? The best answer, I and others have argued, is that we are human beings, living, bodily organisms of a particular species, namely, *Homo sapiens*.

Now one might ask "By contrast with what? What are the other options?" One possible answer: you and I are essentially a soul; or, you and I are essentially disembodied minds, or centers of consciousness; or, again, you and I are some part of the living human being, such as the (functioning) brain.

In various places, colleagues of Professor Arkes, such as Robert P. George and Patrick Lee, have responded to such dualistic claims (dualistic because they imply that you and I are one thing, our bodies another) with a variety of arguments. I would urge all readers to investigate Lee and George's book *Body-Self Dualism* for a number of rigorous criticisms of these views (it should be noted, however, that neither Lee nor George, nor I, nor Professor Arkes would deny that you and I *have* a soul). In place of such arguments, here I wish to offer some reflections of a different order that could lead one to the claim about our bodily nature made above.

Consider the following lines from a play that Professor Arkes can quote, at length, and by heart (I have seen him do so), *Romeo and Juliet*. Romeo has just set eyes on Juliet for the first time:

> Did my heart love till now? forswear it, sight!
> For I ne'er saw true beauty till this night.

Is it not clear that Romeo has fallen in love, as we say "at first sight"? And is this such an impossibility that we should scorn it as mere poetic license? One does not have to be a soft-hearted romantic, I think, to acknowledge the real possibility that one's heart could love with such immediacy. Yet what does love at first sight imply? Only that one human person has looked upon another and *seen that very person*, indeed, come to *know* that person sufficiently to love him or her. But how could this be were we something other than our bodies? For then the body of the other would be a screen, obscuring the presence of the "real" person – the soul, or the mind. There could be no love at first sight were dualism true; only love at first inference.

For this, and for many other sound reasons, the answer given above is best: you and I are essentially human beings. And this claim, it turns out, has tremendous consequences for our primary topic, the rights of the unborn.

When did you and I begin to exist?

Most defenders of the unborn believe that the following answer to this question is true: Unless you and I are the product of monozygotic twinning (unless, that is, we are one of a pair of identical twins), or of human cloning, then we began at fertilization, when a human sperm penetrated an oocyte and both ceased to exist, giving rise instead to a single celled zygote. This zygote was itself a single, whole, individual member of the species *Homo sapiens*, genetically distinct from its parents, and possessed of a developmental program by which it was able to be the executive of its own growth and development to the next stage of human existence: the embryonic stage, then the fetal stage, then the infant stage, and so on.

What is the best evidence for this claim? Professor Arkes notes it himself in *NRRC*; it is the evidence of contemporary embryology, and the scientific authority of those who study human development and the development of other organisms, such as mice. Consider the following, representative, passage, from K.L. Moore and T.V.N. Persaud's *The Developing Human*:

> *Human development begins at fertilization* when a male gamete or sperm (spermatozoon) unites with a female gamete or oocyte (ovum) to produce a single cell – a zygote. This highly specialized, totipotent cell marked the beginning of each of us as a unique individual. The zygote, just visible to the unaided eye as a tiny speck, contains chromosomes and genes (units of genetic information) that are derived from the mother and father. The unicellular zygote divides many times and becomes progressively transformed into a multicellular human being through cell division, migration, growth and differentiation.[2]

There are, of course, those who object to such claims. Some argue, for example, that because the early embryo is capable of twinning, it cannot therefore be considered *one* individual organism. Others argue that within the zygote or early embryo itself, there is insufficient unity for

2   Keith L. Moore and T.V. N. Persaud, *The Developing Human* 7th ed. (New York: W.B. Saunders, 2003), 16.

the embryo to be considered a living *whole*. But such claims are impossible to sustain.

Take, for example, the phenomenon of twinning. Does the possibility of some one thing becoming two mean that it was not one thing to begin with? No one who has ever snapped a stick in half could believe that. Nor, in the domain of living things, have many scientists been tempted to believe that amoebae, which reproduce precisely by splitting, were not individual organisms prior to splitting. (The phenomenon of twinning *does* suggest, however, that *some* human beings came to exist later than fertilization, namely, when an embryo divided, or budded, resulting in two embryos where once there was only one.)

It is not any more plausible to consider the embryo a mere collection of cells, insufficiently unified to be considered one organism. For one thing, the transition of perhaps thousands of cells into a single organism several days *later* than fertilization must be seen as an extremely implausible event with no explanation; what could cause this mere aggregate to become *one thing*? Moreover, contemporary embryologists find an enormous amount of activity, much of it coordinated, amongst the various parts of the developing embryo, activity oriented toward ensuring the embryo's survival and growth. Nor is this coordinated activity the same in all cells; there is a division of labor among the cells even of the very early embryo, and a distinction of role seems evident even from the first cell division. The embryo does not, that is, appear to biologists as a mere heap or aggregate of undifferentiated cells.[3]

As I noted earlier, the two questions just addressed, concerning our essential nature and the time at which we began to exist, are questions concerning the way things are. They are not yet questions of ethics, or of politics or law. But one implication, itself also within the realm of what is, and not of what ought to be, should be noted. As Professor Arkes points out, in speaking of abortions (and the same is true of research that destroys human embryos), "these surgeries destroy human lives," where "human lives" means precisely: the lives of actual, living,

---

3   For interesting evidence regarding this point, see Helen Pearson, "Your Destiny, From Day One," *Nature* 418 (2002): 14–15.

human beings. This is a consequence of the utmost significance in thinking about the rights of the unborn.

Which human beings are deserving of fundamental forms of moral respect?

We turn now to questions of ethics, as the key concepts of question 3 make clear. That question asks about moral *respect*, and, in particular, about the *fundamental forms* of moral respect. This, in turn, implies that there are some forms of respect that are *not* "fundamental." And indeed, this is true.

Consider, for example, the forms of respect owed to the readers of this book, and the author of this essay, in virtue of what they are contingently or accidentally. Some of the readers of this book are students. As such, they are owed certain forms of respect that are not owed to me: the unbiased grading of essays, for example, and the timely return of submitted work. I, on the other hand, as a professor, am owed somewhat different forms of respect: my students should address me as "Sir," or "Professor," for example, titles unnecessary when they address their peers.

Similarly, many readers, as well as this author, are citizens of a particular state and country. Such status, if they are also of a certain age, entitles them to certain rights, such as the right to drive, the right to vote, or the right to purchase alcohol. Respect for their status as citizens requires that other agents not try to stop such readers from exercising these rights.

Yet we do not consider all rights, and all forms of respect, to be dependent upon a status that a person might or might not possess. The right not to be killed, for example, if one is not currently a threat or guilty of a capital crime, the right not to be enslaved, and the right not to be raped are all rights that indicate fundamental forms of moral respect that are not owed in virtue of some contingent status such as profession, or even citizenship. What, then, is the criterion for entitlement to such fundamental forms of moral respect?

Here we come upon one of the key themes of Professor Arkes's work. For, noting rightly that the rights that come and go in consequence of some achieved or conferred status are a result of *decisions* or *conventions*, Professor Arkes asks whether *all* rights, and *all* forms of moral respect must be similarly dependent. And he finds testament to a contrary thought in the words of the *Declaration of Independence*, and in the wisdom of Abraham Lincoln: it is enough to be a *man*, a *human being*, to be the subject of the most fundamental, *natural*, rights – or rights are, after all, no more than a façade, a cover for the exercise of the power of whoever is in charge.

Put one way, we could say that fundamental rights (which Professor Arkes calls "natural rights") are correlated with what we – you and I – fundamentally or essentially are. As we are essentially human beings, we are bearers of fundamental rights precisely insofar as we exist as human beings – i.e., from the time we came into being, whether at fertilization, for the majority of us, or at twinning, for some of us. Nor will we cease to possess such fundamental rights until we cease – at death – to exist as human beings.

Put a different way – and in a very Arkesian manner – we can say that all human beings are created *equal* with the fundamental rights of *persons*. We do not *achieve* the moral status of personhood and the rights that go along with that status; rather, we are persons from the moment we first begin to exist until the moment of our death. And we are persons equal to and with every other living human being.

Interlude: Persons

It will be noted that until the very last paragraph of the previous section, I have avoided speaking of "persons," in favor of discourse about "human beings." There is a strategic reason for this. Many opponents of the rights of the unborn believe that no being is owed fundamental moral respect until it is able, more or less at will, to engage in reason, deliberation, and choice. Such active capacities, these thinkers hold, are the criteria for *personhood*. Thus, an embryo is not, but often becomes, a person, and a comatose or demented elderly person is not, but usually was once a person.

Such views introduce precisely the form of inequality among human beings discussed in the previous (and the following) section: some human beings are, and some are not, persons, and thus not all human beings are entitled to equal moral respect. It is only when we keep our eye firmly on our fundamental equality *vis-à-vis* our humanity that we can establish a regime of *equal* rights, rights based, to be sure, on the *root* capacity that members of the species *Homo sapiens* have for reason, deliberation, and choice. This capacity can, of course, be blocked or damaged, by internal or external factors; yet it makes sense to see species membership as the ground for this capacity in all beings that have it, and thus to treat species membership as the ground for fundamental moral respect.

But after having made this identification, of human nature as the ground for moral status, the language of personhood is very easily and reasonably re-established. For persons just are those beings with root capacities for reason, deliberation, and choice; and persons just are those beings that, in consequence, are owed our most fundamental forms of moral respect. It follows, contrary to the deniers of rights to the unborn, demented, and permanently comatose, that *all human beings are persons*.

Is the fundamental moral respect we are owed compatible with being killed, or used, at the discretion of others?

The short answer to this question is, of course, "No." And it is perhaps above all in Lincoln's principled response to Stephen Douglas, in their great debates about slavery in the nineteenth century, that Professor Arkes finds the keys to a pro-life ethics in American history. Lincoln asks: Can anything that an owner wishes be done to his negro slave, as the owner may do what he wishes to his hogs? Lincoln answers in the affirmative, with the following proviso: "*if* there is no difference between hogs and negroes" (emphasis added). In point of fact, it depends

> . . . upon whether a negro is *not* or *is* a man. If he is *not* a man, why in that case, he who *is* a man may, as a matter of self-government, do just as he pleases with him. But if the negro *is* a man, is it not to that extent, a total destruction of self-government, to say that he too shall not govern *himself*?. . . If the negro is a *man*, why then my ancient faith teaches me that 'all men are created equal;' and that there can be no moral right in connection with one man's making a slave of another.[4]

4   Abraham Lincoln, Speech at Peoria, IL, 1854, quoted in Arkes, *NRRC*, 17.

The two propositions that answer our two ethical questions are both expressed by Lincoln in this passage: *all* human beings – all "men" – are owed the most fundamental forms of moral respect; and those fundamental forms of respect above all militate against making one man a mere object of use for another, against treating another human being as some *thing* whose fate rested rightly in one's own hands, as the disposal of one's property rightly does.

Professor Arkes burrows a bit more into the essence of these claims. These claims must be false, for example, if there is no such thing as human nature. They must similarly be false if there are no objective moral norms governing our treatment of human beings. And, finally, they must be false if human reason has not the capacity to guide us toward these objective moral norms. If there is no such thing as human nature, then Lincoln's (and Jefferson's) claims to fundamental equality are misguided – it will be a matter of power, typically political, to say what beings should be treated as human, and what not. If there are no objective moral norms then it will again be a matter of power to delineate the boundaries of what will count as acceptable treatment of the beings that we have decided to count as human. And if reason is incapable of grasping moral truth, then expression of moral norms can be little more, in reality, than an expression of sentiment or desire. A steady slide into some form of relativism is thus in place as soon as Lincoln's claims – axioms, Professor Arkes would call them – or our capacity to know them, are denied.

These moral claims have direct and immediate implication both for the morality of abortion, and for the morality of research that destroys human embryos for the sake, e.g., of the obtaining of embryonic stem cells. The case is perhaps clearest in regard to the second of these two issues, for here human beings in the earliest stages of their existence are being taken apart for the sake of obtaining some of their cells, to benefit exclusively the health of *other* human beings. This is treatment of embryonic human beings as things with a vengeance.

But the case is clear also in the case of abortion. For in most cases of abortion, it is the intention of the mother and of the doctor to *end the life* of a human being, not because that human poses a grave threat to another, or because he or she is guilty of a capital crime, but because the child will in some way or other interfere with the purposes of the woman: she does not, e.g., wish to be a mother, or to put aside her career, or to accept the financial responsibilities of care for another. The life of one human being is thus subordinated to the desires, ends, and projects of another, and this is surely not treating the unborn human being as one's equal, or as deserving of fundamental moral respect.

One aspect of the genius of the Born-Alive Infants' Protection Act was its bringing to the surface of this often concealed intention in abortion. The goal of successful abortion is not simply to render someone not-pregnant; else there would be little objection to extending legal protections to the infant in the unlikely event that the abortion should be botched, and he or she should be born alive. But the protest against such protections indicates the truth of the matter, a truth incompatible with the moral claims just discussed (other truths brought to light by the Act will be discussed later in this essay).

What are the fundamental purposes of the state?

Human beings, we have seen, are subjects of *natural* rights, rights that precede the existence of any institution or convention established by men. Of course, not all rights are like this; we have seen examples of such rights in the claims to respect that are owed in virtue of someone's particular status as a teacher, a student, or citizen. And, as the example of citizenry makes clear, some such rights are precisely established by a political society for its members.

These rights are clearly of great importance, and there can be little peace or justice without some established set of liberties and entitlements that mark off how *we*, *this* set of persons in *this* political society, are to understand ourselves as a community and comport ourselves together in our mutual dealings.

But such rights are not our most fundamental rights nor can their institution be considered the most fundamental purpose of political society. Rather, the fundamental purposes of the state are correlative to our most fundamental rights as persons; the state exists precisely to protect those rights in a way impossible, or inadequately fair or efficient, in the absence of political authority. Thus, among the primary purposes of the state – the purposes for which the state exists in the first place – is: the defense and protection of the natural rights of all human beings – all persons – within its borders. This is not a purpose, therefore, limited in application only to citizens, or to the law-abiding or morally upright: it includes, in addition, immigrants, even illegals, and criminals. Nor is it a purpose limited in application to the productive, the healthy, the strong, or the intelligent: it includes, in addition, the aged and infirm, the profoundly demented and disabled, and those youngest members of our moral community, human beings in the embryonic and fetal stages of development.

Professor Arkes rightly identifies the protection of these natural rights as "those ends for which governments were instituted in the first place," and builds a theory of *constitutional* government from this insight.[5] A just constitution takes natural rights both as its ground and its end. Citing the early American jurist James Wilson, Professor Arkes elaborates:

> In his famous lectures on jurisprudence, James Wilson argued, as a central point, that the purpose of government was not to create new rights. The aim, rather, was to secure and enlarge the rights that we already possessed by nature. The purpose of any legitimate government – and the purpose, then, of any constitution devised for a legitimate government – was to secure those natural rights. Even in the state of nature, there was no "right to do a wrong." We had never possessed a "right" to kill or rape. . . . At the same time, human beings possessed, even in the state of nature, a right not to suffer those kinds of wrongs. That right did not arise, then, when men and women entered into civil society; it was not a right created by the government. Again, the function of the government was not to invent rights of this kind, but as Wilson said, to secure and enlarge them.[6]

So, a state that allows any human beings, even those at the earliest stage of development, to be killed as a solution to the difficulties – even tragedies – of others, fails in its fundamental mission, and this is true of the state that permits abortion. The continued legal permission of

5   Arkes, *Natural Rights and the Right to Choose*, 21.
6   Ibid., 20–21.

abortion is thus an injustice and a failure of the state's fundamental mission. Similarly, a state that allows the destruction of any human beings, even embryonic human beings, as a solution to the problems of disease and disability among *other* human beings similarly fails in its fundamental mission, and this is true of the state that permits, much less funds, embryo-destructive biomedical research. A just state, we may conclude from the five-step argument, is one that gives *legal* protection to the fundamental *moral* rights of all persons within its boundaries.

The Law and the Unborn in Non-ideal Circumstances

The argument so far serves to establish that unborn human beings *are* within the scope of the human community, and thus are also within the scope of the moral community. And the claims about the most fundamental purposes of the state serve to establish both that the unborn should rightly take their place within a just society's legal community, and that any legal regime that permits the killing of human beings who themselves pose no threat and are guilty of no crime is seriously deficient. The argument could rest there.

But we live in troubled times in which the state – that it to say, its legislators – are not at liberty to move decisively to protect the unborn from violence. A series of decisions by the Supreme Court have decisively, for the time being at least, effected precisely the opposite protection: the protection of those who seek to end the life of the child in the womb from virtually any form of interference. What should right-minded legislators and citizens do under such circumstances? What purposes can pro-life citizens and lawmakers hope to achieve when the law falls so far short of its primary purpose? And what authority does the law, under these conditions, have?

These questions are vast and difficult, requiring both theoretical acumen and the virtue of prudence, and they cannot be adequately addressed here. But I do wish to close this essay with a discussion of three related points concerning the law in the world in which we live that Professor Arkes has articulated in his work. These considerations can serve to guide the considerations, practical and theoretical, of citizens and legislators who pursue an end to unjust discrimination against unborn human beings.

The three points are as follows: First, the law must be a teacher; this is, in fact, a function of the law in good times and in bad, under healthy legal regimes and unhealthy, except, perhaps, under the worst possible regimes in which no faith remains in the law itself. Second, under unhealthy legal regimes, the law must be turned to the pursuit of "modest first steps," steps that will, *by practical and conceptual necessity* lead towards a healthier condition of the law. This aim of the law would, of course, disappear were the end of these modest first steps to be achieved. Third, corruptions of the life and logic of the law, such as those corruptions that permit abortion and encourage the destruction of human embryos, are corruptions of the law, and of political society *as a whole*: as a conceptual matter, these corruptions cannot be limited to the damage they do to the unborn, but in fact threaten to undermine the entire fabric of the law as an institution whose primary purpose is the protection of natural rights.

In the remainder of this paper I briefly explore what is meant by these three related claims.

The Law as Teacher

Imagine a society, all of whose laws were just, and in which no law essential to the protection of the natural rights of its citizens was absent or deficient. In this society, as well, the law is fairly and efficiently administered. And then imagine the very opposite sort of society, one in which the laws systematically favor some over others, allow unjust discrimination, even to the point of unjust killing, rape, or enslavement of some disenfranchised class of persons, and in which even good laws are unfairly or only occasionally enforced. And imagine each society not just at a time, but as it exists over several generations, as children are born and raised under such legal regimes, coming to accept and internalize the demands made or not made, the values recognized or not recognized, by the legal fabric of their society.

Such thought experiments make clear that the law does not *simply* create a stable pattern of behavior – just or unjust – over time, although it does do that. Rather, the law also creates a culture, and it does this precisely insofar as it instructs the citizens of a society as to the moral code that will govern its people and therefore constitute its cultural out-look and framework. As Professor Arkes puts it:

> As the classical philosophers recognized, the law teaches. When the law forbids, say, acts of racial discrimination, it removes those acts from the domain of private choice or personal taste, and forbids them to people generally and universally. . . . As the public absorbs the understandings of right and wrong contained in the laws, the character of the public becomes shaped, for better or worse. That, as Aristotle understood, was the vast promise and the vast danger of politics; and it was the condition that could never be removed. The law could never stop teaching lessons of right and wrong. . . . Law there must needs be, and the men and women who shape the laws must, perforce, be teachers of morality.[7]

A legal regime, therefore, that permits the killing of innocent human life does *more* than simply permit an injustice against some class of persons: it *teaches* the legitimacy of this injustice, and thus erodes its citizens' understanding of the nature of justice. In this case, of course, the primary "lesson learned" concerns the moral claims about the equality of all human beings, and the legitimacy of treating human persons as things. Thus, the wrongness of the law is not simply a matter of its practical consequences; a permissive abortion law that – somehow – resulted in *fewer* abortions would still express precisely the wrong moral to the nation's citizens. And a citizenry whose culture is founded on a radical misunderstanding of justice is, to that extent, a weakened, and even, for reasons that I will explore shortly, an *unfree* people.

Modest First Steps

In the face of this double travesty – the wrong done to the unborn, and the misshapen moral norms inculcated by the law to its subjects – what can be done? Professor Arkes has advocated a strategy of "modest first steps" that addresses both of these difficulties.

In *Natural Rights and the Right to Choose*, Professor Arkes details the progress of two different, and limited, challenges to abortion law.

---

7   Ibid., 3.

One concerned the attempt to restrict the form of abortion known popularly as "partial birth abortion," a procedure in which the body of the child is delivered and the head left in the birth canal. The skull is then punctured and the cranial matter suctioned out before the head is removed. The other challenge was eventually to come to fruition in the Born-Alive Infants' Protection Act. That act's primary purpose was to ensure that infants born alive as a result of a *failed* abortion were to be treated as full persons before the law, and given the protections due to persons.

Professor Arkes expresses a considerable preference for the Born Alive strategy, and finds, in the various travails of the partial birth abortion strategy, justification for his views. Partial birth abortion is, after all, an abortion, and it was only to be expected that judges with a vested interest in maintaining the abortion license would find fault with a law that proposed no principle, but only the grotesquery of a means, as a reason for restricting one procedure out of many.

By contrast, the Born Alive Infants' Protection Act was grounded in a principle that could only be rejected at great peril; yet a principle that did indeed have consequences for the wider abortion license. The principle was this: a living human being, exposed to the world, and whether born because of a failed abortion or because of a successful birthing, is no less a person for the circumstances of his or her arrival, or the desires of his or her parents and their doctors, than any other; and thus such living human beings – in this case infants – are entitled to all the legal protections which it is the fundamental purpose of the state to offer.

This principle could be rejected, it is obvious, only at the expense of the full-bore acceptance of the moral and legal legitimacy of infanticide, a step for which few judges, legislators, or citizens, pro-choice or not, were ready. Its passage and judicial security was thus far more secure than that of the partial birth abortion ban. But the principle at work in the Born Alive Infants' Protection Act was not substantively different – not, in fact, different at all – from the principles articulated in this paper that show legally permitted abortion to be a grave injustice at law. Like Senator Lindsey Graham's bill, the Unborn Victims of Violence Act, the Born Alive Infant Protection Act could neither be easily rejected, nor could its conceptual implications be easily avoided.

This modest first step, therefore, moved the law in a direction that would, as a *practical* consequence, presumably save lives; yet it also created a conceptual impetus that might conceivably move the law in a different direction altogether from that in which it had been trending. The modest first step was thus also an eminently teaching moment of the law, bringing to light a tension in the thought of those who both deplored infanticide and applauded abortion.

Law in Crisis

In the state of affairs depicted in the previous paragraphs, a state of affairs in which a principle is introduced, like a camel's nose into the tent, into the law with a view both to practical and conceptual effect, we see the mirror image of a state of affairs which has vexed Professor Arkes and his colleagues for some time now. For Professor Arkes sees a different understanding at work in contemporary abortion jurisprudence than the principle that all human beings are created equal, and possessed of equal natural rights. Rather, the dominant understanding is one that rejects the ideas of natural rights, of human nature, and of moral knowledge. Thus,

> The question of "what human beings are protected by the law now as human beings" is a question that must turn entirely on the positive law, for there are apparently no objective standards that yield an answer objectively true. It is no longer taken for granted, as an axiom of law, that there really are human beings, with a distinct nature as moral agents, which fits them distinctly for law and political life. The question, "What is a human life?" becomes a question for political authority, and the question will have to be answered then without the consultation of any standards of moral judgment outside of the opinions held by those who exercise power.[8]

But this, Professor Arkes warns, is an inherently unstable situation, for if this is the understanding that undergirds the *right* to abortion, or any other right at all, then *these* rights, like the rights of the unborn, and,

8   Ibid., 145.

indeed, like all rights, are in reality incapable of moral vindication. The deep assumption that only judicial, or legislative decision (or, for that matter, the votes of a majority, or the edicts of kings) grounds rights means, in the end, that there are no natural rights at all.

Professor Arkes contends, then, that contemporary abortion jurisprudence undermines the very notion of natural rights. But in doing so, he likewise contends, that same jurisprudence likewise undermines the ideas of law, of political society, and of constitutional government. For, as we have seen, all these ideas are, in Professor Arkes's work, tied precisely to the fundamental task of the law, namely, the protection of those natural rights of man that precede, in their existence, political authority, and serve as that authority's ground and end.

Professor Arkes's point about the corruption of law could, perhaps, be put like this: as Aristotle noted, the end of constitutional government is a rule of law, and not men. For the rule of law, where the law is guided and shaped by and around the natural rights of men, is a law for men, though not by men. In its limitation by objective moral norms, the law provides a standard against which the desires, wants, and power-plays of mortal men are to be judged, and against which those desires may on occasion be found wanting and called to account. Such a rule of law is thus an order of liberty for human persons, for no human being is made subject, as such, to the rule of another, but only to the rule of law and right.

But this order is subverted in contemporary jurisprudence, and in any politics that takes as its axiom the Protagorean claim that "man is the measure." For the "man" in question is always some particular man or men, and it is the lives of others that are measured by these particular men. But that, unlike the rule of law, is in fact a form of servitude, of subordination, to the will of others, a subordination known in our own day by the unborn, as in another day it was known by African slaves and their descendents. But it is, argues Professor Arkes, a subordination built into the contemporary understanding of law; no human being is thus, in principle, untouched by this understanding; and the citizenry of a polity whose laws are built on this understanding is thus, to that extent, no free people at all.

The stakes of the abortion debate – the debate over the status of the unborn in the human community – are thus of overwhelming significance. For the problem of abortion is, in fact, not *one* problem. It is, on the one hand, the problem of a massive injustice done to the weakest and most vulnerable members of the human community; but it is also a challenge to the existence of our own – or that of any comparable society's – *political* community, the fabric of which is undermined by an unsustainable and manufactured "right to choose." It is only in the legal recognition of the moral rights – the natural rights – of the unborn, that this two-sided tragedy of law, politics, culture, and morality, can finally be exorcised and the promises of the Declaration of Independence finally be realized.

Chapter 15:
Being Personal These Days: Designer Babies and the Future of Liberal Democracy
Peter Augustine Lawler

We are – big, big time – about change, change we can believe in. We're the species that can take nature personally and do something about it. We have personal or individual objections to the limited and precarious character of our biological existence. Nature, I can say, is cruelly indifferent to my personal existence. Nature doesn't care about me as a person. Nature is out to replace ME. We're the animals who care about ME, who think in terms of personal identity, who can orient themselves around the insight that each person is unique and irreplaceable. Each of us is an animal who refuses, to some extent, to be reduced to merely a part of a species or a part of some impersonal natural process.

My purpose here is to give a glimpse into the future of *thinking personally* in the emerging era of biotechnology, with some focus on what are called designer babies and the search for genetic justice. It's really quite wonderful both what we persons can do for ourselves and what we can imagine what we can do for ourselves and those persons we love. There's no substitute, of course, for beginning with an account of the emergence of the person.

Personal Evolution

It's plausible to say that the theory of evolution was completely true until our species showed up on this planet. Impersonal natural evolution continues gradually to be displaced by conscious and volitional evolution – evolution caused by members of our species with ME in mind.

All of nature has been altered by our personal willfulness, and it's almost true to say that it's impossible to find anything that's purely nature or merely impersonal on our planet anymore. This development is far from completely recent. We've engineered whole species – like dogs and pigs and cows and chickens – into existence for our personal convenience and even our personal vanity in mind. Although the human species hasn't been changed by nature in any fundamental way since it showed up, it's changed the rest of nature with itself – with the human person – in mind. And now we're on the edge of the biotechnological revolution which promises to allow us to change our own natures with me in mind.

Our scientists tell us that we're pretty much like the dolphins – cute and smart dependent rational social mammals. And we are like the dolphins in some ways, of course. But now the very being of the dolphin depends on us, but not the other way around. For now, we think they're cute enough and smart enough and entertaining enough to protect, while the tuna are ugly enough and dumb enough – not to mention tasty and nutritious enough – to die. But we could easily switch things up and take the dolphin out –perhaps as a threat to our species self-esteem – and gain a strange Rousseauian or Buddhist appreciation for the noble simplicity of the tuna. The dolphins don't have what it takes to be out to get us, because they don't have what it takes to be in technological rebellion against their natural existence. Our being will never be dependent on them. One reason is that they can't think personally enough to raise the question of being. Another is that they are not equipped to act freely enough to consciously and willfully change their own natures. Although we don't know exactly what is going on in the heads of those brainy dolphins, they aren't displaying any discontent with their merely natural existences. Dolphins aren't about changing nature with the perpetuation of the existence of particular dolphins in mind.

The evolution of nature, we can't help but see, produces ontological differences or different kinds of beings. Being changed when the plant emerged from the rock, as biology emerged from physics. How life – and so the distinction between life and death and life and nonlife – emerged from inanimate nature remains a mystery to us. Being changed again when the animal emerged from the plant; all the capabilities and behavior turned the distinction from life and death into birth and death. And being changed again when the social, rational, free or technological animal who can raise the question of being, take things personally, love personally, be aware of, reflect on, and rebel against personal contingency and mortality emerged. I've mentioned that there's no dolphin technology worth mentioning. But neither are there dolphin physicists, priests (or preachers), presidents (or princes), poets, or philosophers, and even dolphin parents aren't that much like our parents. And of course there's no dolphin safe sex.

The last ontological difference, of course, is easily the most important one. The questions that surround the mystery of being, including who we are, what we are, and who or what God is couldn't be raised without us. Actually, we really know that the "what" questions couldn't be raised by anyone but a "who," a being with a name who can name. (Certain other animals have names and even know them, but we give them their names to personalize them, with very limited success, in our own image.) And so despite the best efforts of many philosophers and scientists, we've never been able to reduce the "who" to a "what," the human person to some impersonal, wholly necessitarian natural process. The "who" is the being open to the "what," and the mystery of the "who" – the person – is much more wonderful than the famous "why is there being rather than nothing at all" issue.

Perhaps the physicists are right that impersonal nature would be perfectly explicable without us, at least if one doesn't dwell too much on the mystery of being or the mystery of life. But everyone knows that physics can't explain the physicists. Perhaps physics, for all I know, can explain the correspondence between the physicist's mind and the invincible laws of nature. But the physicist isn't a mind; he's a whole human being – a person – who can't be reduced to a body or mind or even some incoherent mixture of the two. The physicist can't explain the uniqueness of the scientific effort of human beings to deny the uniqueness of our species – and especially particular members of our species – in the cosmos. We don't look to the physicist to explain the undeniably truthful and undeniably personal and undeniably wonderful experience of the particular human being existing for a moment between two abysses. We can look to penetrating psychologists from

Aristophanes to Pascal to Nietzsche to Walker Percy to remind us that the physicist's attempt to lose himself in an impersonal account of nature is really, in part, an always partly failed attempt to divert himself from what he really knows about himself, the "who," the particular being with a name who can name.

Physicists from Aristotle onward have said that the most wonderful things in the cosmos are the stars, because of the majestic regularities of their impersonal, inanimate behavior. The Bible says that nothing we can see is more wonderful than the behavior that characterizes the personal destiny of the particular human being. But maybe we can wonder most of all about the behavior of the being who can so easily know what moves the stars but seems to remain an elusive, even impenetrable, mystery to himself. Aristotle, following Socrates, says we're most deeply moved by wonder, and the Bible says we're most deeply wanderers or pilgrims in this world. Surely the truth is that because we wonder we wander or because we can wander we wonder. It's because of our personal detachment that we're open to the truth and we always fall short of integrating ourselves into the natural our physicists and biologists so perfectly describe. That doesn't mean being personal means that we're nothing but absurdly purposeless leftovers or miserable aliens stuck inside our puny, particular selves. Sure, we have miseries not given to the others species that flow from our contingency as wonderers, but we're also given joys – such as wonder and deeply personal love – and responsibilities – such as those that flow from being open to the truth and taking responsibility for the very future of life on our planet – not given to the other species.

As Harvey Mansfield points out in his *Manliness*, from the very beginning members of our species devoted huge amounts of time and resources to religion as a way of explaining and securing their personal significance. Our personal concerns intensified with the coming of Biblical religion, particularly Christianity. For the Christian, natural theology and the civil theologies of the Greeks and Romans wrongly reduced the person to merely part of nature or part of the political community or did not account for the whole person as a unique and irreplaceable being. For the Christian, the person retains his personal identity in his relationship with the personal God, and for the Christian there's no doubt about the infinite worth of the particular person made in the image of the personal Creator. Not only that, Christian writers such as St. Augustine focused personal concern on the anxious misery that comes with being a self-conscious mortal. The only reliable freedom from that experience of contingency comes through hope in salvation from the limits of my merely biological being by a personal God, in the Creator who lovingly sustains my personal being against the nature indifferent to my existence. God knows and cares about who I am, just as I am.

For many Christian theologians, death is not even our natural end, but a punishment for sin. So we're not really mortals, and death is not an invincible reality to be accepted. It's not enough, for the Christian, to say that I have compensations for my personal death through memories of my glorious deeds or through my children. Citizens of Rome were looking in the wrong place when they sought security in their country; Rome, for instance, didn't care about any of them in particular, and the glory that was Rome didn't save any particular Roman from oblivion. Death is the reality that Jesus struggled against and conquered for us, and so he secured each of our personal identities as images of God forever. Jesus, we might say, restored us to who we really are as more than beings who can be described by the laws of nature applicable to all the other species.

We can say that the modern, technological project for the conquest of nature, the decision by men like Bacon and Descartes to focus human efforts on pushing back our natural limitations, on imposing our personal will on impersonal nature, is based on the Christian focus on personal identity without the Christian belief in personal, supernatural salvation. The modern, technological goal is the overcoming of natural scarcity, most of all the scarcity of time that plagues the lives of particular persons. The goal is indefinite longevity or freely personal lives of any sense of definite duration. The goal is to keep us from being defined by or obsessed with time, to keep us from being able to count the days that make up my particular life. In the absence of the personal God, we persons experience ourselves more than ever as temporal, ephemeral, contingent beings, and we work harder than ever not to be defined by that experience.

The Christian focus on personal identity, absent the personal God, caused reformers to believe that History – or human political, revolutionary efforts – could eventually achieve in this world what God promised in the next. The idea of History – which peaked, of course, with Marxist communism – caused particular persons existing today to be sacrificed in huge numbers for the perfect freedom of the persons of the future. But everyone knows these days that Marxism was both cruel and confused. For the same reason persons can't be regarded as primarily nature or species fodder or "city" fodder, they can't be regarded as primarily "History fodder." Not only that, we now know that History with a capital H was quackery; there is no merely political or revolutionary cure for what ails us by nature.

But it seems that we're now back on the more sensible modern, technological track. We now know of no higher standard than securing the being of the persons alive right now. We're now clear that we have no right not to say anything but all persons have human dignity and human rights, and the point of life is to sustain them in their personal identities as long as possible. That means, of course, that they have the duty to do what they can to sustain themselves, to protect themselves as well as possible from all the "risk factors" that surround them. In that sense, we're more pro-life than ever.

The most obvious positive effect of technological progress – combined with personal freedom – is the extension of the average life to near 80. There have always been occasional exceptions among members of our species to the natural rule of reproduce, raise one's children, and soon thereafter die. What's new is the average person now has a new birth of freedom, a generation or really more when his kids are grown and he or she is finally on his or her own. This fact seems to confound the evolutionary theorists. This long period of postmenopausal flourishing among our females, for example, simply does not exist among the other mammals.

What we have here, in truth, is a real technological victory over nature. It's a very limited victory – so far the oldest of the old are no older than they were in the past and hardly anyone reaches three digits in age – but real nonetheless. And we have the new biotechnological hope that some combination of genetic manipulation, regenerative medicine (which promises to either to fix up or generate replacements for our key bodily organs) and perhaps nanotechnology will finally start to move persons in the direction of indefinite longevity. We have the hope, in other words, that we can really change our natures in ways that keep us from being so defined by time and death. There are some who say that the first person to live to be a thousand is alive today. (It's as certain as certain can be that it's not me.)

There are actually, of course, two new facts that make the population of the most technologically advanced countries older than ever. Not only are people living longer, they are having fewer children. And it's pretty much the case that the countries that have the most longevity have the least fertility. Persons, we might say, are tending to do what they can to choose not to be replaced. They're not doing their duty to the species or for that matter to their country (the birth dearth is obviously a growing national security problem in some European countries and maybe Japan), because persons aren't thinking of themselves as parts of anything greater or larger than themselves. Americans are getting older too, although we stand out in still doing our duty in generating sufficient personal replacements. But if you take out first-generation immigrants and observant religious believers, our birth rate is the same of, say, the France that is gradually fading away.

So one result of our diminishing personal concern about extending my personal being toward others through love and beyond my biological demise is a new moral – or very judgmental – focus on personal health and safety. Unprecedented personal longevity and personal security depend upon me taking maximum personal responsibility for keeping myself around. The emerging medical and other technical means for achieving those goals are worthless unless I really use them. I have to be determined to apply them in my own case. It's irresponsible for ME not to act on what I can know when it comes to diet, exercise, supplements, drugs, safe sex, and so forth.

More than ever, we blame people who die young for their irresponsibility. We're much less accepting of the thought that death is the intention of nature or God's will or just bad luck. We used to have the romantic thought that only the good die young. We now think we can see that it's the case more often than not that it's the stupid and self-indulgent who die young.

We can even appreciate that our separation of sex from reproduction – which, we can imagine, will eventually become perfect through biotechnological progress – is much more pro-life than it first seems. It's first of all about keeping me alive, but its general intention is to keep everyone around at any particular time alive as long as possible. Now it's still true, horrifyingly true, that we still use abortion for eugenics. We're getting almost perfect in inducing moms to choose against defective models – such as babies with Down syndrome. And we still let women choose abortion when their personal virtue or contraception fails them. But anyone with eyes to see can be pretty optimistic that the era of abortion, at least or especially eugenic abortion, is coming to an end. One of our real goals is to make sex perfectly safe. Another is to fix the allegedly defective fetuses in the womb or, even better, to be very careful about only implanting embryos that have been certified defect-free. Relatively unsophisticated Americans like you and me still admire Sarah Palin's loving choice of the gift of her beautiful Down's son over abortion.

We still can and should regard Down babies as lovable gifts of God. But who could deny it would be better to correct such natural defects if possible, and that it's perverse and irresponsible, if we have the techno-means to do something about it, to regard Down syndrome as an unalterable gift? If some kind of biotechnological eugenics – and not abortion or the killing of particular persons – were the cause of the disappearance of Downs children, who would be against it?

Being Personal in American Thought Today

American sophisticates usually speak of personal significance in terms of the theory of John Rawls. Rawls has become, many think, *the* political philosopher of our liberal democracy. Our friendly French observer Pierre Manent, in a review of Rawls in *First Things*, seems perfectly right that "Rawls does *not* qualify as a political philosopher," because he "*presupposes* the validity, truth, and excellence of our democratic principles and institutions." All he really does is "ingeniously tinker with parochial details." What Rawls really claims to do is articulate with rigorous consistency what sophisticated Americans already believe. His limited goal, he says, is to articulate a "political liberalism."[1] But the truth is that, in his mind, political liberalism is one aspect of a comprehensive liberalism based on the principle that there's nothing worth knowing or protecting but the security and autonomy of the free person. Any religion, for example, that contradicts that principle is not only unjust but unreasonable. Rawls' aim is to educate people on how to live comprehensively liberal or coherently personal lives, to help people in being personal – nothing more and nothing less – these days.

What Rawls and Rawlsians think they know for certain is both modern and Christian: All persons deserve equal respect, and that respect that doesn't depend on their intelligence, moral excellence, or productive accomplishments. And no person can be used as a means to the better life of other human beings or as a mere part of some great whole (such as a country). That's because the person is not fundamentally a natural or biological being; the person is free from nature in the way members of the other species aren't. Every person is equally significant and equally irreplaceable. As rational agents responsible for who they are, persons are free, unlike the dolphins, to chart their own destiny and act morally. Rawlsians almost never think that anything they know is specifically Christian, and so they can or should think of themselves as post-Christian guardians of the personal insight about who we are.

That's not to say that Rawls thinks that persons aren't dependent on nature. He generally assumes in *A Theory of Justice* that "the [inegalitarian] distribution of natural assets is a fact of nature" with which we are stuck. We persons have no choice but to work with what nature has arbitrarily given us. It's certainly "not in the advantage of the less fortunate to propose policies which reduce the talents of others." I don't have more if you have less, and it's senselessly self-destructive to reject anything any of us has been given by nature to better secure ourselves as persons. But that doesn't mean that each person's natural abilities are his or hers to be used as he or she pleases; no moral being can affirm some absolute right to self-ownership. That's because no person deserves – or has

---

1   John Rawls, *Political Liberalism* (New York: Columbia University Press, 2007).

earned on his or her own – his lucky breaks in the natural lottery. We can and should regard "the greater abilities" some of have "as a social asset to be used for the common advantage," because what distinguishes me by nature is not, from a moral point of view, my own.[2]

It would be better, Rawls almost suggests, if we, in the name of equality or justice, could redistribute what persons had been given by nature, if we could redistribute natural gifts against natural randomness and on behalf of personal justice. But we can't, of course, figure out how to take extraordinary mathematical ability from one person and give it to another who's numerically challenged in order that they both have equal quantitative skills. And it's far from clear any person would really want that. It's not in my interest to surrender what I've been given, and it's not anyone's interest to have no one around who excels in the skills required for science and technology – from which we all benefit – to progress. From a personal view, we most of all want more than what nature has given us; it remains, Rawls claims, "in the interest of each to have greater natural assets." Who would have no use at all for what we now regard as extraordinary mathematical ability? We persons really have two objections to impersonal nature – it's both arbitrary and stingy.[3]

That fact obviously has eugenic implications. Rawls claims that "the parties want to insure for their descendants the best genetic endowments (assuming their own to be fixed)." That means, of course, that a just society would aim to correct genetic conditions that undermine personal security and flourishing, and that would include providing genetic enhancements that promote personal success. Precisely because nobody earned their winnings in the genetic lottery, we have to think of biotechnology in terms of making nature itself less arbitrary or more just by raising everyone higher. The Rawlsian goal is to give every person equal access to an enhanced or engineered genetic endowment. We should do everything we can, Rawls says, to improve "the general level of natural abilities," as well as "to prevent the diffusion of serious defects."[4]

2   John Rawls, *A Theory of Justice*, revised edition (Cambridge: Harvard University Press, 1999), 92.

3   Ibid., 92.

4   Ibid., 92.

The (sort of) Rawlsian legal philosopher, Ronald Dworkin, says straight out in *Sovereign Virtue* that we're ethically commanded to struggle against blind or personally indifferent nature with our "conscious designs in mind," "to make the lives of future human beings longer and more full of talent and hence achievement."[5] We must consciously redesign nature with the freedom and security of persons in mind. As David Schaefer observes in *Illiberal Justice*, the Rawlsian moral "exhortation that we work to overcome the moral arbitrariness of nature" requires "the exercise of what the biologist Edward O. Wilson calls 'volitional evolution.'"[6] The more evolution is in our willful hands, the more it will serve (as it clearly does not in its impersonal, natural form) our personal purposes.

Until the possibility of genetic enhancement (especially after the sequencing of the human genome), we couldn't take responsibility for natural inequality. And so we had to begin with the fact that people are who they are by nature – a fact that arbitrarily limited our personal freedom or made our imperfectly free world imperfectly moral. Rawls, of course, laid a value judgment on nature by articulating the duty of the naturally well endowed to the naturally unfortunate, but the unfortunate, unfortunately, were stuck with remaining somewhat unfortunate. Now we seem to have the responsibility to start thinking about changing nature to produce genetic justice – not by dragging anyone down but by raising everyone up.

Certainly, this possibility will weaken the libertarian (or Randian) position: I have a right to everything I've been given by nature and everything I've mixed my labor with or earned. I have no duty to the envious or allegedly "unfortunate" who want to drag me down. Surely my natural rights can't include my ability to use my property to make myself even more naturally better or more enhanced than others, and certainly we can't have a few using money or power to be able to buy themselves out of the natural equality described by our Declaration of Independence. How can we be devoted to the proposition that all men

5   Ronald Dworkin, *Sovereign Virtue* (Cambridge: Harvard University Press, 2000), 452.

6   David Lewis Schaefer, *Illiberal Justice* (Columbia, MO: University of Missouri Press, 2007), 128.

are created equal if we're free to creatively negate that fact? Personal evolution – based as we think it is on the uniqueness and irreplaceability of every human being – can't be understood to be at the service of a few persons at the expense of others.

One scenario is that genetic enhancement might be regarded as no different from the way we now view elective cosmetic surgery – expensive and not covered by health insurance. The result might be the emergence of a "genobility" based on the obsolescence of the empirical foundation of democratic equality. The aristocrats of old thought of themselves as different kinds of beings from most human beings, but they deluded themselves. The new aristocrats might come to think of themselves as radically better because they *are*. They will have the power to get themselves the genetic right to rule.

As Alexis de Tocqueville points out in *Democracy in America*, however, we modern democratic persons refuse to defer to the privileged claims of aristocrats even or especially when they're deserved. So Fukuyama concludes that "it seems highly unlikely that people in modern democratic societies will sit around complacently if they see elites embedding their advantages genetically in their children."[7] If all the significant social positions were occupied by children whose parents could afford expensive genetic treatment, and most people's children had no significant chance for success no matter hard how they worked, then we might finally have the revolution that comes when most people think they have nothing left to lose. The Marxian prediction of the emergence of inexorable division of labor that reduced the great mass of people to, relatively speaking, nothing would finally become true. But it's highly unlikely that things will ever go that far.

Much more likely, of course, is the emergence of government programs aimed at making the current level of enhancement available to every particular person. "If banning biomedical enhancements would be foolhardy and if restricting their use to socially desirable ends would require a repressive police state," Maxwell Mehlman sensibly concludes in *The Price of Perfection*, "the only alternative is to make sure

---

7   Francis Fukuyama, *Our Posthuman Future* (New York: Farrar, Strauss, and Giroux, 2002), 158.

that enhancements are available, not only to the well-off but to everyone." We now agree that "basic education" has become a right, because without it success is almost impossible. Why would at least "basic enhancement," so to speak, be any different? In deciding what enhancements to make generally available, it makes sense to say, Mehlman goes on, that "the government decision-maker might look to John Rawls's notion of 'primary goods' – those that every rational person should want."[8]

Maybe it will be easy enough to limit the universal genetic entitlement to what genuinely contributes to health, security, and autonomy on which rational agency depends. Because biomedical enhancement would spare many from the ravages of particular diseases and other physical disabilities, it can't really be compared to cosmetic surgery. It should be covered, it seems, by any health care plan as easily the most effective kind of preventive medicine. And our children and our children's children can be presumed to have consented to our species' permanent, germline enhancement, if that becomes possible. Nobody can argue that any person would be better off with worse health or a shorter lifespan or fewer or weaker capabilities. We can, from a Rawlsian view, presume that consent from all future generations; persons will *always* be for changes to nature that make them more free, responsible, and rational. It would surely be personal exploitation to choose for dependence, debility, and every early death for persons whom we could allow to escape those indignities.

People still take unreasonable pride in their natural gifts, and the members of any meritocracy – even or especially a natural meritocracy – can't help but often have an unreasonable sense of entitlement. Enhancement will serve justice both by equalizing those gifts and making it clearer than ever that being who we are depends on the conscious intention of other persons. Justice is served by eroding the sense of entitlement that the gifted now have to genes better than most. Maybe we can actually *make* ourselves better Rawlsians, as Rawls himself expects. The conscious pursuit of genetic justice will bolster the

8   Maxwell Mehlman, *The Price of Perfection* (Baltimore: Johns Hopkins University Press, 2009), 222.

otherwise languishing social and dutiful dimension of personal or individual consciousness. The belief that our liberties and capabilities are the gift of a personal God has faded almost into insignificance, but now we have a new foundation – in a way both natural and socially constructed – for personal responsibility to other persons.

There is, however, another way of thinking about enhancement. Today, we don't blame people all that much for being less productive than others. We know there are natural differences, and so we know that even if everyone were virtuous enough to be all that he or she can be outcomes would remain unequal. Our general, Hobbesian tendency to equate dignity with productivity – or personal power – can't help but be moderated some by compassion or pity. It is also moderated some by our dedication to the proposition that all men are created equal, meaning that all persons are of infinite and irreducible worth. The equal significance of persons, only the most heartless libertarian denies, should be some limit on meritocratic inequality. It's true enough, though, that we can already feel the pressures of meritocracy eroding our pity, and that's why we're more anxious than ever about personal productivity.

Today, we already see ambitious and loving parents using the available enhancements, most of all, to give their kids an edge in the competitive race that is life. Parents of very short kids use growth hormones to make their kids more fit for production and even reproduction. The mainstreaming of the ADD drug Adderall is all about keeping kids focused on personal success. Not only does it help them pay attention in mind-numbing classes, studies show it keeps the kids' heads in the game that is the boring standardized test.

More generally, we see that the use of cosmetic neurology and cosmetic surgery so far is mostly about making oneself look younger and smarter, feel more positive, be more engaged and engaging, think more clearly, and remember more precisely. We can see that enhancement is mostly about enhancing the personal productivity that contributes to personal security. Personal safety requires a lot more than being healthy and avoiding diseases. Designing parents aren't really, as some claim, trying to instrumentalize or commodify their kids in their own eyes. It's because they love them as particular persons that they're so paranoid about securing their contingent personal existence in an increasingly hostile environment.

If our genetic endowments were biotechnologically equalized, the race of life would become much tougher and more judgmental. Personal failure would be connected more clearly to one's own lack of industry and dedication. And nobody would be smart enough to soar above others without trying very hard. The result might well be less pity for those who fall behind, and perhaps a greater sense of ownership of one's success. "Nature or God didn't give me my edge, I did" would actually make more sense than ever; people would have more reason than ever to take proper pride in what they've accomplished.

If everyone becomes pretty equally gifted, then gifts no longer make the difference. A person with an enhanced memory and powers of concentration still has to study. And if our physical capabilities were equalized, we'd still have to train to excel. How hard and smart a person studied or trained would make all the difference (abstracting, for the moment, from environment).

In *The Case Against Perfection*, Michael Sandel writes, in (despite himself) a kind of Rawlsian spirit, that "if our genetic endowments are gifts, rather than accomplishments for which we can take credit, it is a mistake and a conceit to assume that we are entitled to the full measure of the bounty they reap in a market economy." We have been given advantages that we did nothing to deserve, and they're a chief cause of our productivity. "We therefore," Sandel goes on, "have an obligation to share this bounty with those who, through no fault of their own, lack comparable gifts."[9] Because a particular person doesn't really earn all of his bounty, he must give share some of it with the unfortunately ungifted.

The engineering of genetic justice, of course, blows that sharing argument out of the water. Now that our gifts are comparable, why do we owe each other anything at all? John Harris gives us the good news that "enhancement provides more to redistribute." Overall there's much more bounty because people are much more capable – "and less need

---

9   Michael Sandel, *The Case Against Perfection* (Cambridge: Belknap Press of Harvard University,2007), 91.

for redistribution," because there's less need to act socially or politically (as opposed to biomedically/technologically) to correct the inegali-
tarian injustice of nature.

Loving Hyperparenting

So far, we've exaggerated the coming personal responsibility by slight-
ing the role of nurture or "being raised" in how a person turns out. Next
to natural gifts, the most important predictor of personal success is the
quality of one's parents. Enhanced genetic justice won't allow parents
and children to relax. These days, we often think that kids who are
genetically gifted don't have to be pushed as hard, and they often don't.
But if the time comes when every child has the same fair natural start,
parenting will be more important than ever. No kid will be smart
enough or talented enough to stand out from the others without being
forced to sweat hard. Parents would have more reason than ever to be
drawn into what Sandel calls "an ever-escalating arms race" of "promoting and demanding all manner of accomplishments from their children" out of loving concern for securing their personal beings as well
as possible. Genetic justice would enhance "the trend toward hyperparenting" in our personally anxious time; parents will feel more and more
personally responsible for their children.

Consider that when today's hyperparents obsess over their children's competitiveness, they tend to think less than ever about them as
future parents, about their moral fitness as nurturing and caregiving
beings. One reason people are having fewer children than ever is that
they take less and less solace in their biological replacements. When
they do have replacements, they're less likely to think of them as beings
who will find a primary purpose in life in generating their own replacements. People these days tend to think of both themselves and their
children as personally irreplaceable, and that turns out to be fuel for
self-obsession, parental paranoia, and parental love.

We have become so *personal* that Darwinian (or species-serving)
explanations of our thoughts, feelings, and behavior actually work less
well than ever. People are more paranoid about both themselves and
their children staying around as long as possible; they're more attuned
to the risks of personal existence. Another reason sophisticated people

are having fewer children is that raising them has become so tough – in the sense of so conscious and volitional.

That's not to say people don't in some ways love their children more than ever. The relational bond between parent and child (or certainly between mother and child) resists both personal and impersonal destruction, and it gets stronger in some ways (as in the case of the increasingly common lonely and isolated single mom) as other social, relational bonds atrophy. People are self-obsessed enough these days to bother less and less about creating new persons. But everything changes, of course, when they loosen up enough (or screw up enough) to do so.

The anxiety about the very being of the gift of the child reflected in the various forms of hyperparenting can be at the expense of love, but those efforts are still mostly about lovingly preserving the being of a person. The parental perception of responsibility for the very being of their child, of course, is some combination of existentialism and high technology. We're more moved than ever by the contingency of personal being in an indifferent universe, and we're more aware than ever that there are steps we can take to reduce personal contingency and enhance personal control.

The limits to the steps to be taken turn out not to be so clear. Those who are not only strong and smart but pretty do have an added edge when it comes to productivity and so personal security. When it comes to enhancements concerned with physical augmentation (or reduction) or eradications of peculiarities thought to be ugly (like a huge nose) or disguising the facts of aging, Carl Elliott observes in *Better Than Well*, our incoherent approach "is to embrace the procedures while passionately criticizing the cultural attitudes that make the procedures seem necessary."[10]

Because it's easier to change the physical appearance of the person than change cultural superficiality when it comes to persons, a Rawlsian might be drawn to embracing an effort to equalize nose or breast size at what sociologists and evolutionary biologists tell us is the most desirable possible level. Rational agents, it's easy to say,

10   Carl Elliott, *Better Than Well* (New York: Norton, 2004), 283.

shouldn't care about physical appearance, and humoring such cosmetic silliness, everyone knows, is an affront to the very idea of personal freedom. But it's too tough to expect persons to succeed by standing out; no person is no less or *more* significant than another. Maybe even relatively trivial forms of genetic diversity are an affront to genetic justice. It's harder than ever to deny, we have to add, that growing old and dying are affronts to personal freedom that we have to work hard to remedy. Sophisticated parents, we can say, are more concerned about indefinitely perpetuating their (youthful, fit) physical appearance than ever, and what they want for themselves, they want for the kids.

There is, after all, a natural cause for our preference for smooth skin over winkles, which only increases in a culture which has lost any sense of what old people are for. Anyway, it's not so clear how many people at any time would have chosen to look (or be) old if they had a way out of it. A just distribution of physical capabilities (which include beauty) would make, say, the singles' bar and the pursuit of a mate much more competitive; successful outcomes might be both more meritocratic and much more ephemeral. Or maybe inward goodness or "the person inside" – instead of skin-deep beauty – would secure more deserved victories than he or she ever has in the past.

We usually don't think of enhancement of any kind as changing the person, but of allowing the person to be more who he or she really is. Mood enhancing drugs like Prozac claim to free me from disabling chemical imbalances to be who I really am, and men who experience themselves as women and small-breasted women who think of themselves as amply endowed now have more opportunity to change with their personal identity in mind.

Personal Change?

Mehlman boldly contends that every argument against biomedical enhancement serves the class interest of the naturally gifted: "By enabling those who are deficient in natural talent to be better at what they do, enhancement means more competition for the gifted." That's why "it is critical for the gifted to attack this [engineered] improvement in performance as unfair, inauthentic, destructive to 'personhood,' and above all, as cheating and unmerited." The gifted who oppose enhancement, Mehlman concludes, only "appear . . . to preserve the role of effort." Their real goal is "to preserve their unearned hegemony."[11] In a genetically just world, hegemony will be more earned than ever. Maybe those over whom hegemony is exerted would have less reason to complain (or whine). The right to rule will have become personal, and so neither conventional nor natural.

Leon Kass objects that a lot might be lost in terms of natural joys and natural purposes, and so there will surely be much less personal fulfillment. Who can deny how much has already been lost as we, in freedom, continue to move away from nature in many ways? But the modern goal seems to be, above all, securing the person against the indifference of impersonal nature, and certainly personal identity will remain as nature continues to recede. The person might be freed up more than ever from the arbitrary limits of impersonal natural determination, as well as freer from the personal supports of tradition and place. He'll be stuck with, as we say these days, being his own person. Or maybe, as we can already see, he or she will seem to be increasingly dependent on his or her parents (or single parent) alone.

What spooks parents most of all about the possibility of "designer babies" is that the children might become somehow *too* enhanced – too different from them – to love them and be lovable. We want our children to be more personally secure than we are, but we don't want them made into gods. Nor, of course, do we want them reduced to beings to be controlled like automatons. There are loving personal limits we routinely assume and readily affirm, when we think about it, to equipping persons with or subjecting persons to "rational control." It makes no sense to say that parents are obsessed with having perfect children. They know that (with the exception, in some cases, of the mysterious personal God) that perfect person is an oxymoron, and even that it's good that persons are dependent, relational, rational beings. Parents want their children to be nothing more or less than good persons.

Parents know well enough that enhancement will not, in the moral

---

11   Mehlman, *The Price of Perfection*, 87.

or spiritual sense, make their children better human beings. Hyperparenting is often based on the perception that a person has to *be* before he or she can *be good*. We live in a time when people think much more clearly about personal security than about personal virtue. That's why no one much is hoping – and that's good, because there is so little reason to hope – that we can engineer ourselves into being more loving (and so charitable and caregiving) or courageous or more realistically open to tough truths we can't help but know. Everyone knows – except, admittedly, some Rawlsian experts – how little correlation there is between being intelligent and being humane or being decent or even between knowing what justice is and being just.

We're getting more and more skeptical of any quasi-Darwinian faith that the "moral sense" will progress as surely as technology as part of our personal evolution. Insofar as sophisticates retain that faith, it's only in terms of personal progress in discrediting the moral illusions of the past concerning God, country, nobility, and nature that caused the sacrifice of persons for some allegedly higher cause. The personal progress we've observed can't be affirmed, it's obvious, in terms of moral excellence, unless we say, with Rawls, that justice is the only virtue persons share in common and even the most wonderful characters of the past were, by our personal standards, unjust.

But it still might be the case that in an increasingly enhanced, genetically just world we will be distinguished by our personal virtue more than ever. That means, to begin with, the bourgeois virtues that lead to personal productivity. But there's no reason to believe that the other virtues – especially those connected with loving caregiving, but also those connected with courage in the face of death and in defense of one's own – will become superfluous either. It'll be more admirable for me to risk one's life for others if he or she could live for an indefinitely long time. And who can deny that personal sacrifice will still be required to protect personal liberty? It'll be tougher but still indispensable for living well to face up to one's ultimate biological finitude. The lonely disorientation that comes from being detached from God – especially the personal Creator – and natural purposes will be more common. And for the growing category of the very old, it will be harder to find happiness through a personal purpose beyond hanging on indefinitely. Their personal struggles in a world repulsed by their very existence will become, soon enough, the stuff of heroic poetry. Being a better person in the moral or spiritual sense may be harder and more of an advantage than ever.

It's also true enough, as David Schaefer complains, that Rawls seems blind to the "Brave New World" fear that biotechnology, at some point, will lead to "changing the essence of humanity" not only for particular persons but "for all succeeding generations."[12] Through germline gene therapy, the fear is, we might tyrannically make all future human persons into beings lacking the freedom and dignity of the persons around right now. In our efforts to free the person from natural limitations, we might transform ourselves into merely determined or merely engineered beings, or at least into beings ignobly freed from being animated by the personal longings that flow from love and death. Can personal identity and so personal relationships (such as marriage and parenthood) really be sustained for an indefinitely long time? Can personal virtue (such as courage) really be possible if death, disease, debility and so forth disappear as ennobling necessities and become accidents that can be prudently avoided through constant attention to risk factors?

We can already see in our time – a time when the average person both lives longer and is more security obsessed than ever – courage has become more scarce. Every sacrifice of life might come to seem Christlike – an optional death suffered out of boundless personal love. Would even Socrates, we can ask, have been up for that kind of sacrifice? His self-sacrifice, we remember, occurred very near what he knew would be the natural end of his singular life. Certainly the sacrifices of Jesus and Socrates were made with the freedom and dignity of future generations in mind, and that couldn't have meant for creating a world where such sacrifices would seem meaningless or insane.

My own view is that those fears are overblown, that we're stuck with virtue. I don't think the Brave New World is coming. My personal claim has been that any impulse toward the perfection of our children will be moderated by personal love. And so I've assumed that love is a

12 Schaefer, *Illiberal Justice*, 28.

personal capability that we've been given by nature, that there's some ground for being a person in nature itself, perhaps because it was created by a personal God.

But that's not actually Rawls's view. He believes that nature has given us nothing personal. His view of personal freedom, in other words, is characteristically modern. We usually trace that distinction between the person and the natural animal to Kant, but it's also found in Locke, who said that nature and nature's God gave persons nothing worthwhile but the capability to freely transform nature.

Rawls's theory, by itself, does point us in the direction of the perfect justice that might come with perfect freedom from nature. For Rawls, "personhood" is basically Kantian. The person exists in some undisclosed location and, from there, exercises control over nature on behalf of who he or she is as a free or unnatural being. The person is a rational agent or essentially not a being with a body insofar as it gets in the way of being rational and exercising free agency, the body is better understood as an impediment to personhood.

Natural enhancements, from this view, can't transform personhood, but only allow the person to be more secure and flourish better as who he or she is in freedom. As Kass explains, the Rawlsian doesn't reflect on what enhanced personal freedom might do to our loves and longings, to the dignified fulfillment we find in doing what comes naturally as the embodied, social animals Mr. Darwin describes.[13] So the Rawlsian, for example, doesn't reflect on what the separation of sex from procreation in the name of personal security might do to personal identity. And a Rawlsian can't explain why there's personal dignity in affirming who we are by nature, in taking responsibility for being men and women who are born, live full of personal longing, and know all along they're born to die.

Having said all this, there's still some Christian wisdom in assuming we can't make ourselves into something better or worse than who we are as persons. We can't, thank God, reduce ourselves to just

---

13   For the best introduction to Kass's thought, see Leon R. Kass, "Defending Human Dignity," *Human Dignity and Bioethics: Essays Commissioned by the President's Council on Bioethics* (Washington, D.C., 2008), 297–332. On this issue, see my *Modern and American Dignity* (Wilmington, DE: ISI Books, 2010).

another "subhuman" species, and we can't raise ourselves to the level of the immortal gods or the personal God. That's why even Christian thinkers such as Gilbert Meilaender embrace the distinction between being personal and being natural; our truest dignity *is* personal.[14] We, of course, are a species, but we're not just another species. Our longings and so our behavior can't be explained in the way those of the other species can. Even with revelation, Meilaender explains, we know "that the individual is not the species," that "the desire that moves us is a desire that cannot rest entirely content with mate and offspring," and no individual "could be simply replaced by those who come after."[15]

We still can correct Rawls by saying that parents are animated by love, and even by saying that charity or caregiving, for persons, is a far higher virtue than justice. It is higher precisely because it's more personal. But we're also stuck with observing that personal concerns have caused us to privilege personal control over natural love, although that choice, ironically, is often animated by love. By neglecting the social or, relational dimension of being personal, we've both made personal existence in this world somewhat more secure and made it seem more contingent – or isolated or detached or ephemeral or insignificant – than ever. To say personal existence has become more contingent in that way is not at all to say it's become unreal, and the very good news is that who we are continues to elude our rational control.

Personal Eugenics

We're also naturally repulsed by the tyrannical idea that biotechnological enhancement is really eugenics – or a way of improving the human "herd" the way we've "improved" so many of the other species. Certainly every such eugenics scheme of the past has been authoritatively discredited. Nobody who reads Plato's *Republic* these days, for example, actually thinks it's just to have government secretly control marriage and reproduction to improve the genetic quality of citizens. We think of people as persons, not citizens; we know they're not

14 Gilbert Meilaender, *Neither Beast Nor God* (San Francisco, CA: Encounter Books, 2009).
15 Meilaender, *Neither Beast Nor God*, 17.

expendable parts of some civic whole. More than ever, we think of choices concerning marriage, sexual partners, and having babies as matters of personal autonomy. The Supreme Court, in *Planned Parenthood v. Casey,* has said, for example, that women, like men, are free to define their own personal identities, and so they're free not to have babies, even babies already in their wombs.

We also, of course, recoil in horror from allegedly Darwinian Progressivist efforts to sterilize the unfit to improve the competitive edge of the species, and even more from the more horrifying Nazi efforts to strengthen and purify the racial identity of the nation. And even those who notice that it couldn't be good that the most accomplished and sophisticated people with the highest I.Q.s and all that aren't reproducing much these days, while those who seem to be a bit short on genetic gifts are doing so in larger numbers, don't think government should do anything to remedy that situation.

Biotechnological enhancement will be different from the old eugenics in all sorts of obvious ways. It will, first of all, really work by transforming nature or as part of conscious and volitional evolution. It won't be another ridiculous effort to consciously direct merely natural or impersonal evolution. It will also be directed toward what's best for every human person. The goal will always be personal or not in any sense coercive or collective. The result must secure the consent of any person intelligently concerned with his or her security or flourishing. Everyone agrees these days that even babies to be genetically modified are ends in themselves. That means the enhancement must be good for the baby as a person and not as part of a family or country or anything else.

We don't even think that the parent's personal opinion about what's best for the child should be the standard. Their judgment must be reasonable from the child's personal view. It's that kind of "reasonability test" that allows courts, for example, to force the Jehovah's Witness parents to allow their children to have blood transfusions. No parent will be able to choose enhancements that will condemn the child to an unnecessarily risky or painful life. Surely parents won't be able to choose deafness for their child in order that he or she be totally integrated into the deaf community to which her deaf parents belong.

There are limits to indulging the parental desire that the child be like them. Some have to do with health and safety, others with restricting genetically the child's freedom to choose his or her own "lifeplan." The point of enhancement is to secure the person as far as possible against alien – meaning first of all natural but also finally political and parental – determination.

"While liberal eugenics is a less dangerous doctrine than the old eugenics," the communitarian Sandel complains, "it is also less idealistic." The old eugenics, "for all its folly and darkness," aspired "to improve humankind, or to promote the collective welfare of whole societies." The new eugenics "shrinks from collective ambitions . . . of social reform." Its more modest and obviously selfish goal is to "arm" children "for success in a competitive society." Its goal, in other words, is nothing more than personal, and so has nothing do with what's best for "humankind" or even a whole society.[16] "People want genetic technology," libertarian Virginia Postrel explains, "because they expect to use it *for themselves*, to help themselves and their children."[17]

A monstrous downside of the old eugenics was the thought that persons with a low quality of life don't even deserve to live. The new eugenic intention seems to be not only pro-life but pro-quality of every life. The choice will be for every person against nature's randomness and indifference.

Ronald Green reassures us in *Babies by Design* that one difference between our liberal, personal eugenics and the schemes of the past is "a strong commitment to reproductive liberty," a right which has become "almost sacrosanct." A combination of "[i]mproved science and a tradition of procreative liberty suggests that democratic societies are unlikely to drift back to the statist control of reproduction that marked the eugenics movement."[18] That's not to deny that the strong social pressure to be productive and keep up generally will motivate parents in the direction of enhancement, just as it motivates them in other ways to ensure their children's success. It's also not to deny that the pressure the

16   Sandel, *The Case Against Perfection*, 78.
17   Virginia Postrel, *The Future and Its Enemies* (New York: Simon and Shuster, 1999), 168.
18   Ronald Green, *Babies by Design* (New Haven: Yale University Press, 2007), 165.

available cosmetic neurology and cosmetic surgery already puts, and will increasingly put, pressure on people to use all available biotechnological means to be smart, pretty, pleasing, and effective.

The decision of some athletes to use enhancements, if regarded simply as a matter of autonomous choice, really does put the pressure on other athletes to do the same to be competitive. The same with actresses who use Botox and various forms of surgery to look young and pretty and ample. The same would also be true of professors who used chemical means to remedy their moodiness and get better student evaluations and publish more. It's even more true, of course, of physicians who use cognitive and mood enhancements to become more effective at diagnosis, surgery, and so forth and save more lives. People may prefer watching "natural athletes" or even "natural actresses" (well, there's little evidence supporting the latter), but nobody is going to choose the "natural" or unenhanced physician who's more likely to kill him.

So Fukuyama is surely right to observe that "my decision to have a designer baby imposes a cost on you (or, rather, your child)," even if reciprocal enhancement won't really make either child better off in the competitive race for the scarce good things of life.[19] But neither of us is likely to leave our kids vulnerable through unilateral disarmament, and we can't expect government these days to enforce some disarmament treaty. There remains a difference, surely, between social and economic pressure and government coercion. The professor retains his right to his "natural moods" as his alleged opening to the truth about being, just as the dean has the right to deny him tenure if he remains, as a result, as unproductive as Socrates.

Fukuyama adds that "special burdens" will be imposed "on people who for religious or other reasons will not want their children genetically altered."[20] The pressure will be on them to do what's required to keep them in the race. Maybe nothing would please proud liberal secularists more than to live in a world where religious people really are much more stupid than they are. But that thought would have to be

19   Fukuyama, *Our Posthuman Future*, 97.
20   Ibid., 97.

trumped by egalitarian concern for the fate of every human person, not to mention by the thought that the unnecessarily stupid and disease-ridden religious people would be dangerous burdens on persons who have acted with more genetic responsibility. In this case, it's hard to see how "social pressure" wouldn't be supplanted by coercion. It'll be too risky to have babies the old-fashioned way anymore. Under the law, safety trumps parental freedom when it comes to children.

We live in a time when personal choice is the bottom line, and we're too chastened by experience and science to be suckered by any larger form of social or collective idealism. But personal idealism, it turns out, can be a source of coercion too. We're not going to let biotechnological enhancement be a source of more genetic injustice than nature has already given us. The poor, surely, will be less likely to voluntarily enhance their children, even if the biomedical technology were made readily available to them. They, after all, already have a distressing propensity to opt out of all sorts of prudential measures already available to improve their health and safety. Can we really allow the poor or the religious to deprive their children of genetic justice? It's not enough for parents to have access to enhancements, just like it is not enough for them to have access to health care, if they don't use them on behalf of their children.

Sandel reminds us that many liberal theorists in the Rawlsian spirit see little difference between biomedical enhancement and a good education in maximizing the child's intellectual capabilities and so personal possibilities.[21] Both good genes and good instruction (including the inculcation of good habits), in fact, are required to make the person as secure as possible. We require parents to send their kids to school. So why wouldn't we require them use any generally available safe and effective means to make it easier for a kid to implement whatever lifeplan he or she has chosen? It's true we allow parents to choose religious schools for their children, but only if they meet minimum standards in terms of indispensable skills. And no dogmatic limitation of personal options taught in religious schools is permanent in the way the genetically challenged person would be limited by his parents' sectarian irresponsibility.

21 Sandel, *The Case Against Perfection*, 78–79.

Green explains that it makes no sense to say that people wrong children by not having them. So nobody has an obligation to be a parent, and that principle extends, in his mind, to the right to have an abortion. But once the decision is made to have the kid, parents should be compelled to avoid "careless reproductive behavior." It just does "too much harm." We can't allow "negligence or thoughtlessness" of any kind to compel kids to live "impaired lives."[22] Unenhanced children will surely end up suing their parents over needless impairment. And there's no reason parents shouldn't be held to account for not taking all reasonable steps to secure the health and well-being of their children.

How parents need to be held accountable is spelled out with rigorous detail by Dworkin. He calls the duty of parents to do what's best for children as persons "the principle of special responsibility." In exercising that responsibility, parents must follow the "first principle of ethical humanism – an objective concern that any life, once begun, be successful." That means that government can command parents to exercise that responsibility through "mandatory [genetic] testing."[23] He admits that it's natural for modern people to be adverse to persons being compelled to submit to procedures against their religious convictions. But that revulsion can't justify irresponsibility when it comes to securing a child's success in avoiding disease, deformity, unnecessary dependence, and early death.

Ordinarily, Dworkin assumes, we think of a woman as enjoying reproductive freedom based on her sovereignty over her body. And he does say, in one place, that, although there's nothing wrong with genetically engineering human beings, it probably will never become common. "Most people," he contends, "delight in the mysteries of reproduction."[24] But his general view is that it's irresponsible to rest content with mysterious randomness when there's the possibility of personal control. Surely parents can't be allowed to revel in that delight in ways that reduce their child's chances for success.

The "flat principle of bodily integrity" embraced by the contemporary defenders of reproductive choice," Dworkin can't help but conclude, "may be one of those artifacts of conventional morality that

22   Green, *Babies by Design*, 213.
23   Dworkin, *Sovereign Virtue*, 450.
24   Dworkin, *Soveriegn Virtue*, 442.

seemed well justified before the possibilities suggested by modern genetic medicine were plausibly imagined, but not after."[25] What seemed like a right turned out to be merely a convention; the false perception depended on our inability to imagine the ways free persons could genetically improve natural bodies. What Green calls our tradition of reproductive liberty turns out, for Dworkin, to be just that, a mere tradition, one that must give way to the progress of science and personal principle. Now or soon enough, "a more fundamental principle for the concern for the lives of everyone" – for securing of the being of every person – trumps bodily integrity.[26] The bottom line remains being personal, which means, first of all, avoiding non-being.

Being pro-life, in other words, is more fundamental than being pro-choice. So today the pro-lifers are all for having unprotected sex and hoping and praying for the best; they're for minimizing persons messing with the mystery of reproduction. The pro-choicers are all for safe sex and planned pregnancies; they want to bring the free person's calculation and control to minimize reproduction's mystery. But soon enough, being pro-life may require the control that comes from separating sex from reproduction, from doing everything we can to enhance or engineer successful persons into being.

The old pro-lifers will become the new pro-choicers. They'll want to be left alone to stay with the old-fashioned or unsafe way of having babies, and they'll have given up trying to impose their convictions by law on others. Concern for particular persons and the safety of us all will be the reason government won't be able to leave them alone.

The pro-choice principle will remain in terms of having children; nobody can force a person to generate replacements for his or her country's or species' or family's sake. But once the decision to create a new person is made, we're responsible for doing what we can to reduce personal risk by achieving genetic justice. We can ever hope or expect that consistent Rawlsians will come to see, tutored by Hadley Arkes and imaging technology, that the fetus both is and at a very early stage of development actually looks like a person.

25 Dworkin, *Sovereign Virtue*, 450.
26 Dworkin, *Sovereign Virtue*, 450.

The growth of personal liberalism, as David Walsh predicts in *The Growth of the Liberal Soul*, will extend personal idealism to its properly inclusive limits.[27] The principle of choice concerning having children may well not extend past conception – either in or outside the womb. At that point, the principle of special responsibility properly takes over: the separation of sex from reproduction that might be required for us to exercise that responsibility with the greatest control in securing genetic justice, as we remove all the allegedly autonomous excuses for the personal extermination that is abortion. Aborting allegedly defective fetuses is obviously the discredited form of eugenics; personal eugenics is about remedying and preventing the defect and making the irreplaceable person as secure and free as possible.

Personal Diagnosis

When and to what extent the pursuit of genetic justice will become possible is a matter of speculation. For now, our perfect knowledge of the genome isn't even translating into quick discovery of causes and cures of the diseases that plague us. But something like "designer babies" must still be regarded as somewhere between possible and likely from a personal point of view. Those who deny the possibility tend to be whole-hog Darwinians, who say that the elusive complexity of impersonal nature will always defeat our best efforts to bring evolution under our conscious, personal control.

These same Darwinians incorrectly say that the human behavior isn't really personal; it can be explained in the impersonal way the species-oriented behavior of all the animals can. They don't even begin to explain why members of our species alone are in such rebellion against their merely natural existence, and they can't explain the emergence of the personal insight that only members of our species are unique and irreplaceable. Many Darwinians believe that the Christian and modern insight that to be a person is to be somewhat homeless or alienated as a biological being is based on some illusion. Even if that's true, it's the source of an increasingly powerful personal evolution – the limits of which seem remarkably indefinite or unclear.

It's in some strange way fitting that our understanding of who the person is is more indefinite than ever. That doesn't mean we are nihilists, of course. Each of us is sure enough that I am not nothing, and my personal struggle is to secure myself in a hostile environment. And my certainty about me extends to you. No sophisticated person denies these days that there's any foundation for public policy higher that the equal significance of every person. The purpose of our "relativism" is to devalue every standard higher than the person for the person's sake. One purpose of Rawls's theorizing is to cut us off from the very impersonal and otherworldly theories of the past, those that devalued the person now existing and sacrificing him or her – as an expendable part – to some whole or to some impossible fantasy about the future.

Our "nonfoundationalism" is about discrediting foundations or standards that don't make the person the bottom line. That the person's security in freedom is the bottom line is the foundation that discredits Nature, History, Tradition, and God. Each of those standards gave illusory or alien content to the person – making the pure person needlessly constrained and insecure. We don't turn to God or History or Nature to explain why the person exists; we, not without reason, are satisfied with basing everything on what we can see and experience for ourselves these days.

As Marx saw (in "On the Jewish Question"), the modern, liberal world is a mixture of personal idealism and competitive survivalism. He really didn't see why, though. Capitalism doesn't empty out personal significance by turning most of us into a commodity. It's because irreplaceable, personal existence seems so contingent that persons must struggle so hard or be so productive. My struggle is not so much against you as against the nature that's out to extinguish us both. We both want to live longer, and we both can through prudent attentiveness to risk factors and biomedical progress. And we both prefer the genetic justice that makes all the available enhancements available to us both. Because many of the means of security and freedom will inevitably remain scarce, interpersonal conflict will remain. It's even true that, despite our egalitarian idealism, the struggle for personal significance will remain. The struggle will, in fact, intensify, because persons will feel more insignificant – but not unreal – as they experience themselves as more on their own than ever.

Tocqueville said that the purely democratic experience of who we are was described by the proto-existentialist Pascal: The person exists for a moment between two abysses. Solzhenitsyn heard just beneath the surface of our happy-talk pragmatism the howl of existentialism. Our efforts at rational control of our natural environment are failing diversions from what the unspeakable truth about how absurd and ephemeral each person's existence really is. Lots of our personal efforts can be explained, in part, as diversions from what we really think we know about each of ourselves. But those efforts are hardly merely diversions; my job is really to secure myself for as long as I can. Real success is possible, although not, of course, permanent success.

The true existentialist can be all fatalistic and relax – maybe even achieving serenity now by living beyond hope and fear when it comes to his impending personal annihilation. But persons, these days, can't learn how to die, if that means, as it did for Socrates, losing oneself in a whole greater than oneself. The person has to do what he or she can to secure himself, his children, and perhaps persons in general. That's what we now mean by personal responsibility.

Today's person is plagued both by being certain that he or she is more than a biological being and that his or her biological death ends not only his or her personal existence but being itself. There's nothing, the person believes, without ME around. The Christian view, of course, is that personal being is a gift of God and continuously secured by the Creator. I am not responsible for my being or the being of my children. Biological death doesn't end all, and, thank God, I will continue *to be* no matter what I do.

It is – as Tocqueville says – that confidence that each of us is somehow immortal or not defined by biological death that both frees us from petty self-obsession as well as for accomplishments (beginning, of course, with children) that stand the test of time better than each of us, as a natural or biological being, does. It frees us, Tocqueville adds, from the heart-contracting error of individualism and for reveling in the present in love with other persons. It frees us for the liberty of personal intimacy and from a paranoid concern for security at the expense of our free pursuit of real satisfaction of our polymorphous erotic longings. That confidence would be inexplicably perverse if it ended technological development or personal evolution, but we can hope it might subordinate that evolution to properly (or relationally) personal purposes.

Contributors

FRANCIS J. BECKWITH is Professor of Philosophy and Church-State Studies at Baylor University, where he is also a Resident Scholar in the Institute for Studies of Religion.

ROBERT P. GEORGE is the McCormick Professor of Jurisprudence, and Director of the James Madison Program in American Ideals and Institutions, Princeton University.

SUSAN MCWILLIAMS is Assistant Professor of Politics at Pomona College in Pomona, California.

DANIEL N. ROBINSON is Distinguished Professor Emeritus of Philosophy at Georgetown University and a member of the philosophy faculty at Oxford University.

LARRY ARNN is President of Hillsdale College in Hillsdale, Michigan.

ALLEN GUELZO is Henry R. Luce Professor of the Civil War Era and a Professor of History at Gettysburg College.

MICAH WATSON is Assistant Professor of Political Science at Union University in Jackson, Tennessee.

JAMES SCHALL, S. J. is Professor of Government at Georgetown University.

DAVID FORTE is Professor of Law at Cleveland State University.

VINCENT PHILLIP MUÑOZ is Tocqueville Associate Professor of Religion & Public Life in the Department of Political Science at the University of Notre Dame.

MICHAEL NOVAK is the George Frederick Jewett Chair (emeritus) in Religion, Philosophy, and Public Policy at the American Enterprise

Institute in Washington, D.C., and Distinguished Visiting Professor at Ave Maria University.

GERARD BRADLEY is Professor of Law at the University of Notre Dame Law School.

CHRISTOPHER WOLFE is Emeritus Professor of Political Science at Marquette University, as well as Vice-President of Thomas International.

J. BUDZISZEWSKI is Professor of Government and Philosophy at the University of Texas in Austin.

JAMES R. STONER, JR. is Professor of Political Science at Louisiana State University.

CHRISTOPHER TOLLEFSEN is Professor of Philosophy at the University of South Carolina.

PETER AUGUSTINE LAWLER is the Dana Professor of Government at Berry College.